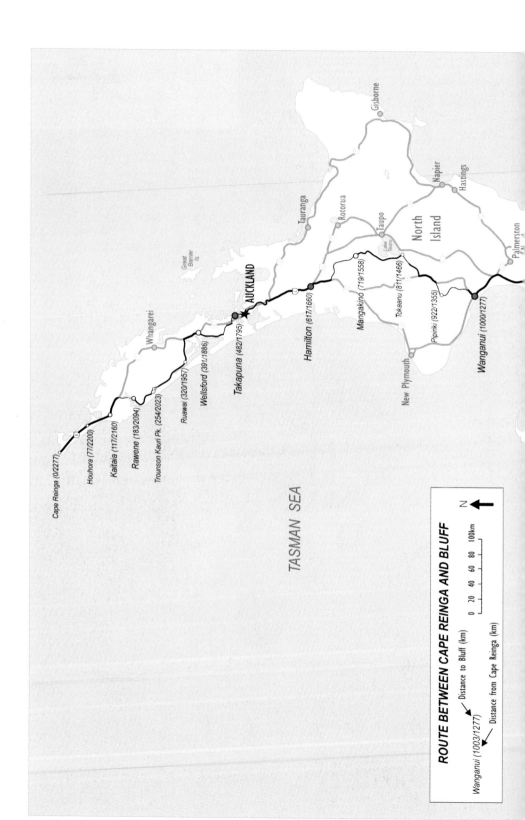

Cape Reinga (0/2277)
Houhora (77/2200)
Kaitaia (117/2160)
Rawene (183/2094)
Trounson Kauri Pk. (254/2023)
Ruawai (320/1957)
Wellsford (391/1886)
Takapuna (482/1795)
AUCKLAND
Whangarei
Great Barrier Is.
Tauranga
Hamilton (617/1660)
Rotorua
Mangakino (719/1558)
Taupo
Lake Taupo
Tokaanu (811/1466)
New Plymouth
Pipiriki (922/1355)
Wanganui (1000/1277)
North Island
Napier
Hastings
Palmerston N.
Gisborne

TASMAN SEA

ROUTE BETWEEN CAPE REINGA AND BLUFF

N

0   20   40   60   80   100km

Wanganui (1003/1277)

← Distance to Bluff (km)
↙ Distance from Cape Reinga (km)

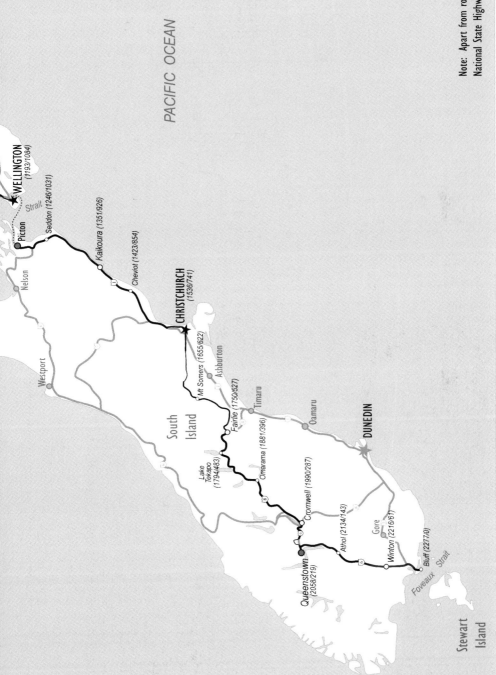

PACIFIC OCEAN

WELLINGTON
(1193/1084)

Picton

Strait

Seddon *(1246/1031)*

Nelson

Kaikoura *(1351/926)*

Cheviot *(1423/854)*

CHRISTCHURCH
(1536/741)

Westport

Mt Somers *(1655/622)*

Ashburton

South
Island

Fairlie *(1750/527)*

Timaru

Lake
Tekapo
(1794/483)

Omarama *(1881/396)*

Oamaru

Cromwell *(1990/287)*

DUNEDIN

Athol *(2134/143)*

Gore

Queenstown
(2058/219)

Winton *(2216/61)*

Bluff *(2277/0)*

Foveaux Strait

Stewart
Island

Note: Apart from route, only
National State Highways shown

For Riley

BIKE
NEW ZEALAND

CYCLING FROM CAPE REINGA TO BLUFF

Paul Salter

AN
EPIC
GUIDE

Epic Guides
PO Box 31053
Milford
New Zealand

www.epicguides.co.nz

1st Edition Published 2006
Copyright © Epic New Zealand Ltd, 2006
ISBN 0-9582256-2-1

Disclaimer and Safety Note:
We produce epic guides for independent travellers. The author and publisher accept no responsibility for the enjoyment or safety of any person using this book or for any errors or omissions. For trip-critical details, where the outcome of conditions different to those described in this guide would be more than an inconvenience, we suggest checking ahead. No guide can identify the limitations of every reader, or, all the potential hazards on a journey; use common sense on your trip and check conditions before setting out. Since cyclists have to share the road with other users, be aware of the potential for traffic accidents.

82 Million years ago; NZ splits from Australia and Antarctica, with the opening of the Tasman Sea

INTRODUCTION

New Zealand's stunning scenery and laid-back lifestyle make this corner of Polynesia a perfect destination for cycle tourists. This guide describes touring the country from Cape Reinga, traditionally considered the top of the North Island, to Bluff at the southern tip of the South Island, an amazing journey of about 2,300km that takes in many of the country's most scenic spots.

Bike touring in New Zealand typically involves changeable weather, hills, and riding on roads that are narrow by Western standards, but the rewards are worth it. In the North Island the tour passes through ancient kauri forests in Northland, the rich farmland of the Waikato, the Taupo Volcanic Zone, and the remote Whanganui River region. In the South Island, the route takes in Marlborough's wine country, a magnificent coast road to Kaikoura, the tussock-covered Mackenzie Country, New Zealand's Southern Alps, and the spectacular lake setting of Queenstown. Organised to visit a mix of big cities, small towns, and out of the way places, this tour gives a great taste of New Zealand.

Consider taking 3 to 4 weeks to do this trip, which is split into 27 stages ranging from 40km to 135km, dividing your time equally between the North and South Islands. Alternatively, you can shorten or lengthen these stages depending on time available, your level of fitness, and the riding conditions, or, do parts of the tour connected with the other forms of transport available, as described in the guide.

The guide is designed to give tourers detailed information on the route and facilities available, as well as some history on places the tour passes, but still be light enough not to weigh you down on uphills. A unique feature of Epic guidebooks are the photographs taken along the route, at 50km intervals in this case, which give riders an idea of countryside and road conditions they can expect on a tour.

The book is split into "Preparations" and "The Journey". The Preparations section has data for cyclists coming from overseas, such as getting to New Zealand with a bike and arrival details, as well as sections on when to tour, what to take, and what to expect on New Zealand roads. Some information for beginner cycle tourers is also included.

The Journey section describes each stage between Cape Reinga and Bluff, laid out over 4 pages, as described on pages 38 and 39. A strip map and elevation profile is included for each stage. The accompanying text has a description of the stage including notes on the general cycling terrain, however individual hills are typically not described. The guide includes listings for some of the campground, hostel, bed and breakfast, motel and hotel accommodation on the route, as well as data on information centres and bike shops.

Options for other routes, which could be connected to this tour, such as the unpopulated East Coast of the North Island, the scenic but wet West Coast of the South Island, and Stewart Island in the far south, are included as suggestions but are not dealt with in detail in this guide. Appendices at the end have more information on topics such as weather conditions, Maori language, and sources for additional data.

New Zealand's main street - State Highway 1 - starts at Cape Reinga, although this far north it's just a gravel road with a lighthouse at the end. This is a great place to begin a journey that will take you as far as the road goes. The tour touches State Highway 1 several more times along the way, although more often than not it follows quieter roads. Fittingly, the end of the road is also the end of Highway 1, at Stirling Point in Bluff.

Good luck and enjoy biking New Zealand.

925 *In Maori mythology, Kupe is the first Polynesian visitor to NZ, 40*
       generations ago, before returning to Hawaiki to extol the new land -
       Tiritiri O Te Moana

TABLE OF CONTENTS

PREPARATIONS

*1315 (+/- 10 years) Mt Tarawera erupts. Fossil pollen, linked to a major
deforestation, is found under the ash from this eruption; a possible sign
of human settlement at the time*

9

THE JOURNEY

NORTH ISLAND

SOUTH ISLAND

1350 Maori oral tradition records the arrival in Aotearoa (Land of the Long White Cloud) of a migratory expedition consisting of 7 canoes. Today, some Maori trace their ancestors back to one of these canoes

1400's Polynesians have settled the Chatham Is, possibly via NZ.
The Chathams Is. tribe elects to settle disputes with a version of
boxing, rather than warfare, and come to be known as Moriori

11

1642 On December 13, someone on Abel Tasman's
Heemskerck sights the Southern Alps, as the ship nears
the West Coast, becoming the first European to see NZ

PREPARATIONS

GETTING TO NEW ZEALAND

Airlines and Bringing a Bike

About 15 airlines currently fly directly to New Zealand. Several others fly to Australia and then connect with New Zealand using partner airlines that are part of the Star Alliance and Oneworld groups. Air New Zealand, the National airline, and Qantas, Australia's largest airline, operate the most flights to New Zealand. Auckland is the main international entry/exit point, although selected flights (mainly Trans-Tasman or Asian) also land in Wellington, Christchurch, and Queenstown. In choosing the airline you fly consider limiting the number of connecting flights to avoid the hassle of collecting and re-checking your bike gear.

Bicycles can be brought on your flight as personal luggage, although your total baggage must still be within the airlines weight allowance. Check the costs for bringing your bicycle - some airlines charge nothing, others charge a significant amount. Most carriers require a bicycle to be bagged or boxed, with the tyres deflated. Some airlines will allow your bike to be loaded unboxed with the pedals removed or turned inwards, the handlebars turned sideways, and the chain covered. Cardboard bike boxes can usually be obtained free of charge from bicycle shops, which normally throw them away after new bikes have been delivered. Pack your touring gear in plastic bags around your bike to protect it in the box. Hard case bike boxes can also be bought.

Entry Requirements

To enter the country you will need a passport that is valid for at least 3 months beyond your planned departure date from New Zealand. A visa (permission to enter the country for a certain period) may or may not be required, depending on your citizenship and intended length of stay. For example, visas are not required for stays of less than 3 months for visitors from America, Canada, Japan, The United Kingdom,

and some European countries (see *www.immigration.govt.nz* for details and other countries in this visa waiver programme). On arrival, immigration officials may also ask to see evidence of sufficient funds for your stay and an onward travelling ticket. Australians do not need a visa to travel to New Zealand and can stay in the country indefinitely.

Passports are issued in your country of origin and may take a while to process, so plan on allowing a decent amount of time before you plan to travel. Keep your passport with you at all times, as it is your most important travel document. It pays to carry a separate photocopy of your passport, and leave another copy at home.

Entry regulations change from time to time so check the requirements with your local New Zealand embassy or consulate before leaving home. Working in New Zealand on a tourist visa is not permitted.

Clearing Customs

On your flight in you will get a New Zealand Passenger Arrival Card that has a Customs section asking if you are carrying any prohibited items (weapons, illicit drugs, indecent material, wildlife products, etc). Other questions include, whether or not you

1640's The Dutch call NZ "Nova Zeelandia", discarding Tasman's "Staten Landt" label as it's clear the land is not connected to Staten Landt (S. America). Oz is called "Nova Hollandia"

are carrying commercial goods, goods for someone else, or more than NZ$10,000 cash or equivalent currency (travellers' cheques are not included and you can bring in more than $10,000 cash, you just have to report it).

The list of agricultural items that must be declared includes, amongst others; food, camping gear and used bicycles. An incorrect declaration results in a $200 instant fine and/or more serious penalties. In particular, ensure your shoes, camping equipment, and bicycle tyres are free of dirt before flying. These regulations are aimed at protecting New Zealand's large agricultural industry (recent unwanted arrivals include the Painted Apple Moth, discovered here in 1999 and only now in the final stages of eradication, and a Fire Ant nest discovered and destroyed at Auckland International Airport in 2001).

Keep in mind your home country's duty regulations when returning with purchases made in New Zealand. Before travelling you can have Customs at your departure point stamp a list of high priced items you are taking with you, if you think your purchases in New Zealand will put the total value of your goods over your home country's duty limit when returning. Also note, there is a $25 departure tax not automatically included in your ticket price, which must be paid when flying out of Auckland.

Health

No special health precautions are needed before coming to New Zealand. In fact New Zealand is blessed by a lack of seriously poisonous animals, except for the rather rare katipo spider (a relative of the Australian redback, and American black widow) found around beach dune habitats.

Water from rivers, streams and remote campground water supplies may be affected by giardia or cryptosporidium and should be treated before use. Tap water in cities and towns is typically excellent quality. Bathing in natural thermal pools carries the slight risk of contracting amoebic meningitis, a serious infection caused by a single cell protozoan that enters the body through the nasal passages. Keeping your head above water prevents this unlikely occurrence.

The mosquito that carries Ross River virus in Australia was discovered in Hawke's Bay in 1998, although there was no evidence it was carrying the disease. In any case prevention of mosquito bites is a good idea.

New Zealand's weather is variable. In hot conditions be aware of the possibility of heat exhaustion, and in the cold and/or wet - hypothermia. Also, see Hazards p.33.

Insurance

Travel insurance is worth having. Comprehensive policies cover medical expenses, airline cancellations, and loss of luggage. Other policies cover these things separately. Check if your existing homeowners insurance covers loss of luggage, and if your existing health insurance covers medical expenses while travelling. Some credit card companies offer free insurance if you use their card to book travel - check with yours. Most travel insurance policies exclude pre-existing medical conditions, and many have exclusions for activities classified as "dangerous" like skiing and motorcycling, so check the policy covers bicycle touring.

Australians and travellers with temporary visitor permits valid for 2 years of more have access to the same public health services as New Zealanders. There is also a reciprocal agreement with the United Kingdom that enables UK visitors to get some public hospital services free.

1769 Cabin-boy Nicholas Young spots land on October 8, beginning Captain Cook's exploration of NZ. Young Nicks Head, at the headland he saw near Gisborne, is named in his honour

15

IN NEW ZEALAND

Discounts

Discounts on travel and entrance fees to tourist attractions are sometimes available for students and seniors (over 65 years of age). A student ID or ISIC card is usually requested before a student discount is given.

An automobile association card from you home country will enable you to get free maps at New Zealand's AA offices (if the club is affiliated with the Alliance Internationale de Tourisme (AIT) or the Federation de l'Automobile (FIA)), and may entitle you to discounts on car rentals and accommodation.

Arriving in Auckland

There is a Visitor Information Centre on the ground floor of the Auckland International Airport Arrivals Hall where you can make accommodation and travel bookings if you have not done this before arrival. You can also buy phonecards and maps there.

The Airport is about 20 km south of downtown Auckland. There are numerous hotels and motels within 5km of the airport, along Kirkbride Rd and Massey Rd (see p.186). Options for getting to downtown, which most locals simply refer to as "the City", include cycling, taking a shuttle, a taxi, a bus, or getting a rental car.

Cycling to downtown from the airport is easily done, however the roads are quite busy and some of the suburbs in the south have a reputation for being rough - mainly at night. See p.185 for a description and map for riding into downtown, and p.32 for information on New Zealand roads and the road code.

Shuttle buses (mini vans that take several passengers and typically tow luggage trailers) will take you door-to-door to your desired destination in the City or suburbs, and may be your best option with a bike if you are connecting with other transport to get to Cape Reinga. New Zealand taxis are typically midsize cars that cannot easily fit a boxed bike (unless you specifically request a station wagon). For rental car information see p.20.

Details on transport to Cape Reinga are on p.37. If you decide to get a connecting flight north you may decide not to go into downtown at the start of your trip as this tour passes through the City later.

A BRIEF HISTORY OF NEW ZEALAND

Select events in New Zealand's history are noted chronologically along the bottom of the pages in this guide and additional information is contained throughout. This section briefly adds some more background.

The islands making up New Zealand were the last major landmasses on Earth (Antarctica excepted) to be inhabited by man, which is probably why much of the country is still so beautiful. For the longest time, these remote islands were home solely to an interesting collection of animals and plants - one that did not include mammals (apart from 3 bat species) due to a split from the supercontinent of Gondwana 80 million years ago before mammals arrived.

Prior to man's arrival, lowland New Zealand was mostly covered by rainforest dominated by kauri in the north, and rimu, matai, and totara in the south. The forest dwellers included a wide variety of birds including Haast's Eagle (the world's largest) and many flightless birds such as moa (one species growing to over 2.5m), takahe, kakapo, and the national bird - the kiwi.

Apart from bats, the first land mammals to arrive were Polynesians, who are

16

1773   Cook refits on the 2ⁿᵈ of his 3 expeditions to NZ, then heads
towards Antarctica - reaching 71o 10' S before turning north

thought to have arrived in the 12th or 13th Century from the Cook Islands or Society Islands. This was the end of a migration their ancestors commenced thousands of years earlier, starting from South East Asia and slowly spreading across the Pacific. The human impact on the islands of New Zealand has been dramatic. When Maori stepped ashore, they brought rats and dogs which, combined with burning of the forests, started a cycle of extinctions. Maori dubbed the land Aotearoa - Land of the Long White Cloud - and developed a unique, tribal culture based on a strong connection with the land and sea, family ancestry, and oral tradition.

The first white men to see New Zealand were Dutchmen, aboard Abel Janszoon Tasman's ships in 1642, although the first Europeans did not land until Captain James Cook's detailed exploration 127 years later. When Europeans started arriving permanently, the rate of land change increased dramatically. Although Maori had hunted moa to extinction by the 17th Century and Haast's Eagle had disappeared, Europeans brought new pests, such as stoats and ferrets, which ate bird eggs and chicks, as well as animals and plants that displaced native populations – as well as bringing their own bird species. With mechanised logging and a ready market, a European timber boom continued the trend of forest reduction and the introduction of muskets, metal, alcohol, and tobacco, significantly impacted the Maori way of life.

As the Colonial era began a treaty was signed with Maori ceding sovereignty to the British Crown in return for Maori rights of possession of property and personal protection - a treaty whose application has been controversial ever since. Tribal warfare amongst Maori became more lopsided in the 19th Century as certain groups acquired guns, and before long discontentment with Pakeha (European) land purchases developed into full scale war in Taranaki and the Waikato. Around this time an economy based on timber and farming continued to grow - then gold was discovered, and several rushes followed.

By 1900, New Zealand was being run by its own Government, although ties with Britain were still strong, and numerous capital projects were being undertaken. In 1907 the country became a Dominion, essentially signalling the end of the pioneer days and starting a gradual trend towards urban living.

New Zealand's participation in the two World Wars, separated by a depression, impacted generations of Kiwis during the first half of the 20th Century, and helped forge a national identity. One piece of good news, in 1948, was the rediscovery of a small population of Takahe (a bird), which had been considered extinct for the previous 50 years, in the mountains of Fiordland near Te Anau.

The 1950's and 60's where generally optimistic times - suburbs blossomed, shops were open 5 days a week only, and home ownership became a reality for many New Zealand families. In 1966 New Zealand's labour force reached 1,000,000.

For almost a decade, from the mid-1970's, PM Robert Muldoon was an aggressive leader who advocated a regulated economy and influenced the attitudes of a generation (some saying "Rob Muldoon before he robs you"). In the 1980's colour TV arrived, pitched battles were fought in the streets during a whites-only South African rugby tour, and KZ7 made New Zealand's first attempt at winning yachting's America's Cup.

The 1990's and early 21st Century have seen continued tensions over the Treaty of Waitangi - the biggest issue in 2004 being ownership of New Zealand's foreshore. On a positive note, New Zealand has now recognised the value of its remaining natural resources, as tourism has become a significant money earner for the country.

1792   A sealing gang left at Dusky Sound in Fiordland becomes NZ's first European encampment.   A trickle of whalers, runaway sailors, and traders follows, settling NZ in the early 1800's

ACCOMMODATION

With tourism being so popular there is usually a good range of accommodation to choose from while touring. Standards are generally high, although some 1960's-era motels are in need of refurbishment. This guide lists some of the accommodation available along the route, however, inclusion is not necessarily a recommendation and there are often other alternatives to choose from. The rates listed are approximate, as costs are always changing, so check when booking. Also, ask if there is somewhere to lock your bike up for the night.

New Zealand's most popular National Parks and tourist towns get busy during school and public holidays and last-minute accommodation can be harder to find during these times (see p.24). Local tourist offices have extensive accommodation listings and can help with bookings.

Motels
Motels have traditionally been the accommodation of choice for New Zealand families taking a car trip, and are ubiquitous in small towns and city suburbs on main routes throughout the country. Motel rooms include a private bathroom and self-catering cooking facilities (stove/microwave, refrigerator, pots, plates and cutlery, etc), providing the type of independence and flexibility many New Zealanders like. There is usually a laundry available. Motels often have several units with double bedrooms and/or pullout sofas for large families - a good option for a group of cyclists.

Hotels
Large hotels are really only found in the bigger cities and resort towns in New Zealand and typically cater to the upper end of the tourist market (i.e. they are expensive). At

the other end of the scale are pub-hotels that offer accommodation upstairs, or out-back, from a public bar. These are cheaper but can have a clientele of noisy hardcore drinkers. Large hotels have rooms with en-suites, with a washbasin, toilet, and shower or bath. In smaller or historic hotels bathrooms may be down the hallway and shared. Breakfast is not always included with the room rate so check when booking. At hotels it can be more difficult to find a place to store bikes, but most hosts will make an effort to find somewhere.

Hostels
New Zealand caters well to backpacker tourists. There are hundreds of good value independent hostels throughout New Zealand as well as hostels in the Youth Hostel Association of New Zealand (YHANZ) network. Hostels provide dormitory and sometimes private rooms, shared bathroom facilities, and cooking facilities (some also provide cheap meals). Dormitory rooms are generally single sex. Guests sleep in their own sleeping bags, or in some hostels you can hire linen. Many hostels have in-house tourist information services and they are a good place to network with budget-conscious travellers. Age is not a factor for staying in hostels.

Bed and Breakfasts (B&B's)
B&B's are not common in New Zealand but the number is slowly growing. Basically these are private homes or farms that take in a few travellers at a time. Typically they are not well signposted but visitor information centres have listings. A bed, linen, and

1800's At the start of European settlement, about half the forest that existed before Polynesian settlement has already been destroyed by fire. Now less than 23% of NZ is covered in natural forest

towels are provided along with bathroom facilities. Breakfast is included in the price and places may do other meals by arrangement. B&B's are usually more expensive than motels and hotels but offer a friendly environment with good local knowledge.

Camping

New Zealand has a great network of campgrounds. These are located in most towns and scenic destinations and one excellent feature is that many have a communal kitchen facility that includes a sink with running water and a stove. Some even have refrigerators. For the minimalist cyclist this can mean leaving the camping stove and fuel behind to save weight and just bringing a billy (pot) for cooking.

Most campgrounds have, at a minimum, tent sites, toilet and shower facilities, and drinking water available. Larger campgrounds, known as holiday parks or motorcamps, also have electric hook-ups and dumping facilities for caravans and motor-homes, laundry facilities, and sometimes cabins. Some hostels also offer camping.

In National and Forest Parks, campsites are usually remoter locations and are less developed with long drop toilets and tank water the norm. Many sites are next to tramping huts. These sites are administered by the Department of Conservation (DOC). Check with them on their current booking procedures.

A far as free camping goes, you basically need to know the status of the place you plan to camp in. The following areas are off limits; private land (without the owner's permission), DOC administered lands and scenic reserves, water supply catchments, and, obviously, areas designated No Camping. Outside these areas you may be able to discretely set up camp for the night.

It can rain hard in New Zealand so plan on having a good quality lightweight tent that doesn't leak (see p.30 for other suggested camping gear).

Other Accommodation

Furnished houses, apartments, and caravans are available for rent, typically by the week, and are advertised in national newspapers. The same goes for baches (pronounced "batches"), New Zealand's name for holiday homes - except in the deep south where they are called cribs. Local tourist information centres have details on these and other options.

TRANSPORT IN NEW ZEALAND

Options for getting around New Zealand (besides your bike), before or after your cycling tour, are listed below.

Coaches

Coaches can be a cheap and relatively fast way to travel around the North and South Islands. Bikes will be carried if room is available (there is a small surcharge and some  carriers require bikes to be boxed). Coach services link major cities and most decent sized towns. A primary provider is InterCity, which has a wide network of destinations. Coaches are air-conditioned and most have on-board toilets for the longer trips. Package bus tours are popular with tourists and you may be able to make arrangements with a particular tour company to carry your bike if you want to join one of these before or after your cycling adventures. In addition, some companies run "hop-on hop-off" bus services, or backpacker buses, on popular budget traveller routes.

1809 All but 4 people on the Boyd are massacred in Whangaroa Harbour, Northland. Most Europeans avoid this area for the next 10 years

19

Trains

New Zealand has a somewhat limited train network with the main service provider, Tranz Scenic, offering only a few long distance passenger routes. The good news is these routes are often very scenic, the seating and carriages are of a good standard, and long-haul trains typically including a viewing car with panoramic windows. Trains run daily from Auckland to Wellington, Picton to Christchurch, and Christchurch to Greymouth over Arthurs Pass. Discounted fares are available for those booking early, students, seniors, backpackers (with a valid card), and the disabled. Bicycles are $10 extra and should be pre-booked. Pedal removal and chain wrapping may be requested.

Schedule and route information is available from Trans Scenic (Ph 0800 802 802, or *www.transcenic.co.nz*). Trans Scenic also offer rail passes that include certain amounts of coach, ferry, and air travel, depending on the type of pass you get - a more flexible way to travel extensively than by rail alone.

Suburban train services are nearly extinct although they do operate in Wellington and in Auckland where the Britomart downtown station opened recently.

Planes

Flying is a relatively expensive way to travel domestically and in a country the size of New Zealand, where you can drive from Auckland to Wellington in little more than a day, may be unnecessary for people wanting to see the country. On the flip side, depending what time you arrive in New Zealand you can fly to the far North that day and be rested and ready to head to Cape Reinga the following day (see p.37).

The biggest domestic carrier is Air New Zealand. Other carriers include Qantas, Origin Pacific, Mountain Air, etc. Bikes can be taken as personal luggage, although there is usually an additional charge (currently $20 on Air New Zealand). Depending on the carrier, airlines may require bicycle tyres to be deflated, handle bars turned sideways, pedals removed or turned inwards, and the chain wrapped, or the whole bike to be boxed. Discounted fares are available by booking in advance, or, if you have flexibility in your travel arrangements, flying standby.

Rental Cars

Renting a car is quite expensive, and renting a campervan is very expensive, but it does provide flexibility on your travels before or after a bike tour. If you hire a car, get one big enough to fit your dismantled bike in or with a roof rack, or get a carry rack. Major rental car companies include Avis, Budget, and Hertz. There are also smaller rental

 companies that offer competitive rates. Check the insurance, deductible, and damage waiver details (your personal auto insurance or credit card company may cover some of these costs).

You'll need a current, full, driver's licence from your home country or an International Drivers Permit (IPD) to rent a car, depending on your home country. The minimum driver age for most rental companies is 21. Drivers under 25 typically have to pay higher insurance rates. Rental plans with unlimited-mileage are best if you plan on driving any distance. Petrol prices have risen recently and 1 litre of unleaded fuel costs about $1.45.

New Zealand's State Highways and major routes are often winding undivided roads. This, combined with the fact that every year there are accidents, often fatal, involving tourists driving on the wrong side of the road, should be taken into account before renting. See p.33 for details on driving in New Zealand.

1814 Rev. Samual Marsden brings horses, sheep, and cattle to NZ, establishing a Church Missionary Society in the Bay of Islands

Ferries

On this tour, ferry crossings on the Hokianga and Waitemata Harbours in the North Island save lengthy cycling detours. Apart from flying, ferries are the only way to travel between the North and South Islands (a fact the unions have used to their advantage numerous times). See p.100 for details on the Inter-Island ferries. Other ferries run trips to interesting offshore islands along this tour route, such as; Rangitoto, Tiritiri, Waiheke, etc (from Auckland), Kapiti Island (from Paraparaumu), Somes Island (from Wellingon), various islands (from Picton), and Stewart Island (from Bluff).

BANKS, ATMS, AND EXCHANGE RATES

Banks are open weekdays from 9:00am to 4:30pm. Most banks cash travellers cheques and change foreign currency (except coins) on the spot.

ATMs (called money machines in New Zealand) are common in cities and large towns. Most money machines give cash advances on major credit cards - the logos on the machines tell you which ones. Depending on your home bank, you may also be able to get account balances and cash directly from your account at home (the balances will show in New Zealand dollars). PIN numbers need to be four digits to do this. The exchange rates for getting cash from money machines are often better than the rates and commissions charged by banks and bureaux de change's for cashing travellers cheques, however check the exact fees for doing this.

Most retail shops and supermarkets offer an ATM option, called EFTPOS, at the register, where money is debited directly from your account. Some, especially supermarkets, also offer "cashback" for getting cash with a purchase.

The then Finance Minister, later Prime Minister, Robert Muldoon supervised the introduction of the decimal currency system in 1967. New Zealand presently uses silver 5c, 10c, 20c, and 50c coins, gold $1 and $2 coins, and $5, $10, $20, $50, and $100 notes (5c coins are to be removed from circulation soon).

At the time of printing one New Zealand dollar buys the following;

Country/Currency	1 $NZ will purchase
American dollar	0.70
Australian dollar	0.92
British pound	0.40
Canadian dollar	0.82
Euro	0.57
Japanese yen	79.1

SHOPPING & PRICES

Normal trading hours are Monday to Friday 9:00am to 5:30pm and Saturday 9:00am to 4:00pm. Some shops open Sunday, particularly food stores and large shopping malls. Late night shopping in main centres is usually on a Thursday or Friday till 9:00pm. Supermarkets, restaurants, service stations, and corner stores have extended hours.

1815 Thomas King, the son of Anglican missionaries, is the first European born in NZ. He dies at 3½ and is buried at Oihi (Marsden Cross)

21

The cheapest food prices are normally in supermarkets, rather than dairies or service stations (which usually sell a limited range of packages food items). Some ballpark prices are listed below;

Loaf of bread	$2.90	Milk (1L)	$1.80
Bananas (1kg)	$2.60	Cheese (500g)	$6.35
Marmite (125g)	$2.25	Beef mince (500g)	$9.95
Small chocolate bar	$1.30	Fish & chips for one	$3.80
Bottled water (500ml)	$1.80	Cup of coffee	$3.00
Sandwich	$2.00	Small Hokey Pokey ice-cream	$1.70
Can of soft drink	$1.30	Potato Chips (45g)	$1.20
35mm film, 36 exp. 400	$9.95	Petrol (1L regular)	$1.45
Diesel (1L)	$1.05	Local phone call	$0.70
Internal letter rate	$0.45	30 min at Internet café	$6.00
Movie ticket	$15	Compact disc	$30
Hostel dorm bed	$20	Motel room	$85
Bicycle inner tube	$10	Bicycle tyre	$30

Major credit cards are accepted. Tipping is not common in New Zealand.

A Goods and Services Tax (GST) of 12.5% is included on most price tags (food is exempt). Visitors cannot claim this tax back when leaving, although it is possible to avoid the tax when purchasing expensive items if the item is shipped directly to your home country.

COMMUNICATIONS

Telephone
A local call from a public phone box costs 50c (calling a cell phone is more). Public phones usually take credit cards and/or pre-paid phonecards (available from corner stores (known as "dairies"), supermarkets, Post Offices, etc). Less common are

combination card/coin phones that take coins from 10c to $2, but do not give change. Some dairies have coin phones from franchised pay phone providers. For local calls you do not need to dial the area code.

For the operator dial 010, for New Zealand directory assistance dial 018, and for international directory assistance dial 0172 (there is a fee for directory assistance). Operator assisted calls (e.g. collect calls) have fees of several dollars. Numbers starting with 0508 and 0800 are toll-free. Calling cards (brought from home, you dial a toll-free number, make the call, and it's charged to your home phone bill) or prepaid phone cards (bought in New Zealand, you dial a toll-free number, enter a code, then make your call) are the cheapest ways to call home from New Zealand. To make international calls from New Zealand; dial 00, the destination country code, area code (excluding 0 if it starts with one), then the number. When calling New Zealand from overseas; dial your international access code, 64 (the country code for New Zealand), leave the 0 off the area code, then dial the phone number.

Another option for your trip is to bring your mobile phone from home (after

1820 At Kerikeri a steel plough is used for the first time in NZ

checking it is compatible with one of New Zealand's mobile phone networks and remembering to get the correct electrical adapter for the charger), or, buy a mobile in New Zealand and purchase pre-paid minutes for it. A mobile phone can be an excellent safety tool in serious emergencies, although network coverage may not extend across the whole country. Emergency calls to 111 are free.

Mail

Post offices, or Post Shops as many are now called, are open Monday to Friday 9:00am to 5:00pm, and Saturday 9:00am to 12:30pm in most towns. The internal letter rate is 45c for standard delivery (2-3 days) and 90c for FastPost (1-2 days depending on where you post from). Postcards and Aerograms to anywhere in the world cost around $1.50. Airmail letters cost approximately $1.50 to $2 depending on the destination. Prices for large or heavy envelopes and packages are more. Check the postal rates given here are still current before posting (see *www.nzpost.com*).

Post Offices in large towns offer a Post Restante service that will receive and hold packages for several months free of charge. Items should include "Post Restante" on the address and you will need your passport, or similar proof of identity, to pick packages up. This service can be a good way to rid yourself of excess weight as you cycle the country (used maps and tourist stuff can be sent to a post office near your departure point for pick-up later), or to send items down the line for pick-up later (see *www.nzpost.com* for details).

The Internet and E-mail

Access to the Internet is quite good for travellers to New Zealand. All major cities and most large towns have cyber cafés or Internet service shops. Most public libraries and many hotels and hostels offer Net access. Most upmarket hotels have dataport connections. New Zealand mains electricity is 230 volt, 50 Hz, using a 3-pin plug.

TV, Radio, and The Press

The major free-to-air TV channels with national coverage are TV1, TV2, TV3, and Prime. Other channels include Channel 4 and Triangle Television. For paying customers, Sky TV arrived in 1990's and after a few years caused a stir when they bought the rights to most live All Black rugby matches.

National Radio, on various frequencies around the country (see *www.radionz.co.nz*), has the best news and weather bulletins. There are numerous other AM and FM stations.

Major newspapers include; *The New Zealand Herald*, *The Dominion Post*, *The Christchurch Press*, and *The Otago Daily Times*. Magazines of note, with news, arts, and entertainment information include; *The Listener*, *North and South*, and *Metro*.

There is a monthly magazine called *New Zealand Mountain Biker* that sometimes has touring information. Other New Zealand magazines with various tour and trip details are *New Zealand Outside*, *Wilderness*, and *New Zealand Adventure*.

EMERGENCY CONTACTS

Dial 111 for Police, Ambulance, and Fire services. In an emergency (e.g. loss of passport, arrest, serious injury) your Embassy, High Commission, or Consulate in New

1820 Hongi Hika, cannibal chief of Nga Puhi, visits King George IV in London. Returning via Sydney, he exchanges gifts he received for muskets, which he uses to dominate Waikato tribes

23

Zealand can help with contacting relatives at home, and if you get into serious trouble may provide a temporary loan which will have to repaid.

Your Embassy can also assist with repatriation in emergencies. Get Embassy listings from the phone book or by calling directory assistance.

HOLIDAYS

Banks, Government offices, schools and most businesses are closed on public holidays and traffic can be heavy on these days near main centres. The Labour Day Weekend is particularly busy on the roads leading into and out of Auckland for example. Public holidays are listed below. Each province also has an annual holiday in addition to this list. Note: If the New Years or Christmas holidays fall on a weekend then they are moved to the following weekdays.

Holiday	Date
New Years Day	January 1
Day after New Years Day	January 2
Waitangi Day	February 6
Good Friday	Late March or early April
Easter Monday	Late March or early April
ANZAC Day	April 25
Queen's Birthday	First Monday in June
Labour Day	Last Monday in October
Christmas Day	December 25
Boxing Day	December 26

Domestic travel and accommodation in tourist areas can be more difficult to book during school holidays. Most New Zealand schools moved from 3 to 4 terms in the 1990's, with the main summer holiday running from mid-December to the end of January. Term holidays are 2 weeks each in early April, early July, and mid-September.

TIME

New Zealand is 12 hours ahead of Greenwich Mean Time (GMT), so midday in New Zealand is midnight in the United Kingdom, and near midnight in most of Europe. [One time zone covers all of NZ except the Chatham Islands, which are 45 min. ahead].

The country goes onto daylight saving time from the first Sunday in October until the last Sunday in March (clocks are put forward 1 hour to GMT+13). Note: If you are visiting from the US, remember New Zealand lists dates by day/month/year (not month/day/year).

WEIGHTS AND MEASURES

New Zealand is a metric country. Distances are reported in metres and kilometres, temperatures in Celsius, weights in grams and kilograms, and volumes in litres or cubic metres (a few imperial measures linger in everyday use, such as people's height - which most people still think of in terms of feet and inches).

Air compressors at petrol stations are free to use and measure tyre pressure in pounds per square (psi). See Appendix D for conversions between metric and imperial units for temperature, distance, weight and volume.

1830's Mission stations start appearing in more populous Maori centres

CYCLING NEW ZEALAND

WHEN TO CYCLE TOUR

The weather is a key factor to consider when scheduling a New Zealand tour. New Zealand is effectively a long skinny land with its northern end nearer warm Pacific latitudes and its southern end in the middle of the cooler "Roaring 40's". As a result the north of New Zealand typically has milder weather, while the south is cooler with more pronounced seasons. However, local terrain, and whether you are on the coast or inland, or at low or high elevation, also significantly affects the local weather.

Being in the Southern Hemisphere, December, January, and February are summer months, while June, July, and August are winter months. You have the best chance of cycling in good weather during summer or the months on either side of summer. During these times the days are longer and, statistically at least, there is less rain and more sunshine, although the changeable nature of New Zealand's climate means touring cyclists need to carry a raincoat and warm top year round.

The usual weather pattern for New Zealand is a succession of highs and lows rolling across the country from the west, bringing good, bad, or indifferent weather, which lasts for a few days, or longer, until another high or low pushes it out of the way. If a summer high gets "blocked" over the country, or is slow moving, you can get prolonged dry weather, with occasional inland thunderstorms.

Broadly speaking, annual rainfall and the number of rain-days is higher on the west side of the North Island, the lower east sides of both islands, and the West Coast of the South Island. For example, the West Coast typically has at least 3,000 mm of rainfall and over 175 rain-days a year, compared to less than 600 mm of rain and fewer than 75 rain-days a year in parts of Central Otago.

Wind speed and direction have a huge impact on cyclists. On a macro-scale, wind moves anticlockwise around highs, and clockwise around lows, in the Southern Hemisphere, but local conditions also affect actual wind speed and direction. The closer the isobars on a weather map the stronger the wind will be. Winds from a westerly direction are common, although Wellington - a city with a reputation for strong winds - is sheltered from westerlies by hills, so northerlies and southerlies are more prevalent. A common pattern is a low moving in from the Tasman Sea with northwest wind ahead of it, and southwest winds behind. In the South Island, incoming westerlies are pushed up over the Alps, cooling the air as it rises and dropping rain on the West Coast. When air descends onto to the east side of the island under hot, low humidity conditions, a front can bring strong northwest winds - known in Christchurch as a nor'wester. When a persistent nor'wester reaches gale force it can blow thousands of tons of topsoil out to sea, cause a spike in psychiatric hospital admissions as people get depressed, and make riding a bike impossible.

On this tour, the north of the North Island, Marlborough, and Canterbury can be especially hot and humid during summer (even when overcast) with the heat lingering into the early evening. Higher elevation areas in the central North Island and South Island High Country (around Burke and Lindis Passes for example) can be hot too but have the greatest potential for cool temperatures, and, rarely, dustings of snow out of season. The summit of Mount Ruapehu in the North Island and the peaks of the Southern Alps have permanent snow caps. Doing this type of tour during winter, or immediately on either side of winter, would require more detailed research and

1835 A group of Maori from mainland NZ looking for a new home commandeer a ship and sail to the Chatham Islands, where they brutally subdue the peace-loving Moriori tribe.

25

preparations for persistent cold weather and wet slippery roads.

In summary, think about doing the tour during summer or a month or two on either side of summer, but be prepared for all types of weather when you go - then, if you strike a decent weather, consider it a bonus. Appendix A contains more weather data.

Weather forecasts are broadcast on National Radio (including mountain and extended forecasts at certain times) and TV, and are available for $1.30/min from Metphone (Ph 0900 999 ** [using the area code for the forecast area as the last 2 digits]). December through February is when most Kiwis take their summer holidays, and these are the busiest tourist times at popular destinations (see p.24 for holiday dates).

CYCLING CAPE REINGA TO BLUFF

NZ is a great place to visit by bike - it's sparsely populated by world standards, has many unspoilt and diverse landscapes within a reasonably compact area, and the locals - more often than not - go out of their way to be friendly.

The route described in this guide is a fairly direct route starting at the beginning of State Highway 1, at Cape Reinga. The far north of New Zealand has a low population, and although Cape Reinga has become a tourist destination in recent years, with daily bus tours from the Bay of Islands and Kaitaia, it is still unspoilt. The first 21km from the Cape to Waitiki Landing are on a hilly gravel road with steeply cambered corners, requiring careful riding to avoid a spill.

Past Waitiki Landing things get easier as the road skirts the Parengarenga Harbour looking out to dazzling dunes of almost pure silica sand. The route down the west side of Northland avoids the busier roads on the east side and passes through kauri forest reserves which are home to the nocturnal kiwi. The route skirts the many inlets of Kaipara Harbour before reaching New Zealand's largest city - Auckland. Beautifully located between two harbours, with a backdrop of bush covered hills; Auckland is known as The City of Sails - despite the 2003 loss of the America's Cup yachting trophy.

The next stage takes main roads from Auckland to Hamilton, following New Zealand's longest river, the Waikato, for much of the way. Although the road is busy the shoulder is wide once you get outside the city, and gradients past Bombay are easy, making it a quick route south. Less busy, but longer, alternate routes can be found.

The route returns to quieter country roads south of Te Awamutu, passing through farmland and timber plantations alongside the Waikato. The central North Island is a volcanic hot spot with stunning scenery, including the giant caldera of Lake Taupo, the thermal area of Tokaanu, and the mountainous cones of Tongariro, Ngauruhoe, and Ruapehu. The tour follows the Whanganui River, which flows off Mt Ruapehu, through the historic Whanganui National Park, past tiny Maori settlements, to Wanganui itself.

Heading south to Wellington, the route eventually rejoins State Highway 1 and traffic gets busier, although it is still a very picturesque ride, with the Tararua Ranges on one side and the coast on the other. Wellington likes to think of itself as the nation's cultural capital, as well its political centre, a reputation strengthened by the opening of the highly regarded national museum, Te Papa, in the late 1990's.

The ferry ride across Cook Strait and through the Marlborough Sounds is superb - if it is not too rough - and the cycling from Picton to Kaikoura follows another magnificent coastline. From the cathedral city of Christchurch the tour heads into the foothills, then the High Country, of the Southern Alps. These mountains mark the

1837 The New Zealand Association is formed to purchase land. It becomes The New Zealand Co. a year later. Land sales are unregulated at this time

Alpine Fault, the boundary between the Indo-Australian and Pacific Plates, which runs the length of the South Island. Passing rivers, lakes and mountains, the tour crosses Lindis Pass into Otago and continues past old gold mining areas to the tourist mecca of Queenstown. The tour eventually reaches the end of the road at Bluff, south of the most southerly city in the world - Invercargill.

The route is in 27 stages ranging from 40 to 135km in length, which can be shortened or extended depending on riding conditions and individual fitness. Food and accommodation are available at the end of each stage, and camping facilities are available at the end of most stages. Bicycle shops are found in major towns en-route, but are typically not present in the smaller rural towns.

The 50km photos in this guide show the type of countryside you'll travel through.

The topography along the route is discussed in general terms in the text and is summarised on the stage profiles. Not every climb is mentioned. The terrain is described (in increasing steepness) as flat, gently rolling, rolling, or hilly. Flat terrain may include a few climbs and descents, but where these are present they are generally gentle. Terrain described as gently rolling includes gentle rises and falls with occasional moderate climbs, but rarely any steep climbs. Rolling countryside includes moderate and some steep climbs, and hilly terrain is just that; hilly and hard going. Of course wind direction, weather conditions and individual fitness are strong influences, and a tough head wind can make even flat terrain hard going. See p.32 for more information on the types of roads, and hazards facing cyclists, in New Zealand.

WHAT TO TAKE

Experienced tourers will have their own ideas on equipment and touring technique, based on what has worked best for them in the past. The following sections include some gear suggestions relevant to this tour and tips for those new to cycle touring.

Deciding on the accommodation that you plan to use will make a big difference to the load you carry. Carrying camping gear gives you the flexibility of choosing to camp, or not, depending on circumstances, and is the cheapest touring option. Cyclists who are confident they can ride under any conditions can decide to stay in motels and hostels that supply linen (credit card touring), meaning they can leave behind sleeping bags and camping gear and travel lighter. A cheap and flexible option, that is also a great way to experience New Zealand, is to mix camping with staying in hostels. Regardless of the accommodation you choose, aim to minimise the amount of gear you will carry. Travelling as light as possible allows you to cycle a decent distance in a day and avoids over-stressing you and your bike. A good rule is to take the minimum gear needed to cover the worst anticipated conditions, then add just enough to be able to live from day to day. A suggested packing list and more details on gear are given below.

A Bike

The tour is predominantly on sealed roads with only a few sections on gravel. Three common types of bicycle suitable for this type of trip are; touring bikes, mountain bikes, and hybrids.

Touring bikes are a variant of road (racing) bikes, that have a wider range of gears (21 or more), sturdier components, and a frame geometry tweaked to be more comfortable for long periods in the saddle and braze-ons for racks. These bikes have 700c wheels, with wider tyres than pure road bikes (e.g. 28mm, or wider).

Touring bike

1837 Possum are introduced to NZ for their fur. They go on to become a major pest

27

Touring bikes have historically been the preferred bike for long tours and are quite capable of handling the gravel road sections of this tour.

Mountain bikes are solid workhorses, with good load carrying capabilities, and a wide range of gearing. The smaller frame geometry of these bikes results in a

different riding position compared to road bikes, which some riders do not find suitable for long rides. Others like the lower centre of gravity and stability of mountain bikes. Mountain bikes have smaller diameter wheels compared to road bikes and fatter tyres that cannot be pumped to the same pressures (making them slightly less efficient, but great on gravel roads). Cyclists who use mountain bikes for touring mainly on sealed roads often replace the

Hard-tail Mountain Bike

knobbly off-road tyres with slick tyres, or tyres with a smooth central strip. The suspension forks and rear-end suspension systems found on many mountain bikes do not offer any significant advantages for long road trips. However, with a mountain bike you do have the option of taking days off along the way, unloading your gear, and exploring the backcountry.

Hybrid bikes are a cross between road bikes and mountain bikes, with 700c wheels, wide tyres, and a reasonably large frame akin to road bikes, but handlebars and componentry similar to mountain bikes. Some riders find this riding position works well.

Another type of bike, which has recently become popular and works well for extended touring, is the

Hybrid bike

cyclocross bike. These are similar to touring machines but beefier, although high-end bikes may not have triple chain-rings, and tyres appropriate for touring would be needed.

Whatever type of bike you take, it should be the right frame size for you, have suitable load carrying capacity, and be reasonably lightweight with quality components.

Small adjustments to the height and position of the handlebars and saddle make big differences to the mechanics of cycling. With a well fitting bike, and some fine-tuning of bars and seat, you should be able to find a comfortable touring position. Toe clips, or better still, clip-in pedals and touring shoes, greatly increase cycling efficiency. [A note on technique here; aim to cycle in a

Cyclocross bike

steady rhythm, avoiding bouts of extreme exertion, by using low gears at higher rpm on hills rather than grinding away slowly in a high gear].

High quality aluminium or chrome-moly touring racks are essential, as a rack failure can seriously stall a tour. Panniers (saddlebags) should attach securely and not lean out excessively when cornering. A handle-bar bag is great for often used items. Use plastic bags to line your bags if they are not 100% waterproof. In NZ, quality bike touring equipment such as racks, panniers and bar bags is available under the brand name Phillips (a Christchurch based Co.), from various bike shops around the country.

Carrying two frame-mounted water bottles works well. Some tourers like to wear hydration back-packs, although your back gets hot wearing one in warm weather.

Mudguards (fenders) are great on rainy days, and rain is likely on this tour, however, with a good set of rain gear you can do without these.

A digital cycle computer that includes daily and total distance functions is a great tool to have, allowing you to estimate times and distances to turn-offs, intermediate

1839 J.C. Bidwell defies a Maori tapu and becomes the first European to climb Mt Ngauruhoe

stops, and the end of each stage. These usually include a sensor on some part of the frame and a small magnet that attaches to a wheel, registering each wheel rotation. The computer should be set for the exact tyre circumference of your loaded bike, with you on it (this can be done with the help of someone measuring the distance it takes for one revolution of the wheel with the magnet on).

Some tourers like to use a GPS (Global Positioning System) unit to provide accurate data on distances to and from waypoints, although this is certainly not a necessity and should not replace a map. The GPS co-ordinates used in this guide are described on p.38.

In New Zealand, bicycles are legally required to have lights for night riding (see p.33). Flashing LCD lights are good in gloomy or low light conditions, even if it is not dark, so drivers can see you better. Touring after dark is not recommended.

Clothing and Equipment

Because New Zealand's weather is so variable you will need clothes suitable for hot, sunny conditions, as well as cold, wet and windy conditions - you'll probably end up wearing both some days.

New Zealand farmers have historically worn a uniform of shorts, black singlet, Swandri® (wool jacket), and Redband® gumboots - adding a raincoat as needed - a combination that can be varied for the conditions and has historically served them well. For cycling in New Zealand this layering principal is worth following too.

Start with a good quality raincoat as your most important item of clothing, for cool morning riding and wet and windy conditions. It should be waterproof, seam-sealed, made of a breathable fabric, and have a stowable hood. A mid-weight fleece top to provide warmth is your second most important piece of clothing. With a good raincoat and a warm top you should be able to survive a cold, wet, night in most places in New Zealand. Lightweight rain pants are a good idea, although some riders take the chance and do without them for summer touring.

Polypropylene (thermal) underwear - longs and a top - are important, allowing you to dress in layers and control your temperature (be particularly aware of getting chilled when you stop riding on cold days). You may want a lightweight pair of fleece pants for nights, cooler days, and keeping sandflies off your legs at night. For warm weather riding, bike shorts and a bike shirt (or T-shirt) are generally sufficient. Bright coloured clothing is recommended to increase your visibility to other road users. A reflectorised sash, even for day use, is a good idea. New Zealand has a mandatory cycle helmet law that requires road cyclists to wear approved helmets, with potential fines for riders who don't. Despite debate on the introduction of this law it is now widely accepted.

Cycling gloves protect your hands by spreading the pressure on nerves and help somewhat in a fall. Wrap-around sunglasses provide protection from wind and dust (some high-end glasses include interchangeable lenses for use on overcast days).

Lightweight, waterproof, overgloves and shoe covers are luxuries for cycling in the rain, but you can do without them - some cyclists put plastic bags over their socks before putting their shoes on for riding in the wet.

If you plan on camping, take a lightweight, good quality tent. You could also consider taking the tent fly, poles, and a plastic ground sheet rather than the full tent, in order to save weight (remember the insect repellent with this option). [Note: never cook inside a sealed tent - this has resulted in deaths from CO poisoning].

A down sleeping bag, and ¾-length Thermarest® or closed-cell foam pad for ground insulation, are ideal. Modern synthetic bags (with compression stuff sacs) also work OK.

The suggested basic gear list on p.30 should be able to be packed into rear panniers, on the top of a rear rack, and in a handlebar bag.

1839 In London, Richard Owen, a Professor of Comparative Anatomy, is shown a bone fragment that leads him to conclude the world's biggest bird, the moa, once lived in NZ

BASIC GEAR LIST

BIKE
Bike with rack(s).. ☐
Panniers and handlebar bag... ☐
Water bottles and cages.. ☐
Cycle computer... ☐
Flashing LCD red rear light and white front light, reflectors.............. ☐

CLOTHING
Raincoat... ☐
Mid-weight polarfleece top.. ☐
Polypropylene underwear (longs and top), hat, and gloves................... ☐
2 T-shirts or cycle tops... ☐
1 Pair of lightweight shorts.. ☐
1 or 2 Pairs of cotton socks.. ☐
1 or 2 Pairs of underwear.. ☐
1 Pair of lightweight longs... ☐
1 or 2 Pairs of cycle shorts... ☐
Cycle gloves... ☐
1 Pair of shoes.. ☐
Sunglasses... ☐
Reflector sash... ☐
Bicycle helmet.. ☐
Rain pants (with elastic cuffs or clip for right leg)........................... ☐

CAMPING
Tent (or tent fly, poles, and ground sheet)...................................... ☐
Sleeping bag and ground insulation mat.. ☐
Small towel.. ☐
Small torch (flashlight) that can double as bike light......................... ☐
Plate and spoon... ☐

TOOLS
Pump, puncture repair kit, tyre levers.. ☐
Spare inner tube.. ☐
Tyre patch or spare tyre.. ☐
Spare spokes (including spokes for the rear cluster side) and spoke wrench... ☐
Cluster removing tool... ☐
Chain breaker and spare chain links... ☐
Spare brake and gear cables... ☐
Spare nuts and bolts (including rack bolts)....................................... ☐
Appropriate Allen keys, wrenches, pliers, screw drivers .... ☐
Zip ties, some duct tape, grease & lube, small rag.............................. ☐

MISCELLANEOUS
Bike lock... ☐
Pocket knife with can opener.. ☐
Small First-Aid kit, foil emergency sheet, sewing kit, matches and candle.... ☐
Plastic bags to wrap gear in wet weather... ☐
Camera with spare battery... ☐
Toiletries and medications (including sunscreen and insect repellent) .... ☐
Maps, small compass, personal documents.. ☐
Water purification tablets or filter... ☐

OPTIONAL EXTRAS
Waterproof overgloves and shoe covers.. ☐
Stove, fuel, billy (lightweight cook pot).. ☐
Rear view mirror... ☐
Additional bike parts and tools (e.g. bottom bracket tool and parts)........... ☐
Lightweight groundsheet and tent pegs to cover bike when camping.......... ☐
Hand-held or bar-mounted GPS... ☐

1839 The NZ Co. purchases 20 million acres from Wellington Maori for the first of its 4 NZ settlements, although a Crown check later indicates the sale is largely invalid

Fluids and Food

Drink plenty of fluid before, during, and after riding. Water thins the blood making it easier for the heart to pump, and water losses amounting to only a few percent of total body weight can drastically reduce athletic performance. Some long-distance tourers ride with one bottle of water and another with a sports drink like Gatorade® or Powerade®, switching between to two to keep electrolytes up.

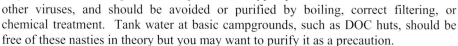

New Zealand's tap water is fine for drinking. Despite the country's clean, green image, water from streams, rivers, and lakes may have the Giardia parasite, the protozoan Cryptosporidium, or other viruses, and should be avoided or purified by boiling, correct filtering, or chemical treatment. Tank water at basic campgrounds, such as DOC huts, should be free of these nasties in theory but you may want to purify it as a precaution.

For most people the volume of food they eat increases while touring due to the rapid rate they are burning energy. Stopping every now and again for snacks (fruit or museli bars for example) and a drink, will help maintain energy levels throughout the day. You may want to avoid the sugar rush and subsequent lethargy that results from foods rich in simple sugars, such as chocolate bars and soft drinks (sodas).

Meal options while touring consist of buying lunches and dinners, carrying food to make your own meals (cooking on a camping stove, at hostels, or in self-catering accommodation), or a mix of both. Self-catering is the cheapest option, but involves carrying more weight. Either way, carry sufficient water and snacks for the day's ride. Backcountry Cuisine, a NZ company, manufactures lightweight, gourmet, freeze-dried meals that you simply add boiling water to in a foil pouch (producing fewer dishes).

Repairs

On a well-tuned good quality bike, carrying an appropriate load, you should have few mechanical problems. However, be prepared and familiar enough with your bike to fix everyday breakdowns, and if you have a major malfunction be able to make sufficient repairs to get to a bike shop. Basic breakdown repairs include fixing a flat tyre, rejoining the chain, and replacing broken spokes. The spare parts and tools you should carry, and know how to use, are in the suggested gear list on p.30.

Try to get lightweight multi-function tools to cut down on weight. If you are riding in a group you can split some of the tools between you (assuming the tools are compatible between bikes), but carry the basics yourself - including a pump and puncture repair kit. Also, before you start the tour check the glue in your puncture repair kit has not evaporated since it was last used, or take the newer peel-and-stick type patches.

Make sure spare spokes are the correct length for your bike and include spokes for the cluster side of the rear wheel, which are usually a different length. Know how the basics of how to tension spokes to true a wheel. Tools and parts for more complicated repairs are useful - if you know how to do major roadside repairs, although the likelihood of this type of malfunction will be minimised with a well-maintained, properly loaded, bike.

It pays to check over your bike each morning on the tour, in particular check tyre pressures, the bolts securing your racks, and the brakes. Once again, make sure your bike is in 100% working order before setting out and test ride it fully loaded before trying to ride the gravel road south from Cape Reinga.

1840 On February 6 in the Bay of Islands, Governor Hobson representing Queen Victoria, and numerous Maori chiefs, sign the Treaty of Waitangi - bringing NZ into the British Empire

31

ROADS AND THE ROAD CODE

Roads

New Zealand's roads are broadly classified as National State Highways, Provincial State Highways, and "other roads". In reality, National State Highways (single-digit route numbers) and Provincial State Highways (double-digit route numbers) can range from motorways in the major cities to remote gravel roads, so just looking at a map can be misleading in regard to the type of road to expect!

Some maps mark roads as main routes, secondary routes, and other routes. Main routes typically link major towns and cities, are sealed roads, and carry the most traffic. These roads vary from multiple lanes each way with a centre divider to, more commonly, one or two lanes each way with no centre divider. Cars travel fast on these roads. Secondary routes are actually quite similar to main routes but usually carry slightly less traffic and are rarely divided. In cities, sections of main routes (and some secondary routes) may become motorways and bikes are not allowed. "Other roads" usually link smaller towns or dead-end in out-of-the-way places. These roads can be sealed or gravel, but traffic still travels quite fast. Even these roads can get busy if their destination is a holiday spot, but more often than not they offer quiet riding.

Chip-seal Road

NZ roads are, in general, narrower than in most countries, possibly a remnant from the early days when it was difficult to push roads through the hilly terrain. However, there is usually some sort of marked shoulder on the left edge of the roadway that provides enough room to ride comfortably on (see the road shots throughout this guide for an idea of the types of road you will be riding). Roads with little shoulder are more likely to be roads classed as "other routes". Stay as far to the left as practical when traffic passes.

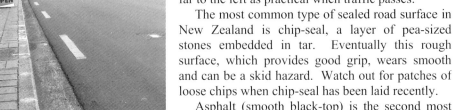

Asphalt Road

The most common type of sealed road surface in New Zealand is chip-seal, a layer of pea-sized stones embedded in tar. Eventually this rough surface, which provides good grip, wears smooth and can be a skid hazard. Watch out for patches of loose chips when chip-seal has been laid recently.

Asphalt (smooth black-top) is the second most common road surface, often used on city streets, high-use roads, and high-wear curves due to its longevity. This surface can be especially slippery for cyclists when wet.

Gravel roads usually consist of gravel, a few centimetres in diameter, which is periodically placed on a dirt base and smoothed out by a grader with a blade. Riding this loose gravel on a loaded touring bike requires concentration. After cars have driven gravel roads repeatedly the gravel tends to get pushed into the sub-grade and several smoother tracks form giving riders some relief - until Transit NZ or the local council re-grades the surface. Ride slower on gravel, particularly going downhill and into corners. Also watch for; potholes, patches of loose gravel (especially if the road has been re-graded recently), and the closely spaced washboard bumps that sometimes form on these roads. In summer, riding on gravel roads with traffic can be a dusty affair.

Gravel Road

1841 John Logan Campbell builds Acacia Cottage, now the oldest surviving building in Auckland. It is later moved to Cornwall Park

The Road Code
The Official New Zealand Road Code, published by the Land Transport Safety Authority, contains rules for car, truck, motorcycle, and bicycle users. Copies can be obtained from bookstores and driver licensing agencies. The road rules are also available on the Internet (www.ltsa.govt.nz/roadcode). Visitors should read these rules prior to riding on New Zealand roads.

Briefly, traffic drives on the **left** so remember to **look right first** when coming to intersections or stepping out onto the road. It is worth consulting the Road Code for the most up-to-date set of road rules, as they sometimes change. Basic rules include;

- At Stop and Give Way signs you give way to everyone
- If you are going straight, give way to vehicles going straight on your right
- If you are turning, give way to all vehicles not turning
- If you are turning left, give way to vehicles coming towards you that are turning right
- If you are turning right, give way to vehicles on your right that are turning right

Despite these rules, cyclists are vulnerable and even with the right of way should remember some motorists may not see cyclists, or may decide they have priority regardless. You can always dismount and walk across intersections if you feel unsafe.

By law cyclists in New Zealand must wear an approved safety helmet. For cycling at night (not recommended for touring) bikes must have a white, yellow, or orange front light, a red rear light, a red or yellow rear reflector, and reflectors on the pedals or the riders lower legs. Lights must be on from 30 minutes after sunset until 30 minutes before sunrise, and be visible from at least 100m.

Other regulations include having your bicycle in good working condition, using a cycle lane if present, and using hand signals at least 3 seconds before stopping or turning (consult the Road Code for details). You are not allowed to cycle on the footpath (sidewalk). For more information on cycling in traffic see the following section on hazards.

All speed and distance signs in New Zealand are in kilometres. For motorists, speed limits are typically 50km/hour in town, and 70, 80, or up to 100km/hour on open roads, as signposted. The open road sign is a black slash on a round white background. Wearing seatbelts in automobiles is compulsory in the front and rear, and New Zealand has strict drink-driving rules. Traffic accidents involving damage or injury must be reported to the Police as soon as possible.

HAZARDS

The weather and other road users are two of the biggest hazards for cycle tourists in New Zealand. As mentioned earlier, be prepared for heat and a beating sun (New Zealand has very high skin cancer rates), as well as cold, wet, and windy conditions, and everything in between. During winter it snows on the inland, high-elevation, sections of this tour from the middle of the North Island south.

In hot weather wear loose light clothing, apply sunscreen, eat snacks and drink water frequently to avoid dehydration (starting early in the day and before you feel thirsty). Avoid extreme exertion and take breaks as necessary. When it's cold, wet, or windy be aware of the potential for hypothermia (a drop in the body's core temperature). Initial symptoms include shivering, slurred speech, irrational or lethargic behaviour, and a loss of dexterity, although if you are going solo these can be harder to

1842 In Auckland, Ligar Canal is constructed, turning the stream running down Queen St into a drain named after the Surveyor General

33

recognise in yourself. To protect against this, dress in layers to stay warm and dry, eat and drink regularly, and don't ride if you are completely tired out. Cyclists can be particularly susceptible to hypothermia when they stop for a rest, or breakdown, as the body can cool quickly. If you get very cold or soaked through, get out of the wind and rain, into warm dry clothes, and have hot drinks - stopping early for the day can be a pleasant break sometimes. Know the symptoms and treatment for heat exhaustion and hypothermia before setting out.

A letter from S. Blume of Illinois, to the editor of *The New Zealand Herald*, while touring New Zealand in 1999, reads…

> *After six weeks and 1,600 kilometres, I have decided to abandon my cycle tour of New Zealand, I value my life too much. I've been run off the roads twice and suffered near misses every day. I don't think drivers learn to drive professionally, rather they are taught by friends or family (while passing a beer back and forth?)….*

A little exaggerated perhaps, but, as in any country, other road users are a significant hazard for cyclists. New Zealand's older roads are often narrow by Western standards - partly due to the tough terrain many roads have to traverse - so cars, heavy vehicles, and cyclists have little room to share. Add the occasional driver clasping a cellphone to their ear and basically you need to be careful.

In city traffic, watch for car doors opening and drivers not anticipating bicycles. When approaching intersections watch for vehicles turning in front of you into, or out of, side roads and do not ride on the inside of vehicles about to turn left (pay particular attention to long vehicles with wide turning circles and poor visibility). When turning right, check it is safe to move to the centre of the road. If it is, move over, and wait for a gap in the oncoming traffic to make the turn. Making eye contact with drivers helps, and using hand signals will make your intentions clearer. At busy intersections it may be safer to dismount and use a pedestrian crossing if you feel unsafe. Be especially careful at roundabouts where drivers are often intent on entering or exiting the roundabout and may not see cyclists.

On open roads stay as far left as practical and expect cars passing by fairly close on your right. Trucks and buses passing at speed can create a draught that requires a firm grip of the handlebars to resist. Also, watch out for logging trucks (more common in the North Island). These often tow trailers that have a set of stabilising wheels on the back of the rear trailer that can sway across the road when the truck overtakes. [The owner of the Takapuna Beach Caravan Park in Auckland hosted a group of Canadian cyclists who had had a run in with a logging truck that sent 4 of them to hospital]. New regulations for logging truck loads have recently come into effect that aim at improving the stability and handling of these vehicles.

On winding roads be especially careful riding around blind left-hand corners, where cars from behind may not see you until they come around the bend hugging the shoulder. Consider pulling off to the side in these types of situations or walking to the other side of the road and walking your bike around the corner. In a nutshell, don't assume drivers will always see you.

In 1999, Transit New Zealand (the body that maintains many New Zealand roads) announced it would stop using a new thermoplastic road marking paint, which it had used for several years on high-traffic roads, as it did not meet skid-resistance specifications. This paint, which was installed molten and stood several millimetres above the road, was linked to the death of a Wellington cyclist who slipped on it and fell into the path of a car. Be on guard for this "plastic paint" which may still be around and, as usual, be careful of normal paint markings which can be slippery when wet.

Most drivers are courteous towards cyclists, a tiny fraction, for whatever reason, are not - these are the ones who honk, drive dangerously, or yell "Hey!" as they drive past. The best policy is to ignore these people, or report them to the Police if they behave dangerously. Recently, a Swiss couple on a bicycle tour had a bottle thrown at them from a passing car, injuring the woman's leg. A youth was arrested and charged for the incident but it  was the end of these cyclists' tour. Thankfully such incidents are the exception and most visitors come back from New Zealand saying how friendly the locals were.

Other hazards include biters and stingers such as bees, wasps (an increasing problem in recent years), mosquitoes, and sandflies. Sandflies (midges) can be bothersome at some campsites. Insect repellent and light coloured clothing with long sleeves will help (some people even don insect-mesh headgear to avoid bugs).

To some dogs a cyclist is something to be chased and snapped at, but this is rare. More of a worry in New Zealand are magpies - black, or black and white, crows - that vigorously defend their territory during breeding season (August to November) by swooping down from behind and flapping around the heads of cyclists reminiscent of scenes from a Hitchcock movie. The distraction can be enough to cause riders to swerve and/or crash, however, these birds do back off once you are outside their territory. Some cyclists report painting two eyes on the back of their helmets helps avoid these attacks.

As anywhere, be conscious of your personal security. A money belt for valuables is a good idea. Don't leaving panniers unattended and lock your bike when leaving it. Tourist Information Centres, or chatting to local policemen, will tell you about unsafe areas to avoid. Having said that, New Zealand is a country where the Police on the street don't carry firearms and most gas stations let you pump petrol before paying.

These hazards aside, riding along a quiet road with the sun shining and a symphony of cicadas in the background, New Zealand can feel like the ultimate cycling destination.

MAPS

Land Information New Zealand (LINZ) is the nation's survey and mapping agency. They produce detailed topographic maps at several scales, available from bookstores, outdoor equipment shops, and internet retailers. Their 260 Series covers the country at 1:50,000 (1cm = 500m, 20m contour interval, 40km x 30km sheets), on several hundred maps, and provides an excellent level of detail (these are the maps trampers typically use) - although a set covering this route would be expensive, heavy to carry, and their size make them cumbersome to use on a bike. If you do want this level of detail you could copy portions of the maps, as needed, and post packages ahead for pick up via Post Restante (see p.23). LINZ also sells a complete, seamless, set of 260 Series maps on CD, called NZTopo. The same maps can be viewed using NZTopo*Online* at LINZ's web-site (www.linz.govt.nz).

LINZ's 262 Series consists of 18 topographic maps covering the country at a scale of 1:250,000 (1cm = 2.5km, 100m contour interval), and these maps have a good level of detail for cycle touring and trip planning.

For this tour, the elevation profiles in the guide show the general trend of the terrain between Cape Reinga and Bluff, so unless you are looking for detailed topo consider using this guide supplemented with touring maps for motorists (widely available from bookstores and motoring organisations) that give good regional perspective and often include tourist information.

BICYCLE ORGANISATIONS AND CLUBS

BikeNZ is a national umbrella organisation encompassing road racing and mountain bike clubs, and cycle advocacy groups in New Zealand. Their web-site has competition dates, results, cycling news, and links to bike clubs (*www.bikenz.org.nz*). Of more use to touring cyclists is the NZ Mountain Biking website (*www.mountainbike.co.nz*), which has a touring bulletin board that includes daily postings from cyclists related to bicycle touring in NZ. They also have a list of bike clubs (road, mountain, and touring). Cycle Action Auckland (an advocacy group) runs fun group rides, on the last Sunday of each month, which generally stick to quieter city roads (*http:\\users.actrix.co.nz\can*).

TRAINING

For reasonably fit riders it is possible to head off without much training, suffer for a few days until your body gets in the groove, and still enjoy this tour, however, for the majority, New Zealand is a topographic country and some training will be a big benefit.

If you are new to cycle touring, doing several short overnight tours will allow you to get the feel for handling a bike loaded with panniers, fine tune your riding position, and assess which items are essential and which might be left behind. Since the first stage of this tour involves riding on hilly, gravel, roads it is important to feel confident on your bike rather than wobbling off from Cape Reinga fully laden for the first time.

In terms of fitness training, plan to build up to a level where you feel comfortable spending a good number of hours in the saddle (with rest stops, of course) and have a weekly mileage over 100km. Include at least a couple of day-rides to the maximum distance you plan on riding in a day during the tour.

AUCKLAND AIRPORT TO DOWNTOWN

As mentioned earlier, roads from the airport into downtown Auckland can be busy and the suburbs the route passes through in the south are not the safest at night, so are not recommended for solo cyclists or tourists arriving late. See p.16 for other options.

A map showing several possible bike routes into downtown is on p.185. The black highlighted route on this map passes One Tree Hill Domain and is a good route if you want to make a short detour to the top of the hill and take in fabulous views over Auckland. From the International Terminal take Tom Pearce Dr to George Bolt Memorial Dr (a huge New Zealand flag flies on a flagpole at this intersection). 4km

from the terminal turn left onto Kirkbride Rd. About 1km along Kirkbride Rd veer right onto McKenzie Rd and continue onto Coronation Rd. Coronation Rd passes through Mangere Bridge town centre and continues on to the waterfront. Continue straight ahead across the old Mangere Bridge (now a foot bridge and cycle path) which takes you across the Manukau Harbour just west of the new motorway bridge. At the northern end of the bridge turn right under the motorway bridge, onto Onehunga Harbour Rd, which curves around and becomes Onehunga Mall heading north. Go left on Neilson St, right on Selwyn Street, and left on Mt Smart Rd. At the Royal Oak roundabout exit Mt Smart Rd onto Manukau Rd heading north. About 500m up Manukau Rd is the entrance to One Tree Hill Domain.

1845 Captain, later Sir, George Grey becomes the third Governor of NZ after stints in Australia and South Africa. He restores order in Kororareka (Russell)

Roads lead around, and up, the cone and you can either return to this entrance, or ride through the Domain and Cornwall Park (on the north side of the volcano) exiting onto Green Lane Rd West and turning left to return to Manukau Rd. One Tree Hill's obelisk, a monument to Maori, is visible from many places in the City, including the ride in from the airport. This is the third highest of Auckland's extinct basalt volcanoes and was once a huge Maori pa (fort) - as evidenced by the extensive terracing on its slopes. Unfortunately, a pine tree that crowned the summit until recently was fatally attacked with a chainsaw in a political protest, and has since been removed.

Manukau Rd becomes Broadway after passing under the Southern Motorway just before Newmarket. Continue through Newmarket and turn left onto Khyber Pass Rd, then right onto Park Rd, which passes the gates to the Auckland Domain and Museum. Park Rd swings left past Auckland City Hospital and becomes Grafton Bridge. Cross the bridge and continue straight, onto Karangahape Rd, briefly before turning right down Queen St into the centre of the City and the waterfront. Cyclists are not allowed on Motorways or across the Harbour Bridge.

GETTING TO CAPE REINGA

Cape Reinga is quite a remote place and most options for getting there involve getting to Kaitaia (the nearest large town), or the Bay of Islands, first. From there, you can ride north or arrange with one of the tour bus companies that take trips to the Cape to drop you off. You can fly, take a coach (bus), or do a one-way car rental to get to Kaitaia, or Paihia in the Bay of Islands. The cheapest option will probably be a coach.

Tour buses for Cape Reinga depart daily from Kaitaia and the Bay of Islands. There are numerous operators, including; Harrisons Cape Runner (Kaitaia, Ph 09 408 1033), Sand Safaris (Kaitaia, Ph 09 408 1778), Tall Tale Travel (Kaitaia, Ph 09 408 0870), Fullers (Paihia, Ph 09 402 7421), Kings (Paihia, Ph 09 402 8288), Northern Exposure (Paihia, Ph 09 402 8644), etc. Choose one that will take bikes, either in a trailer or the luggage compartment underneath the bus. Be prepared for your gear to get dusty on the gravel roads up to the Cape. Some of these bus tours include driving on the hard sand of Ninety Mile Beach and connecting with State Highway 1 via Te Paki Stream, 17km south of Cape Reinga. [Note: The Te Paki Stream track has water crossings and patches of quicksand, and is not suitable for unguided tourists].

If you want to ride to the Cape, follow the directions for the Cape Reinga to Kaitaia stage (p.42) in reverse. Expect a 2-day ride, with the last 21km on a rough gravel road.

GETTING BACK FROM BLUFF

If you are not taking the ferry from Bluff to Stewart Island, and your cycle tour is over, you will need to head back to Invercargill - where air, bus, and rental car services are available for onward travel. Options include, riding the 30km back to Invercargill or arranging transport for you and your bike with one of the local minibus operators such as Blue Star Taxis (Ph 03 218 6079), Spitfire Shuttle (Ph 03 214 1851), or Lynette Jack Scenic Tours (Ph 025 338 370).

From Invercargill, you can fly to the main centres. Alternatively, you can take a bus to Dunedin and connect with other transport options, including train services north and several flights a day to Auckland. A car (preferably a station wagon if you have bikes) or camper van rental is another option for heading north. If you are going to Dunedin, the Southern Scenic Route touches the coast several times and passes through the Catlins Forest Park, a remote part of New Zealand with outstanding natural beauty.

Distance from the start of the stage to a particular destination, including the facilities at that location*:

c = camping
h = hostel or backpackers
b&b = bed and breakfast
m/h = motel and/or hotel
i = information centre
bike shop = bicycle shop

* Note these details can change so check ahead if necessary.

For GPS users, co-ordinates to the right are rough latitude/longitudes for these areas in the NZGD84/2000 datum, which is equivalent to the WGS 84 (World Grid) datum supported by most GPS units).

A description of the stage.
This section often includes general comments on the hillyness of the stage; ranging from flat through gently rolling, rolling, and hilly (see p.27 for details).

This section typically includes more in-depth information on New Zealand history or culture, and often relates to something on that particular stage.

A timeline of various dates in New Zealand's history.

---

1 CAPE REINGA TO HOUHORA HEADS

Cape Reinga to;			
Waitiki Landing	21km	c, h	34 31.6, 172 40.7
Te Kao	45km	b&b	34 39.3, 172 58.3
Houhora	69km	c, b&b, m/h	34 47.8, 173 04.4
Houhora Heads	77km	c, h	34 49.3, 173 08.9

If asked, most New Zealanders would probably say Cape Reinga is the top of the North Island, but the northern tip is actually Surville Cliffs near North Cape, 34km to the east and slightly more to the north (the area is an ecological reserve and a permit from the Department of Conservation (DOC) is needed to visit). Despite this geographical technicality, Cape Reinga has traditionally been a special place for both Maori and Pakeha (Europeans). It is definitely a dramatic location - a steep ridge jutting out to where the Tasman Sea meets the Pacific Ocean; a patch of sea marked by swirling water and waves, as swells travelling from opposite directions crash into each other.

According to Maori mythology Reinga is the "Place of leaping", where the spirits of the deceased slip into the underworld, at a sacred old Pohutukawa tree at the foot of the Cape, to start their journey back to the homeland of Hawaiiki.

The lighthouse here is the most visited in New Zealand, with over 100,000 people making the trip each year. Cape Reinga is also the start of State Highway 1, a route that runs to Bluff at the southern tip of the South Island, and a road this tour takes a number of times.

The only services at the Cape are a tiny shop that doubles as a souvenir and snack shop.

Heading south from the Cape, State Highway 1 is gravel for slightly over 20km, to Waitiki Landing. In the middle of summer this can be a hot and dusty ride - even the trees are coated with dust from passing cars. By early afternoon traffic tends to increase as visitors arrive from the south by tour bus and car. Even without the heat and the traffic the road is a tough one to ride, with steeply cambered corners, corrugations, and patches of loose gravel, so ride carefully - especially going downhill on a loaded bike. If you want to stay near Cape Reinga and miss some of the afternoon traffic take Tapotupotu Road to the left, 3km south of Cape. A steep 2km ride takes you down to a basic campground at beautiful Tapotupotu Bay.

There are a couple of long hill climbs on the gravel section to Waitiki Landing, as the road traverses scrub covered ridges and swampy valleys. 17km from Cape Reinga is the Te Paki Stream turn off. The streambed here is shallow, despite patches of quicksand, was used up until a few years ago to provide public vehicle access to and from Ninety Mile Beach. The track is now limited to commercial tour operators who drive buses on the hard-packed sand of Ninety Mile Beach as part of their Cape Reinga trips.

The first stop of significance after the Cape is Waitiki Landing, which has a campground with cabins, a store and Post Office. After Waitiki you lose the crunch of gravel under your tyres and the sealed route passes through farmland, following the western edge of Parengarenga Harbour. Out to the east, on the sandspit across the harbour, are dazzlingly white dunes of almost pure silica sand where godwits

42

---

congregate before their annual migration to Siberia. At the southern end of the harbour is Te Kao - a small settlement with a school, store, and lodge accommodation.

South of Te Kao the road is rolling, with some pleasantly flat sections. Roadside stalls with honesty boxes along this section sometimes sell rock melons and fruit - good places to stop for a break. 57km from Cape Reinga is Rarawa Beach Road, where there is a DOC campground at the end of a 4km gravel road. Past Ngataki, is the turn-off to Henderson Bay, a good surf beach with backpacker accommodation.

At Waihopo the road reaches the northern end of Houhora Harbour and the passes through the settlements of Houhora, Pukenui, and Rano in rapid succession, before the turn off to Houhora Heads. The Heads are opposite Mount Camel - the distinctive headland at the entrance to the harbour.

Houhora Heads makes an interesting stop. The Subritzky homestead here was the first one to be built on the Aupouri Peninsula, back in 1860, when access was via the sea only. The Wagner Museum next door was the largest private historical collection in the South Pacific, before it closed a few years ago and the contents were dispersed. The museum had Maori artefacts, gum-digging gear, everything an early settler in Northland would use or collect. One curious item was a mollusc-encrusted plank from the Boyd, a ship that was attacked and sunk by Maori in Whangaroa Harbour (southeast of Doubtless Bay) in 1809. The attack was apparently retaliation for the flogging of a Maori chief, and resulted in the crew and passengers, apart from 1 woman and 3 children, being killed and in some cases cannibalised. Three months later a group of whaling ships arrived and killed about 60 Maori thought to be responsible for the murders. The 4 Boyd survivors were rescued and taken to Australia. This unfortunate incident was widely publicised and resulted in Europeans generally avoiding the Far North for the next 10 years.

There is a pleasant campground at Houhora Heads, on the waters edge, near the old homestead. If you don't feel like riding the 2km detour from State Highway 1 to Houhora Heads, there is accommodation near the intersection of SH1 and Houhora Heads Rd, at the Houhora Chalets Motor Lodge, and a good range of services and accommodation at Pukenui, 3km before this intersection.

Maui, The Fisherman

According to Maori myth, Maui, who lived in the ancestral homeland of Hawaiiki and was less than a god but more than a man, went fishing one day with his older brothers. After telling them to go further out - a lot further out than they had ever been before - they started to fish.

His brothers were amazed that after only a few casts their canoe was full of fish. Then Maui took out his hook. He had fashioned it from the jawbone of his grandmother and used his own blood as bait. His cast went deeper than his brothers' did and after a momentous struggle the peak of a roof appeared. Maui had hooked a house, and as he continued pulling land appeared beneath it and they could see he had caught a truly massive fish; "Te Ika-a-Maui" (the North Island). According to the myth, Maui's canoe was "Te Waka-o-Maui" (the South Island), and its anchor "Te Punga-o-Maui" (Stewart Island).

Maui told his brothers to wait while he went to make an offering to the gods for his catch, but while he was gone they started cutting up the great fish, which in turn thrashed around

44

1850 Edward Eyre (in Australia, a heroic explorer and colleague of George Grey) is appointed Lieutenant-Governor in NZ. Eyre makes the first European ascent of Mt Tapuaenuku (Inland Kaikouras) but is fired after falling out with Gov. Grey

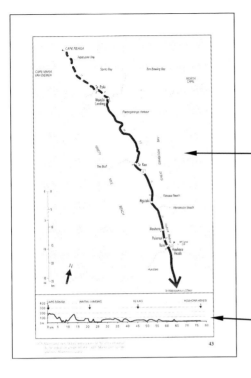

A strip map for the stage. The route is shown as a black line.

The thickest map lines are Motorways (bicycles not permitted). Progressively thinner lines show National State Highways (single digit routes, shown on these strip maps in large shields), Provincial State Highways (double-digit routes), shown in smaller shields, and other roads. Gravel roads are dashed, although their length can vary as new sections are sealed and ill-maintained sections become pot-holed and gravelly again.

Progressively larger circles show small settlements, towns, large towns, and cities. Major city areas are shaded. Some small settlements have no services.

Spot heights are in metres. Map distances are to the nearest km.

A profile for the stage. The y-axis scale is the same throughout the guide, the x-axis scale varies.

- the gashing and writhing producing deep gouges (valleys) and humps (mountains). The fish's head was "Te Upoko-o-te-ika-a-Maui" (Wellington) and it's tail "Te-Hiku-o-te-ika-a-Maui"(the Aupori Peninsula).

Maui went on to other heroic endeavours including capturing the sun in a net and clubbing it into submission to make the day longer, and stealing fire from the fire-god for his own use, before he was finally killed by Hine, goddess of death, while trying to obtain immortality.

Camping:
Tapotupotu Bay DOC Campsite, Tapotupotu Bay, Contact Department of Conservation, Ph 09 430 2907, T$9 ⊕ Waitiki Landing Campground and Cabins, Waitiki Landing, Ph 09 409 7508 ⊕ Rarawa Beach DOC Campsite, Rarawa Beach, Contact Department of Conservation, Ph 09 430 2007, T$9 ⊕ Pukenui Holiday Park, Lamb Rd, Pukenui, Ph 09 409 8803, T$9, Bunk $13, Cabin $30 ⊕ Wagner Holiday Park, Houhora Heads Rd, Houhora Heads, Ph 09 409 8564, T$9, Cabin $35

Hostel:
Northwind Lodge Backpackers, Henderson Beach, Ph 409 8515, S$20 ⊕ Pukenui Farm Backpackers, Lambs Rd, Pukenui, Ph 09 409 7863, S$15, D$34 ⊕ Pukenui Lodge Historic Hostel, Cnr SH1 & Wharf Rd, Houhora, Ph 09 409 8837, S$20 ⊕ Houhora Heaven Backpackers Hostel, Houhora Heads Rd, Houhora Heads, Ph 09 409 8564, S$20 ⊕ Others: See Waitiki Landing Campground, Pukenui Lodge Motel

B&B:
Te Kao Lodge, Te Kao, Ph 09 409 7881 ⊕ The Roach House, Pukenui, Ph 409 8824, D$70 ⊕ Deepwater Lodge, Pukenui, Ph 409 8573, D$100

Motel/Hotel:
Pukenui Lodge Motel and Youth Hostel, Cnr SH 1 & Wharf Rd, Houhora, Ph 09 409 8837, D$90, Dorm$18, D$23 ⊕ Houhora Chalets Motor Lodge, Cnr SH1 & Houhora Heads Rd, Houhora, Ph 09 409 8860, D$85

i:
Far North Information Centre, Jaycee Park, South Rd, Kaitaia, Ph 09 408 0879

A selection of accommodation along the route (see p.18). Addresses, phone numbers, and ball-park rates are included.

T = Tent
Dorm = Dormitory Bed
S = Single
D = Double

Note: rates are approximate - check when booking. Inclusion is not a recommendation. In small places check accomodation is still offered.

Also lists tourist information centres (i:) and bike shops.

6km: Cape Reinga

50km: Between Te Kao and Ngataki

Photos of the stage, taken every 50km, give an idea of the terrain on the tour. The accumulated distance for these photos includes the minor detours required to ride to and from accommodation and nearby shops.

1852 An attempt to colonise the sub-Antarctic Auckland Is. (450km south of Stewart Is.) is abandoned after 3 tough years

39

1852 A Constitution Act is enacted, moving most of the decision making from an appointed Governor to an elected House of Representatives

THE JOURNEY

1852 A large totara tree atop One Tree Hill in Auckland is cut down. Several pine trees are later planted

41

1 CAPE REINGA TO HOUHORA HEADS

Cape Reinga to;			34 25.6, 172 40.7
Waitiki Landing	21km	c, h	34 31.1, 172 50.4
Te Kao	45km	b&b	34 39.2, 172 58.2
Houhora	69km	c, b&b, m/h	34 47.8, 173 06.4
Houhora Heads	77km	c, h	34 49.5, 173 08.9

If asked, most New Zealanders would probably say Cape Reinga is the top of the North Island, but the northern tip is actually Surville Cliffs near North Cape, 34km to the east and slightly more to the north (the area is an ecological reserve and a permit from the Department of Conservation (DOC) is needed to visit). Despite this geographical technicality, Cape Reinga has traditionally been a special place for both Maori and Pakeha (Europeans). It is definitely a dramatic location - a steep ridge jutting out to where the Tasman Sea meets the Pacific Ocean; a patch of sea marked by swirling water and waves, as swells travelling from opposite directions crash into each other.

According to Maori mythology Reinga is the "Place of leaping", where the spirits of the deceased slip into the underworld, at a sacred old Pohutukawa tree at the foot of the Cape, to start their journey back to the homeland of Hawaiiki.

The lighthouse here is the most visited in New Zealand, with over 100,000 people making the trip each year. Cape Reinga is also the start of State Highway 1, a route

that runs to Bluff at the southern tip of the South Island, and a road this tour takes a number of times.

The only services at the Cape are a tiny shop that doubles as a souvenir and snack shop.

Heading south from the Cape, State Highway 1 is gravel for slightly over 20km, to Waitiki Landing. In the middle of summer this can be a hot and dusty ride - even the trees are coated with dust from passing cars. By early afternoon traffic tends to increase as visitors arrive from the south by tour bus and car. Even without the heat and the traffic the road is a tough one to ride, with steeply cambered corners, corrugations, and patches of loose gravel, so ride carefully - especially going downhill on a loaded bike. If you want to stay near Cape Reinga and miss some of the afternoon traffic take Tapotupotu Road to the left, 3km south of Cape. A steep 2km ride

Cape Reinga Lighthouse

takes you down to a basic campground at beautiful Tapotupotu Bay.

There are a couple of long hill climbs on the gravel section to Waitiki Landing, as the road traverses scrub covered ridges and swampy valleys. 17km from Cape Reinga is the Te Paki Stream turn off. The streambed here is shallow and, despite patches of quicksand, was used up until a few years ago to provide public vehicle access to and from Ninety Mile Beach. The track is now limited to commercial tour operators who drive buses on the hard-packed sand of Ninety Mile Beach as part of their Cape Reinga trips.

The first stop of significance after the Cape is Waitiki Landing, which has a campground with cabins, a store and Post Office. After Waitiki you lose the crunch of gravel under your tyres and the sealed route passes through farmland, following the western edge of Parengarenga Harbour. Out to the east, on the sandspit across the harbour, are dazzlingly white dunes of almost pure silica sand where godwits

1855 Shepherd, James McKenzie, formerly of Ross-shire Scotland, is caught in South Canterbury driving 1,000 stolen sheep into a huge, previously unknown, High-Country basin

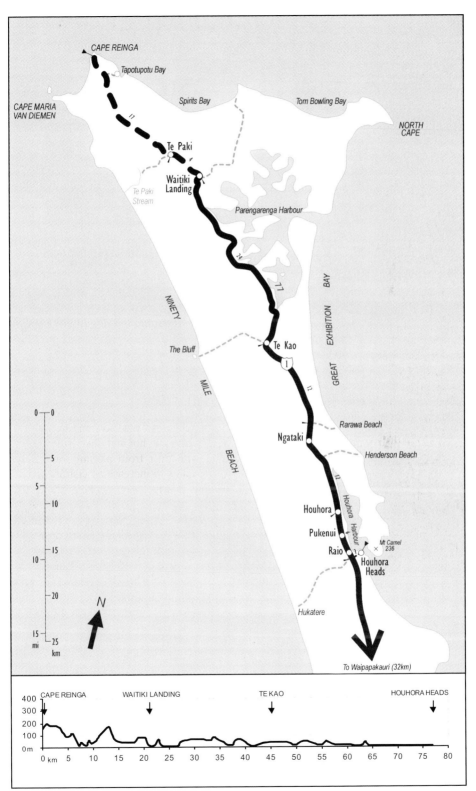

CAPE REINGA

Tapotupotu Bay

Spirits Bay

Tom Bowling Bay

CAPE MARIA
VAN DIEMEN

NORTH
CAPE

Te Paki

Waitiki
Landing

Te Paki
Stream

Parengarenga Harbour

NINETY

The Bluff

Te Kao

EXHIBITION

BAY

GREAT

Rarawa Beach

MILE

Ngataki

Henderson Beach

BEACH

Houhora

Houhora Harbour

Pukenui

Raio

Mt Camel
236

Houhora
Heads

Hukatere

N

To Waipapakauri (32km)

CAPE REINGA	WAITIKI LANDING	TE KAO	HOUHORA HEADS

400
300
200
100
0m

0 km 5   10   15   20   25   30   35   40   45   50   55   60   65   70   75   80

*1858 Maori and non-Maori populations in NZ are estimated
to be equal at about 60,000, with Maori decreasing
and non-Maori increasing*

43

congregate before their annual migration to Siberia. At the southern end of the harbour is Te Kao - a small settlement with a school, store, and lodge accommodation.

South of Te Kao the road is rolling, with some pleasantly flat sections. Roadside stalls with honesty boxes along this section sometimes sell rock melons and fruit - good places to stop for a break. 57km from Cape Reinga is Rarawa Beach Road, where there is a DOC campground at the end of a 4km gravel road. Past Ngataki, is the turn-off to Henderson Bay, a good surf beach with backpacker accommodation.

At Waihopo the road reaches the northern end of Houhora Harbour and the passes through the settlements of Houhora, Pukenui, and Raio in rapid succession, before the turn off to Houhora Heads. The Heads are opposite Mount Camel - the distinctive headland at the entrance to the harbour.

Houhora Heads makes an interesting stop. The Subritzky homestead here was the first one to be built on the Aupouri Peninsula, back in 1860, when access was via the sea only. The Wagner Museum next door was the largest private historical collection in the South Pacific, before it closed a few years ago and the contents were dispersed. The museum had Maori artefacts, gum-digging gear, and everything an early settler in Northland would use or collect. One curious item was a mollusc-encrusted plank from the *Boyd*, a ship that was attacked and sunk by Maori in Whangaroa Harbour (southeast of Doubtless Bay) in 1809. The attack was apparently retaliation for the flogging of a Maori chief, and resulted in the crew and passengers, apart from 1 woman and 3 children, being killed, and in some cases cannibalised. Three months later a group of whaling ships arrived and killed about 60 Maori thought to be responsible for the murders. The 4 *Boyd* survivors were rescued and taken to Australia. This unfortunate incident was widely publicised and resulted in Europeans generally avoiding the Far North for the next 10 years.

There is a pleasant campground at Houhora Heads, on the waters edge, near the old homestead. If you don't feel like riding the 2km detour from State Highway 1 to Houhora Heads, there is accommodation near the intersection of SH1 and Houhora Heads Rd, at the Houhora Chalets Motor Lodge, and a good range of services and accommodation at Pukenui, 3km before this intersection.

Maui, The Fisherman

According to Maori myth, Maui, who lived in the ancestral homeland of Hawaiiki and was less than a god but more than a man, went fishing one day with his older brothers. After telling them to go further out - a lot further out than they had ever been before - they started to fish.

His brothers were amazed that after only a few casts their canoe was full of fish. Then Maui took out his hook. He had fashioned it from the jawbone of his grandmother and used his own blood as bait. His cast went deeper than his brothers' did and after a momentous struggle the peak of a roof appeared. Maui had hooked a house, and as he continued pulling land appeared beneath it and they could see he had caught a truly massive fish; "Te Ika-a-Maui" (the North Island). According to the myth, Maui's canoe was "Te Waka-o-Maui" (the South Island), and its anchor "Te Punga-o-Maui" (Stewart Island).

Maui told his brothers to wait while he went to make an offering to the gods for his catch, but while he was gone they started cutting up the giant fish, which in turn thrashed around

1859 Austrian geologist Ferdinand von Hochstetter notes coal deposits in Huntly

- the gashing and writhing producing deep gouges (valleys) and humps (mountains). The fish's head was "Te Upoko-o-te-ika-a-Maui" (Wellington) and it's tail "Te-Hiku-o-te-ika-a-Maui"(the Aupori Peninsula).

Maui went on to other heroic endeavours including capturing the sun in a net and clubbing it into submission to make the day longer, and stealing fire from the fire-god for his own use, before he was finally killed by Hine, goddess of death, while trying to obtain immortality.

Camping;
Tapotupotu Bay DOC Campsite, Tapotupotu Bay, Contact: Department of Conservation, Ph 09 430 2007, T$9 ◆ Waitiki Landing Campground and Cabins, Waitiki Landing, Ph 09 409 7508 ◆ Rarawa Beach DOC Campsite, Rarawa Beach, Contact: Department of Conservation, Ph 09 430 2007, T$9 ◆ Pukenui Holiday Park, Lamb Rd, Pukenui, Ph 09 409 8803, T$9, Bunk $13, Cabin $30 ◆ Wagner Holiday Park, Houhora Heads Rd, Houhora Heads, Ph 09 409 8564, T$9, Cabin $35

Hostel;
Northwind Lodge Backpackers, Henderson Beach, Ph 409 8515, S$20 ◆ Pukenui Farm Backpackers, Lambs Rd, Pukenui, Ph 09 409 7863, S$15, D$34 ◆ Pukenui Lodge Historic Hostel, Cnr SH1 & Wharf Rd, Houhora, Ph 09 409 8837, S$20 ◆ Houhora Heaven Backpackers Hostel, Houhora Heads Rd, Houhora Heads, Ph 09 409 8564, S$20 ◆ Others; See Waitiki Landing Campground, Pukenui Lodge Motel

B&B;
Te Kao Lodge, Te Kao, Ph 09 409 7881 ◆ The Ranch House, Pukenui, Ph 409 8824, D$70 ◆ Deepwater Lodge, Pukenui, Ph 409 8573, D$100

Motel/Hotel;
Pukenui Lodge Motel and Youth Hostel, Cnr SH 1 & Wharf Rd, Houhora, Ph 09 409 8837, D$90, Dorm$18, D$23 ◆ Houhora Chalets Motor Lodge, Cnr SH1 & Houhora Heads Rd, Houhora, Ph 09 409 8860, D$85

i;
Far North Information Centre, Jaycee Park, South Rd, Kaitaia, Ph 09 408 0879

0 km Cape Reinga

50 km Between Te Kao and Ngataki

1859 The Pencarrow Lighthouse, on the Wellington side of Cook Strait, is NZ's first permanent lighthouse

2 HOUHORA HEADS TO KAITAIA

Houhora Heads to;

Waiharara	17km		*34 57.1, 173 11.2*
Waipapakauri	28km	b&b	*35 01.5, 173 13.7*
Awanui	33km	m/h	*35 02.9, 173 15.4*
Kaitaia	40km	c, h, m/h, i, bike shop	*35 06.6, 173 15.7*

This is a good stage if you are feeling sore after your first day's riding, and tackling the Far North's gravel roads, and are ready for a short day along flat to gently rolling roads. Alternatively, if you are feeling fit, you can combine this stage with the following one to reach Rawene in one long day (106km).

Leave Houhora Heads and ride the 2km back to the Houhora Heads Rd/State Highway 1 intersection (the distances given below are from this intersection). State Highway 1 continues down the Aupouri Peninsula with the huge Aupouri plantation forest off to the west, and swampy lowlands leading to the east coast on the other side. At 7km there is the tiny settlement of Motutangi, which has no services. 10km further on, next to Lake Waiparera, is the small settlement of Waiharara, which has a solitary butchery and store that has been around for over 70 years. The little Catholic church 1km before Waiharara has a monument to the many Dalmatian settlers that arrived in this area in the late 19th Century to dig for kauri gum. Local names include Martinovich, Brljevich, Unkovich, and Subritzky. The Far North's early pioneers had to be tough. Families lived in tents or makeshift huts while the men roamed the scrub and swamps for gum (see p.48) or eked out farms. The women, dressed in heavy Victorian dresses, maintained the family and - even in this colonial outpost - managed to starch collars white.

At Waipapakauri, which is Maori for "kauri in the swamp", a turn-off to the west provides vehicle access to the south end of Ninety Mile Beach, down a 7km road (there is a campground and a lodge, near Lake Ngatu, about halfway down the road). A marathon is run every year along this stunning beach, which is actually 56 miles (90km) long.

3km after Waipapakauri is the Ancient Kauri Kingdom factory, where swamp kauri is turned into furniture and wood products. With logging of living kauri strictly controlled, there is quite a market for this wood. The 30,000 to 50,000 year old buried logs are remarkably well preserved in the waterlogged local soils, and the gnarled stumps that are pulled out are worth thousands of dollars each for the volume of wood they contain.

Highway 10 from the Bay of Islands joins State Highway 1 at Awanui, 5km south of Waipapakauri, and the volume of traffic increases noticeably. Awanui, the first sizeable town after leaving Cape Reinga, has service stations, stores, and motels. The final 7km into Kaitaia is flat cycling. In the distance, past Kaitaia, you can see the Maungataniwha Ranges, a major climb on the next stage.

Kaitaia, with a population of about 5,000, is the commercial centre of the Far North and has a fairly good range of services. The town serves the local dairy farming, timber industries and, increasingly, the tourist trade. Commerce Street, the main drag, is a mix of locals going about their business, farmers stocking up, and tourists coming and going. The Far North Information Centre is at the south end of the main street in Jaycee Park.

In the 1830's the area around Kaitaia was hostile territory, with a number of warring tribes. The Reverend Joseph Matthews, who was interested in establishing a Christian mission north of the Bay of Islands, was scouting in the area in early 1830's when he

1860's Bicycles are imported and used in NZ for the first time

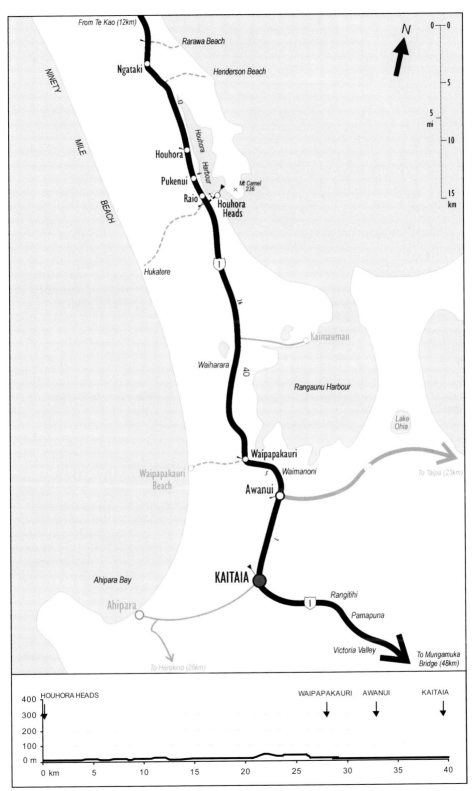

From Te Kao (12km)
Rarawa Beach
Ngataki
Henderson Beach

NINETY
MILE
BEACH

Houhora
Harbour

Houhora
Pukenui
Raio
Houhora
Heads
Mt Camel
236

Hukatere

Hukatere

1

Kaimaumau

Waiharara

40

Rangaunu Harbour

Lake
Ohia

Waipapakauri

To Taipa (23km)

Waipapakauri
Beach

Waimanoni

Awanui

KAITAIA

Rangitihi

Ahipara Bay

Pamapuna

Ahipara

1

To Herekino (26km)

Victoria Valley

To Mungamuka
Bridge (48km)

N

0 — 0

5

5
mi

10

15
km

HOUHORA HEADS
400
300
200
100
0 m

WAIPAPAKAURI AWANUI KAITAIA

0 km   5   10   15   20   25   30   35   40

1860   Elizabeth Pope reportedly starts a gold rush after
finding gold while washing her husband's shirt in the
Whakamarina River west of Picton

was captured by local Maori who planned to kill him. Their chief however, was impressed by Matthews' courage and faith, released him, and invited him to stay. Land for the Kaitaia Mission Station was purchased and the town was founded in 1837 (St Saviours, on Church Road, was built in 1840).

The Kauri Gumdiggers

The Aupouri Peninsula at the beginning of the 20th Century was a hive of activity. An eclectic bunch of prospectors, most equipped with 15 foot probing rods, could be found scouring the swamps and sandhills looking for kauri gum. In fact, the value of the kauri gum extracted by these "gumdiggers" in the Auckland Province, from the mid-19th Century to the start of the 20th Century, made gum the region's second most valuable export, behind timber. As a result, kauri made an enormous contribution to the development of the Auckland region in the pioneer days, until the trees and gum became scarce and exports of gold and farm produce became more economically important.

The reason kauri gum was so valuable was that it was a crucial ingredient in the production of varnish and linoleum, before the advent synthetic substitutes in the mid-1920's. In pre-European times Maori also valued kauri gum for tattooing, chewing (after soaking it in water and puha juice), and making torches.

Kauri gum washed up on a North Island beach

The gum was formed from sap seeping from the tree when it suffered an injury, such as a branch breaking, leaves being damaged, or bark ripping off. The sticky, sweet smelling resin would engulf the wound and harden in crystalline chunks that could reach several feet in diameter.

"Fossil gum" can be found anywhere kauri has grown in the past, either directly on the ground, or buried by subsequent soil deposition. "Tree gum" was also harvested early on, by climbing the huge trees and cutting notches at intervals up the trunk to bleed resin - a practice that often killed the tree and was eventually outlawed in 1905.

The open, sandy and swampy areas of the Aupouri Peninsula made it a prime digging target, along with areas on the western side of the Wairoa River and pockets of coastal and low-lying land from the Bay of Islands to Auckland. By the late 1910's the Far North was the centre of gumdigging activity, with extensive Crown gum reserves, and diggings around Spirits Bay, Parengarenga Harbour, the eastern side of the Peninsula from Te Kao to Houhora Harbour (where State Highway 1 now runs).

After the surface gum had been collected, diggers would use short spears to locate the shallow buried gum. When this gum became harder to find the probes got longer. In the early years of the 20th Century "The Joker" was devised to enable deeper probing. This was a coil of wire that fitted around the spear just behind the tip, causing a larger diameter hole to be formed when it was pushed, and allowing the probe to go deeper (up to 20 feet) but still maintain it's sensitivity to detect gum. In swamps, talented diggers could use a hook on the end of their spear to grab and pull the gum out.

The diggings were typically bleak places, with the surrounding manuka and scrub burnt off to gain access, piles of upturned soil, and the landscape dotted with

1860 Julius von Haast is appointed Provincial Geologist

gumdiggers temporary lean-to's, tents, and corrugated iron shacks. As gum became harder to find in the dug-over areas the diggers would move on. Like miners, these hard working men who worked the earth for a living had a reputation for drunken revelry. There was also tension with other settlers when diggers trespassed and left patches of land unusable, spotted with deep holes and piles of upturned earth.

The diggers working the Far North came from all walks of life and races, and included full-time diggers and part-timers who supplemented their incomes when other work was slow. One group that made a lasting impact on the industry were Dalmatian immigrants from the Adriatic coast. These hard working settlers often teamed up to drain swamps, allowing for the extraction of much more gum, which, in the opinion of individual diggers, lowered gum prices (the maximum price for gum reached about £60/ton around the turn of the century). By the 1890's, Dalmatians made up a large part of the gum digging labour force, and were often resented by the other diggers for their lack of English, teatotalling, thriftiness, and ability to collect most of the gum in the areas they worked. Under pressure from British diggers the Government introduced The Kauri Gum Industry Act, in 1898, creating British-only gum reserves, and licenses which were more expensive for aliens and could only be obtained after 3 month's residency. Despite these setbacks many of the Dalmatians who made the far North their home flourished, and families with Dalmatian ancestry still have a strong presence in the old gum digging areas.

The Kauri Museum at Matakohe, between Ruawai and Wellsford, has an extensive collection of all things kauri.

Camping;
The Park, Waipapakauri Ramp, 90 Mile Beach, (7km west of Waipapakauri, 18km NW of Kaitaia), Ph 09 406 7298 or 0800 367 719, T$9, Dorm $20 ◆ Ahipara Motor camp, Takehe St, Ahipara, (14km west of Kaitaia), Ph 09 409 4864, T$9, Cabins ◆ Kaitaia Motor Camp, 69A South Rd, Kaitaia, Ph 09 408 1212, T$10

Hostel;
Kaitaia YHA,160 Commerce St, Kaitaia, Ph 09 408 1275, Dorm$19, D$23 ◆ Mainstreet Lodge, 237a Commerce St, Kaitaia, Ph 09 408 1275, Dorm$20, D$42 ◆ Others; Kaitaia, Ahipara, See Camping

B&B;
Waipapakauri Bed & Breakfast, Domain Rd, S.H. 1, Waipapakauri, Ph 09 408 7433 ◆ Others; Ahipara

Motel/Hotel;
Norfolk Motel, S.H. 10, Awanui, Ph 09 406 7515 or 0800 266 736, S$75, D$85 ◆ Awanui Hotel/Motel, S.H. 1, Awanui, Ph 09 406 7012 ◆ Kaitaia Historic Hotel, 15-33 Commerce Street, Kaitaia, Ph 09 408 0360, S$40, D$52 ◆ Wayfarer Motel, 231 Commerce St, Kaitaia, Ph 09 408 2600 or 0800 118 100, D$85 ◆ Others; Awanui

i;
Far North Information Centre, Jaycee Park, South Rd, Kaitaia, Ph 09 408 0879

Bike Shops;
Cycle Sport 'N' Heat, 175 Commerce St, Kaitaia, Ph 09 408 2460 ◆ Limited spare parts at The Warehouse, 11 Matthews Ave, Kaitaia, Ph 09 408 6095

100 km Between Houhora Heads and Waipapakauri

1861 Samuel Butler and John Baker cross Whitcombe Pass, an important early route to the West Coast

3 KAITAIA TO RAWENE

Kaitaia to;

Mangamuka Summit	24km	*35 11.4, 173 27.4*
Mangamuka Bridge	38km	*35 14.2, 173 32.7*
The Narrows Wharf	66km h	*35 23.1, 173 31.6*
Rawene	66km c, b&b, m/h	*35 23.9, 173 30.2*

This stage includes a climb of about 300m over 5km to the top of the forested Mangataniwha Ranges, before dropping down past several small settlements to the shores of the Hokianga Harbour, where there is a ferry crossing to Rawene.

Leaving Kaitaia, State Highway 1 starts out flat to gently rolling and passes productive dairy farms. After 18km the road passes a stream and the Raetea Forest Recreation Area, and after another kilometre, or so, starts climbing. The road winds upward through the Mangamuka Gorge Scenic Reserve, a beautiful piece of bush regenerating after early European logging, and full of ferns. After 4km steady climbing Mangamuka Summit is reached and there is a rest area. There have, in the past, been instances of undesirables causing trouble along this relatively remote forested section, so roadside camping in the bush is not recommended.   The ride down the southern side of the ranges is a glorious, twisting, 8km descent with several picnic areas. Near one rest stop there is a soda spring which locals believe has curative properties.

The downhill ends 31km from Kaitaia as the road gently rolls through patches of farmland and bush, and passes a distinctive Ratana Church.   This largely Maori religion blends Christianity with traditional Maori beliefs and was started in the 1920's by faith healer Tahupotiki Ratana and, although the sect's popularity has waned, still carries influence in Maori politics.

At Mangamuka there is a marae and, a bit further down the road, a cemetery where graves from the local Otere family dominate. 3km after Mangamuka is Mangamuka Bridge, which consists of a pub, petrol station, and dairy - a tiny settlement, but big enough to have its own local radio station. The route leaves State Highway 1 here and heads towards Kohukohu, 26km away (it is another 4km from Kohukohu to the Rawene ferry wharf).

At Mangamuka Bridge turn right off State Highway 1, onto Mangamuka Road, and follow the yellow AA signs to Kohukohu. The route is soon following the Mangamuka River, a pretty stretch of road lined by bush and toetoe grass (also known as cutty grass). The road climbs briefly, passing distinctive limestone formations at Mangataipa Scenic Reserve, before reaching the mangrove-rich tidal portions of the river 5km from Mangamuka Bridge. From here the road heads inland again for several kilometres to a junction, 10km after Mangamuka Bridge, before turning back towards the Mangamuka River, joining it just before it empties into a channel of the Hokianga Harbour.

The road hugs the shoreline to the settlement of Kohukohu, which consists of a hotel, post office, store, and butchery. Down the road, at The Narrows, cars wanting

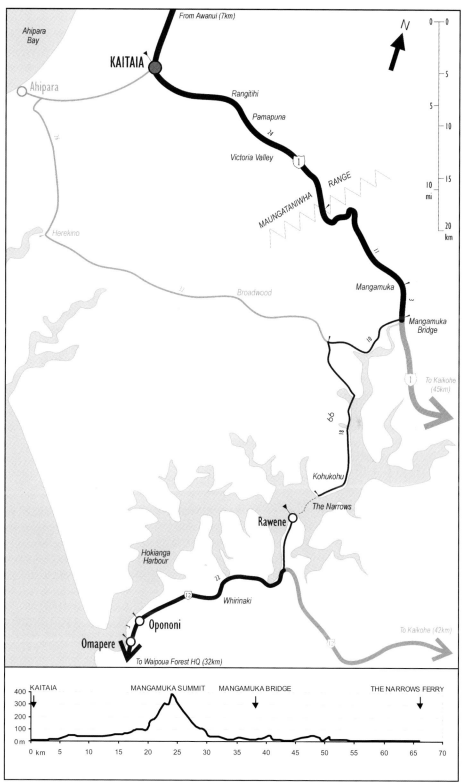

Ahipara Bay

KAITAIA

Ahipara

From Awanui (7km)

N

0 — 0

5

5

10

15

10
mi

20
km

Rangitihi

Pamapuna

24

Victoria Valley

1

MAUNGATANIWHA RANGE

Herekino

11

Mangamuka

3

Broadwood

22

Mangamuka Bridge

1 To Kaikohe (45km)

66

18

10

Kohukohu

The Narrows

Rawene

Hokianga Harbour

22

12

Whirinaki

Opononi

Omapere

To Waipoua Forest HQ (32km)

12 To Kaikohe (42km)

KAITAIA   MANGAMUKA SUMMIT   MANGAMUKA BRIDGE   THE NARROWS FERRY

400
300
200
100
0 m

0 km   5   10   15   20   25   30   35   40   45   50   55   60   65   70

1863 Prussian born Gustavus von Tempsky becomes a leader in The
Forest Rangers - a volunteer group during the Waikato Wars,
which fought Maori on their own terms in the bush

51

to take the Rawene ferry can expect a queue during the peak summer holiday periods, but pedestrians and cyclists usually get straight on. A few years ago ferry masters on this run were reprimanded for doing "donuts" with the ferry, at the request of some of the passengers during late night crossings. Things got out of hand during one spinning session when a van was thrown through the front barrier of the boat. Luckily, the van, and its occupants, stayed aboard, although the driver had to be restrained from taking on the ferry captain. Such antics have since ceased.

Ferry sailings from The Narrows, and directions to bike friendly accommodation

Hokianga Harbour is the place legendary explorer Kupe, from Hawaiiki, is said to have first landed his waka (canoe) in Aotearoa. The harbour is the result of a drowned river valley, formed from the confluence of the Mangamuka, Waihou, Waima, and other rivers, and served as an important transport route for Maori and early European settlers alike. During the kauri rush of the 19th and early 20th Centuries the harbour was being criss-crossed by flat bottomed sailing scows that would come across the treacherous Hokianga Bar to load kauri. The boats beached themselves at prearranged spots at high tide and when the tide dropped bullock teams hauling freshly cut logs from the bush would come onto the beach allowing the logs to be directly loaded onto the scows. When the tide came in, the boats were floated off and readied themselves for the return trip across the Bar.

Rawene is a pleasant little town built on slopes leading down to the harbour edge. The town has a long history of fishing and farming, with the earliest European settlers in the area arriving on a New Zealand Company expedition in 1826 (although many of them later left for Sydney), making Rawene New Zealand's third oldest settlement. The town has numerous shops including a supermarket and several cafés, a post office, campground, b&b's, and the Masonic Hotel - one of New Zealand's oldest hotels (pubs). Another interesting building in Rawene is Clendon House, built in the 1860's for James Clendon - a trader whose family lived in the house for over 100 years.

Opo statue, main street Opononi

1863 Dr James Menzies, Superintendent of Southland, introduces rabbits to Bluff for the benefits of meat and sport. Millions of dollars are subsequently spent controlling rabbit grazing in NZ

Opo, The Friendly Dolphin

In the 1950's most New Zealanders heard of Opononi, down the road from Rawene, for the first time, when a young bottle-nosed dolphin - nicknamed Opo - made the town home in the summer of 1955/56.

She was first spotted by fishermen - a lone dolphin, about a year old - surfing the bow waves of their boats in the Hokianga Harbour. People at the time remembered someone had boasted about shooting a dolphin recently, and it was speculated this might have been Opo's mother. Whether it was or not, Opo was shy at first but grew more precocious with time, allowing her back to be scratched with an oar or rubbed with a mop. Soon, she started frequenting the town wharf, then the town beach, allowing people in the water to get nearer and nearer. By early 1956 Opo was tossing balls back to spectators and gently playing with children in the water. She seemed to have a special affection for one 13-year-old girl, always going to her in the crowd and towing her for rides through the water.

Soon, Opo, and Opononi, were national news and the town's hotel and campground were booked solid, as thousands made the trip to see the friendly dolphin. Fears started to grow that so much attention could actually be detrimental to Opo. At the same time some of the local fishermen were complaining the dolphin was scaring fish away, and some Maori believed Opo was a taniwha (a water monster) sent by Kupe. In response, the Government passed a law limiting the amount of interaction people could have with Opo.

In a sad irony, Opo was found dead the day after the law came into effect - washed up on rocks. The reason for her death was never conclusively established, but there were widespread rumours that she had been killed by fishermen using explosives to fish. Her body was bought back to the beach and she was buried by the town hall in a ceremony that drew national attention. A statue of Opo, with a child riding or her back, is on Opononi's main street, by the wharf.

Camping;
Rawene Motor Camp, 1 Marmon St West, Rawene, Ph 09 405 7720, T$10, Cabin$20pp

Hostel;
The Tree House, 168 West Coast Rd, Kohukohu, Ph 09 405 5855, S$25, D$46 (1.5km W of The Narrows ferry wharf)

B&B;
Searells B&B, Nimmo St West, Rawene, Ph 09 405 7835, S$45, D$80 ◆ Old Lane's Store Homestay, Rawene, Ph 09 405 7554 ◆ Hokianga Blue Studio, Rawene, Ph 021 263 1171 or 09 405 7675

Motel/Hotel;
Kohukohu Hotel, Beach Rd, Hokianga Harbour, Kohukohu, Ph 09 405 5808, S$40 ◆ Masonic Hotel, Rawene, Ph 09 405 7822 ◆ Others; Rawene

150 km Between Mangamuka Bridge and Kohukohu

1864 Followers of the Pai Marire (Hauhau) cult cannibalise Rev. Carl Volkner at Opotiki. After further incidents, including one at Pipiriki, Governor Grey deems the Hauhau "fanatics" and orders troops to suppress them

53

4 RAWENE TO TROUNSON KAURI PARK

Rawene to;

Opononi	22km	c, h, b&b, m/h	*35 30.3, 173 23.5*
Omapere	25km	h, b&b, m/h, i	*35 32.0, 173 23.4*
Waipoua Forest HQ Jct.	57km	c, i	*35 39.2, 173 34.2*
Trounson Kauri Park	71km	c	*35 43.2, 173 39.0*

After Rawene, the route passes through several coastal towns along the southern shore of Hokianga Harbour, before turning south and climbing towards Waipoua Forest - an area that contains some of New Zealand's last remaining truly massive kauri trees.

A short climb takes you out of Rawene. The road is gently rolling next to a tidal estuary before joining State Highway 12, which leads to Opononi, Dargaville, and further south. 9km out of Rawene there is a tough 2km climb, followed by a pleasant

descent with views away to the jagged hills of Waima Forest. There is another hill at 16km, steep and winding for 1km. From the top of this hill it's another 6km into Opononi. Waitemarama Gorge Rd, on the left before Opononi, is the turn off for a YHA youth hostel.

Keep an eye out for the old Whiria Pa site, on a hill to the right, 3km before Opononi. Pa were fortified Maori villages (as opposed to open villages called kainga), that the locals lived in for safety or retreated to in times to war.

Mangroves between Rawene and Opononi

Opononi is a popular tourist stop that comes alive each summer. The town looks across the Hokianga Harbour to immense sand dunes at North Head. The dangerous Hokianga Bar, where many ships have come to grief trying to enter the harbour, is marked by rip currents, sand bars, and breaking surf. Opononi has a small museum, hotels, motels, a backpackers, and several stores, although no bike shop. The town became known throughout New Zealand in the summer of 1956 when a single dolphin, nicknamed Opo befriended the locals (see p.53 for more details). There is a statue of Opo in the main street, near the town wharf which local kids enjoy jumping off.

2km past Opononi is Omapere, another sandy beach with numerous accommodation options, several shops, and a tourist information centre. Leaving Omapere, there is a tough 1km climb to a stunning rest area, looking out over the harbour to the North Head dunes and beyond. This climb is the first of 3 short steep climbs, the last of which is followed by a pleasant downhill, then gently rolling terrain to Waimamaku (37km from Rawene). There is a store, homestay, and backpackers here.

The climbing starts again 2km past Waimamaku, as the road heads into the Parataiko Ranges. Rugged terrain, scarred by landslides, closes in around the road. The bush starts 43km from Rawene as the road continues winding upward. After another kilometre the route officially enters Waipoua Forest, which, along with the neighbouring Mataraua and Waima Forests, makes up the largest surviving kauri forest in New Zealand. Soon after entering the Forest the road summits at 387m and starts dropping. 46.5km after Rawene there is a short walking track off the right, leading to *Tane Mahuta* ("Lord of the Forest") - the largest living kauri in terms of volume [the tallest kauri is *Hokianga*, in Omahuta Forest, and the oldest is *Te Matua Ngahere*, also in Waipoua]. *Tane Mahuta* is thought to be about 2,000 years old.

When Europeans arrived in New Zealand they quickly recognised the potential of

54

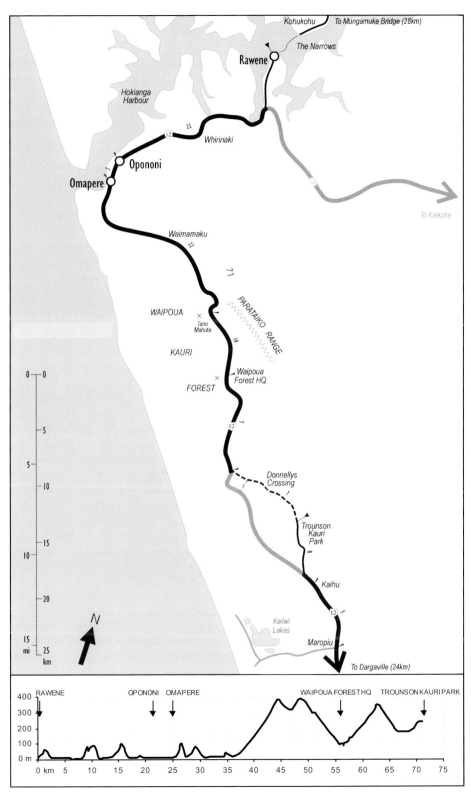

Kohukohu   To Mungamuka Bridge (28km)

The Narrows

Rawene

Hokianga
Harbour

Whirinaki

Opononi

Omapere

12

To Kaikohe

Waimamaku

PARATAIKO RANGE

WAIPOUA
× Tane
Mahuta

KAURI

Waipoua
Forest HQ
×

FOREST

12

Donnellys
Crossing

Trounson
Kauri
Park

Kaihu

Kaiwi
Lakes

Maropiu

To Dargaville (24km)

0 — 0

5 — 5

5 — 10

— 15

10 — 20

15 — 25
mi   km

N

| RAWENE | | OPONONI | OMAPERE | | WAIPOUA FOREST HQ | TROUNSON KAURI PARK |

400
300
200
100
0 m

0 km   5   10   15   20   25   30   35   40   45   50   55   60   65   70   75

1865 NZ's first newspaper, goes on sale for 1 penny

the younger kauri trees for ship's spars, and the solid older ones for the huge quantities of lumber they contained. This, combined with the desire to clear the land for farming, led to forest cutting and burning which peaked around 1905, but continued well into the 20th Century - leaving less than 10% of the kauri forests that existed before man arrived. Typically, an axeman would cut a notch in the trunk the direction they wanted the tree to fall while two-man crosscut sawing started on the otherside. Iron wedges were hammered in behind the saw to keep the blade moving. Once the tree fell, the head was lopped off and the trunk cut into pieces for transport by bullock teams and/or bush railways, or, in some cases, by flooding logs downstream from behind a kauri dam. The Crown purchased Waipoua Forest in 1876, but intermittent logging continued until 1952, when the Waipoua Forest Sanctuary was established.

The road through the forest is a beautiful one, with abundant birdlife, tall kauris and other impressive native trees such as northern rata, kohekohe, and taraire forming a canopy over ferns, nikau palms, and young kauri. 57km into the stage there is a turnoff to the right, to the Waipoua Department of Conservation Visitor Centre, which has a lodge, cabins, and campsites (lodge and cabin bookings should be made in advance). The Visitor Centre has excellent historical and biological displays. There is also a large grassed area with a good swimming hole. Trounson Kauri Park campsite is about 14km further south, via gravel side roads off State Highway 12, so if you particularly dislike riding on gravel consider staying at Waipoua and avoiding the side roads to Trounson on the following stage.

Past DOC's Waipoua Visitors Centre the road climbs until breaking out into farmland again, with glimpses of the ocean off to the west. 7km after the Waipoua Visitors Centre is Katui Road, the turn off to Donnelly's Crossing and Trounson Kauri Park (7km distant). [Note: If you don't plan on visiting Trounson continue on State Highway 12]. Katui Road is gravel and can be a rocky ride if it hasn't been maintained recently. 5km down the road, at Donnelly's Crossing, which consists of a few ramshackle houses and dumped car bodies, make a right turn onto Trounson Park Road for the final few kilometres to the campground.

Trounson Kauri Park consists of campsites and small cabins on the edge of a magnificent stand of kauri (The campground is closed between Easter and Labour Weekend). The cabins at Trounson Kauri Park can be booked at Waipoua DOC Visitors Centre).

Trounson Kauri Park

The solid stands of trees full of birds in this small fragment of kauri-podocarp forest give visitors a glimpse of what northern New Zealand must have been like before man arrived, and sleeping in the campground you can hear, if you're lucky, a rare sound these days - the call of a wild kiwi.

The park is a 445-hectare reserve, surrounded by land now cleared for farming, resulting in the Department of Conservation considering the reserve a "mainland island". Originally, in 1890, when it became obvious almost all the kauri forests in Northland would be cut down, the Government set aside a mere 3 hectares as a reminder of what once existed. A neighbouring landowner, James Trounson, donated 22 more acres and later sold another 360 hectares to the Government to make up the majority of today's park.

Kauri (*Agathis Australis*) is endemic in New Zealand and grows from about Te Awamutu, north. Today, the remnants of the forests that have survived logging support a habitat with many smaller tree species growing under the kauri canopy, and in the case of epiphytes, on the kauri itself. These plants in turn support the birds that can be heard calling within a healthy kauri forest - the kokako, kaka, and kakariki.

1868 The first railway track in NZ is run in Christchurch. NZ eventually adopts a narrower gauge than Australia and the US due to the hilly terrain and tight corners

Since 1995, DOC has been actively eradicating introduced predators in the park, such as weasels, stoats, and feral cats. This has allowed the re-introduction of native North Island pigeons and robins, and other endangered species, such as the North Island brown kiwi and kokako. The park is also home to the long-tailed bat, one of the two bat species remaining in New Zealand, and, near the campground, a colony of glow-worms.

There is a 30-minute loop walk through the park. Keep an eye out for fantails as you walk - an acrobatic little bird that trails walkers, looking for insects that might be disturbed. During summer, night-walks through the park are offered, where you may hear kiwi shuffling around in the undergrowth, using nostrils on the end of their beaks to sniff out bugs and grubs. Unfortunately, all 5 of New Zealand's kiwi species are threatened, and numbers have continued to decline in recent years (the population is estimated to be about 70,000). Thankfully, brown kiwi chicks in Trounson Kauri Park are surviving better than elsewhere, and numbers are actually increasing here.

Camping;
Opononi Beach Holiday Park, S.H. 12, Opononi, Ph 09 405 8791, T$11, Cabin$50 ◆ Waipoua Campground, 1km off S.H. 12, Waipoua Forest, Ph 09 439 3011, T$8, Cabin$14pp, Bookings required ◆ Trounson Kauri Park Campground, Ph 09 439 3011, $T8, Open Labour Weekend to Easter.

Hostel;
Opononi YHA, 140 Mountain Rd, Opononi, Ph 09 405 8815, Dorm$19, D$50 ◆ House of Harmony, S.H. 12, Opononi, Ph 09 405 8778, Dorm$18, D$40 ◆ Globetrekkers Lodge, S.H.12, Omapere, Ph 09 405 8183, Dorm$18, S$35 ◆ Kauri Creek Backpackers, Waimamaku, Ph 09 405 8448

B&B;
Opononi Dolphin Lodge, S.H.12, Opononi, Ph 09 405 8451 ◆ Harbourside B&B, S.H.12, Omapere, Ph 09 405 8246 ◆ Others; Opononi, Omapere, Waimamaku

Motel/Hotel;
Opononi Resort Hotel, SH 12, Opononi, Ph 09 405 8858, D$100, Dorm$20 ◆ Omapere Tourist Hotel/Motel, Main Rd, Omapere, Ph 09 405 8737, D$100 ◆ Others; Opononi

i;
Hokianga Information Centre, S.H. 12, Omapere, Ph 09 405 8869 ◆ Waipoua Forest Visitor Centre, Waipoua Forest, Ph 09 439 3011

200 km Just before Opononi

250 km Between Donnellys Crossing and Trounson Kauri Park

5 TROUNSON KAURI PARK TO RUAWAI

Trounson Kauri Park to;

Kaihu	8km	c, h	*35 46.2, 173 41.8*
Maropiu	13km		*35 48.6, 173 43.7*
Dargaville	37km	c, h, b&b, m/h, i	*35 56.5, 173 52.1*
Tokatoka	54km		*36 03.6, 173 58.0*
Ruawai	66km	c, h	*36 08.1, 174 01.4*

From Trounson Kauri Park the route drops, almost continually, for about 15km, before flattening out and following the Kaihu River plain to Dargaville. From Dargaville on, the route is pancake flat, across the plains of the Wairoa River.

The route re-connects with Highway 12 8km from Trounson (3km before the road joins the Highway there is another campground; the Kauri Coast Holiday Park).

Kaihu has a pub, service station, and store. 6km down the highway is a turn-off to Kai Iwi Lakes, about a 14km detour on gravel roads. These freshwater lakes have formed in sand dunes where buried ironstone pans prevent rainwater from escaping. The lakes are very pretty and a popular destination for power boaters and jet skiers. There is camping available at the adjacent Taharoa Domain, and chalets for hire on nearby farms.

Highway 12 south crosses the fertile flood plain of the Kaihu River to Dargaville where the river joins the much larger Wairoa River, which eventually flows into the Kaipara Harbour. As Highway 12 enters Dargaville it swings left onto

Between Trounson Kauri Park and Kaihu - good news for cyclists

River Rd, crosses a bridge over the Kaihu, and follows the main street into town (Normanby St, which in turn becomes Jervois St).

Dargaville is a town of about 4,500 set on a bend in the wide, brown, Wairoa River (a river the locals like to say flows upside down). An Irishman, Joseph Dargaville, who had kauri timber business interests in the area, founded the town in 1872. Many Dalmatian settlers arrived in the 1880's when the area was still largely forested, and there was even a Jugoslav consulate. Back then the river was a busy thoroughfare, packed with log rafts being floated downstream and sailing ships off-loading supplies and loading timber for delivery to Onehunga, southern ports, and Australia. Large sawmills lined the banks of the Wairoa, processing large quantities of kauri and, as this became rarer, kahikatea. However, by the 1920's logging had all but eliminated kauri as an economic resource and much of the river traffic ceased. When the mills closed the populations of these small settlements dwindled, although Dargaville managed to hold its own better than the others. Today, plantation forests are an important industry in the area, along with farming, and to a lesser degree, tourism (as travellers opt to take a quieter route north compared to State Highway 1). The town has had its problems recently though, with high unemployment and a nationally publicised firebombing of a local dairy. There are campgrounds near town, and at Bayleys Beach (14km west of town).

An interesting stop in Dargaville is the Maritime Museum in Harding Park

1876 The Provincial System is abolished in favour of more centralised government, although the use of province names persist in geographic and sporting usage

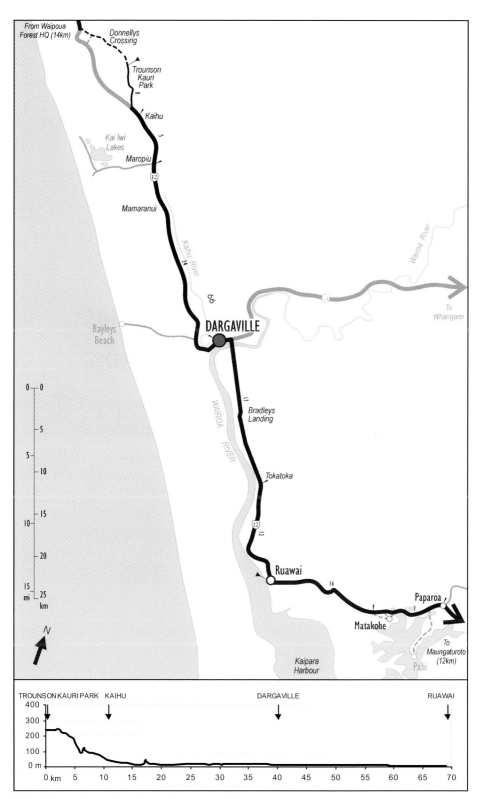

From Waipoua
Forest HQ (14km)

Donnellys
Crossing

Trounson
Kauri
Park

Kaihu

Kai Iwi
Lakes

Maropiu

Mamaranui

Kaihu River

DARGAVILLE

Bayleys
Beach

WAIROA RIVER

Wairoa River

To
Whangarei

Bradleys
Landing

Tokatoka

Ruawai

Paparoa

Matakohe

Pahi

To
Maungaturoto
(12km)

Kaipara
Harbour

N

| TROUNSON KAURI PARK | KAIHU | DARGAVILLE | RUAWAI |

TROUNSON KAURI PARK KAIHU   DARGAVILLE   RUAWAI

400
300
200
100
0 m

0 km   5   10   15   20   25   30   35   40   45   50   55   60   65   70

(instead of going left when entering town go right on River Rd, then left onto Mahuta Rd at Mt Wesley Corner. The museum entrance is a short distance up Mahuta Rd on the right). The museum has relics from the numerous ships wrecked while trying to navigate the infamous Kaipara Bar. There is also as a good collection of Maori and Pioneer artefacts, the largest known piece of Kauri gum, and the masts from the *Rainbow Warrior* (see p.68).

Leave Dargaville by continuing east along Jervois St, then right onto Grey St, which crosses the Wairoa River and heads south. Highway 12 runs through the Wairoa River flood plain, which is a big dairy farming and kumara (sweet potato) growing area and the flat straight roads to Ruawai make for easy cycling, unless there is a headwind. The route passes the barely noticeable settlements of Mititai, Tokatoka, and Raupo, before reaching Ruawai. At Tokatoka there is a tavern and the road makes a few turns as it squeezes between the river and the 173m high peak of Tokatoka Peak. The pyramid shaped hill was the heart of a volcano 20 million years ago. Since then the majority of the cone has been worn away, leaving only the vent plug.

Ruawai is a small farming based town that is a centre for kumara production. You can buy a 10kg bag of these red-skinned yellow-fleshed sweet potatoes for $10, or try kumara pancakes at the Travellers Lodge backpackers on Highway 12, just before the main street. This backpackers also has tent sites. Ruawai has several stores, a service station, fish and chip shop, etc. If you arrive on a Friday, the Volunteer Fire Brigade has an open invitation for visitors to join them at their regular Friday night social.

Kumara

The sweet-potato known as kumara (*Ipomoea batatas*) has been grown in New Zealand since Maori arrived with it, along with taro and yam, hundreds of years ago. The quick-maturing and hardy nature of kumara made it a staple for many tribes and it was successfully grown as far south as Banks Peninsula. When Europeans settlers came, they too appreciated the flavourful qualities of kumara. Today, despite plenty of other choices available, kumara still takes pride of place in most Maori hangis and Pakeha Sunday roasts.

90% of New Zealand's kumara are grown in the rich river plain soils around Dargaville and Ruawai - earning Dargaville the nickname "Kumara Capital of New Zealand".

For Maori, the appearance of the kowhai's yellow flowers at the end of winter indicated it was time to start planting kumara. Frost-free coastal plains or sunny, north-facing, slopes were the preferred planting locations, to improve yields of this essentially tropical crop.

In true organic fashion, some tribes reportedly used trained seagulls to guard their plots from the ravages of the kumara caterpillar. Several varieties of kumara were grown, although none reached the size of those obtained from today's commercial operations. After harvesting, the kumara were stored in rectangular pits excavated specifically for kumara storage, and covered to allow maturation of the tubers to continue (remnant kumara pits are often archaeologists first clue of a Maori settlement nearby). Cooking was usually by slow steaming in an earth oven (hangi), where the kumara and other food items were wrapped in leaves and buried

1878 The first NZ bicycle manufacturer, T. Boyd, sets up shop in Christchurch

between hot rocks.

European kumara farming dates from the 1850's when fatter varieties were imported from the Americas. These days, kumara farming in Northland typically involves sowing seedbeds at the end of winter. Young shoots are then transplanted into growing fields in spring and early summer. From mid-summer on, the kumara are harvested, either by hand or machine, and stored in temperature controlled rooms which allow the tubers to continue turning starch to sugar. The kumara are then taken out of storage as needed, washed, graded, and packed for shipping. Modern varieties available today include orange, gold, and red kumara, with a perennial favourite being the Owairaka Red.

Being rich in fibre, Vitamins A, B6, and C, and potassium, iron, and calcium; kumara are currently being advertised by the horticulture industry as a healthy inclusion in their "5+ A Day" vegetable marketing plan.

To sample the local product, consider staying at the Travellers Lodge in Ruawai, which serves kumara pancakes. Alternatively, many kiwi pubs serve kumara fries, and upscale restaurants are increasingly offering kumara either mashed in various dishes or as a soup. You can also try cooking it yourself (most supermarkets carry at least one variety) or, if you get the chance, try kumara the original way - from an authentic hangi.

Camping;

Kauri Coast Top Ten Holiday Park, Trounson Park Rd, Kaihu, Ph 09 439 0621 or 0800 807 200, T$11, Cabin $30, Motel $70 ◆ Kai Iwi Lakes Camp, Kai Iwi Lakes Rd, Ph 09 439 8360, T$16, Bookings at Kauri Coast Information Centre, Dargaville ◆ Bayleys Beach Motor Camp, 22 Seaview Rd, Bayleys Beach (14km W of Dargaville), Ph 09 439 6349, T$9, Cabin$30 ◆ Dargaville Holiday Park, 10 Onslow St, Dargaville, Ph 09 439 8296 or 08000 114 441, T$9, Cabin $17pp

Hostel;

Kaihu Farm, S.H.12, Kaihu, Ph 09 439 4004, Dorm$18, S$35 ◆ The Greenhouse, 13 Portland St, Dargaville, Ph 09 439 6342, S$25, D$30 ◆ Travellers Lodge, 64 Jellicoe Rd, Ruawai, S$15, D$30 ◆ Others; Dargaville (see Motel/Hotel)

B&B;

Waterlea, Kai Iwi Lakes Rd, Ph 09 439 0727, D$80 ◆ Others; Kai Iwi Lakes

Motel/Hotel;

Dargaville Motel, 217 Victoria St, Dargaville, Ph 09 439 7734, $D80 ◆ Commercial Hotel, 75 River Rd, Dargaville, Ph 09 439 8018, S$25, D$65, Dorm $20 ◆ Parkview Motel, 36 Carrington St, Dargaville, Ph 09 439 8339, D$75 ◆ Motel Hobsons Choice, 212 Victoria St, Dargaville, Ph 09 439 8551, $D100 ◆ Others; Kaihu (see Camping), Dargaville

i;

Kauri Coast Information Centre, Normanby St, Dargaville, Ph 09 439 8360

Bike Shop;

Nearest is in Whangarei (56km E of Dargaville) Hedgehog Bikes, Ph 09 438 2521, 29 Vine St, Whangarei. Limited spare parts at The Warehouse, Victoria St, Dargaville, Ph 09 439 3120

300 km Between Dargaville and Ruawai

1879 Rewi Maniapoto, a distinguished leader against the British at Orakau during the Waikato Wars, receives a hero's welcome in Auckland. A monument to him is erected at Kihikihi and he receives a government pension

61

Ruawai to;

Matakohe turn-off	16km	c, b&b *(at Matakohe)*	*36 07.5, 174 10.3*
Maungaturoto	35km	b&b, m/h	*36 06.6, 174 21.3*
Brynderwyn	43km	m/h	*36 05.8, 174 25.8*
Kaiwaka	51km	m/h	*36 10.2, 174 26.8*
Wellsford	71km	b&b, m/h, i *(limited info at museum)*	*36 17.7, 174 31.4*

This stage leaves Ruawai and skirts the northern fingers of the Kaipara Harbour, before rejoining the busy State Highway 1 for 28km to Wellsford.

The first 9km from Ruawai are flat and provide a pleasant warm up for the day's riding. 5km from Ruawai the road crosses the Awaroa River and, 4km later, starts gradually climbing for 1km. The climb passes a couple of grain silos then gets steeper for another 2km before descending to rolling countryside which continues to Wellsford.

The Kauri Museum at Matakohe is a short signposted detour off Highway 12, about 16km past Ruawai. The museum has the country's most extensive collection of kauri logging equipment and kauri gum, as well as other colonial exhibits, and is well worth checking out, especially if you didn't stop at any other museums in Northland.

To bypass Matakohe, continue on Highway 12. After the Matakohe turn-off the road climbs briefly then descends to the Matakohe River, then crosses another ridge before dropping to Paparoa Stream and the township of Paparoa. This pretty little settlement was established in 1862 and has some solid old buildings including an old Post Office (now a backpackers), pub, service station and store. Just before Paparoa is a turn-off to Pahi (6km south), a small fishing community at the mouth of the Pahi River.

After Paparoa the route has a couple of steep climbs. Maungataroto is another small stop with a pub, service station, and store. The milk tankers you have probably seen passing deliver to the dairy factory here. The café here has good local pies.

At Brynderwyn, 43km from Ruawai, the Kauri Coast Route and Highway 12 end, and the route re-joins State Highway 1. There is a service station and café at the intersection here, along with a memorial to Joseph Coates made from stone from the foundations of Waterloo Bridge, London. Coates was Prime Minister from 1925-28 and was born at Matakohe. This stretch of State Highway 1 is busy with speeding cars and trucks, and the road is narrow in places (white crosses dotted along the roadside serve as reminders of fatal traffic accidents). The ride to Wellsford includes some quite long (over 1km) climbs, as the route passes farmland, exotic forest, and, occasionally, native bush reserves.

Kaiwaka (8km from Brynderwyn) has shops, a service station, and accommodation. There is a turn off here to Mangawhai and Mangawhai Heads - popular beach resorts with campgrounds 14km to the east (Mangawai back to Wellsord is another 20km). Te Hana (24km from Brynderwyn, 4km before Wellsford) has shops and a service station.

Wellsford is reached after a final 2km climb, the last section being the steepest. This is the biggest town en-route since Dargaville, and has a fairly good range of services (but no bike shop, although the hardware store sells repair kits) The town started out as a collection of gum-diggers huts then grew as farming in the area developed. It now serves as a service centre for the area and for travellers on State Highway 1. Interestingly, the early farmers discarded the old Maori name for the area and adopted Wellsford - not because of any well or ford nearby but based on the first letters of their surnames; Watson, Edgar, Levet, Lester, etc. The town's A&P Show is held every year in November.

1880 The Zealandia Cycle Works begins building bicycles in Christchurch, later becoming NZ's largest manufacturer

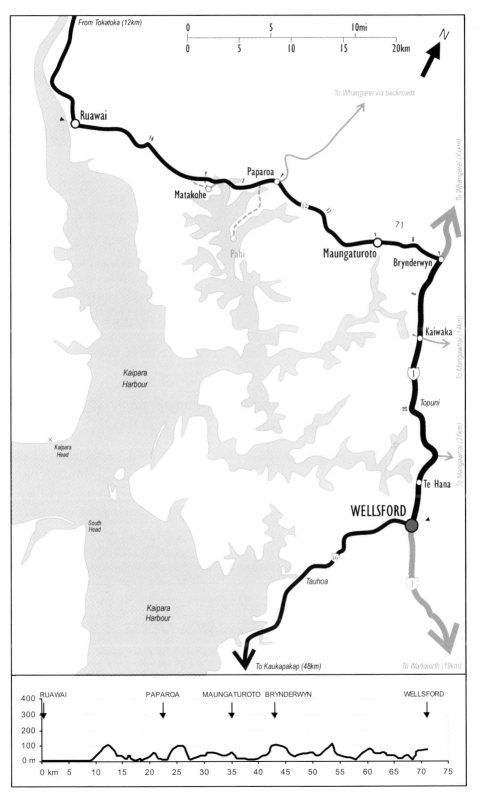

From Tokatoka (12km)

0   5   10mi
0   5   10   15   20km

N

To Whangarei via backroads

Ruawai

16

Paparoa

Matakohe

12

To Whangarei (Xxkm)

Pahi

71

Maungaturoto

8

Brynderwyn

8

Kaiwaka

To Mangawhai (14km)

1

Topuni

10

To Mangawhai (27km)

Kaipara
Harbour

Te Hana

Kaipara
Head

WELLSFORD

South
Head

16

Tauhoa

1

Kaipara
Harbour

To Kaukapakap (48km)

To Warkworth (19km)

| | RUAWAI | | PAPAROA | MAUNGATUROTO | BRYNDERWYN | | | WELLSFORD |

400
300
200
100
0 m

0 km   5   10   15   20   25   30   35   40   45   50   55   60   65   70   75

1882   The first shipment of frozen meat leaves NZ, the trip
from Dunedin to London taking 98 days

New Zealand's National Game

Kiwis love their rugby with a passion that, according to folklore, sends the New Zealand stock market down after the All Blacks lose an important match. True or not, a set of goal posts marks almost every school and the edge of most towns. Rugby arrived with immigrants, who were just learning the game themselves, after William Webb Ellis, a pupil at Rugby School in Warwickshire "with a fine disregard for the rules…took the ball in his arms and ran with it", in 1823.

By the 1860's various versions of Association football, Victorian rules, and rugby were being played in New Zealand by settlers looking for a diversion from the stresses of breaking in a new land. The teams were commonly pub-based, with 30- or 40-men sides, few rules, and matches that sometimes lasted for days. Charles John Monro is considered the father of rugby in New Zealand. The son of New Zealand's Speaker of the House, Monro was sent to Christ's College in England on his 16th birthday in 1867. He returned with the rules of rugby in his suitcase and convinced the Nelson Football Club, which had been playing Association and Victorian rules, to switch to rugby. Monro's old high school, Nelson College, was also encouraged to try the game and on 14 May 1870 the school fielded fifteen players against the Nelson Club side in the country's first rugby match. (The term "First Fifteen" has become ubiquitous in every New Zealand secondary school, describing the school's top rugby team).

Clubs formed throughout the country over the next few years as settlers moved into new areas, but not everyone was impressed by the game. In 1875 *The Otago Daily Times* reported "some beautiful spills and scrimmages…afforded considerable amusement to the spectators…" but finally decided rugby was "…a rough and dangerous game". An Auckland player did die after an 1877 match, with the coroner describing rugby as "…worthy of savages". Another paper felt "…bull-baiting and cock-fighting have more to commend them…". Despite the bad press, several clubs formed the Canterbury Rugby Union in 1879, and other unions soon followed. In 1884 New Zealand's first national team toured New South Wales, winning all 8 matches. The 1888 New Zealand Native Team was the first Kiwi sports team to tour Britain. Away for over a year, they played 107 matches and started the tradition of the Maori war dance - the Haka.

The 1905 "Originals" team were seen as ambassadors for the colony. Farewelled by PM Richard Seddon, Deputy-PM Joseph Ward, and the opposition leader, William Massey, this team earned the nickname "All Black" due to their uniforms, or possibly from a miss-print after the team was described as "All Backs" because they were so fast (no-one is certain which). The 1920's saw the first All Black star,

Rugby Test; New Zealand vs. England

19-year-old George Nepia, who played in all 38 matches of the "Invincibles" tour, with tough tackling and a flare from fullback that stunned spectators. Unable to earn a living from the amateur game, or his small East Coast farm, Nepia was forced to convert to rugby league (a professional game at the time) to feed his family, although a war-time amnesty allowed him to return to rugby union for his final playing years. Aside from money, the more explosive issues of race and

1882 The first of several, unsuccessful, barrier fences are erected to control the spread of rabbits

politics were creeping into top-level rugby during Nepia's time. Teams to South Africa were banned from bringing "coloured" players, a demand the New Zealand union acquiesced to, and Nepia was omitted from the 1928 touring team.

By the 1970's the rugby-mad South Africans were willing to make an exception to their apartheid policies and the star of the All Black tour was a kiwi of Samoan descent; Bryan Williams. In 1981 sports and politics collided head-on in New Zealand when the Springboks (South Africans) toured. An election year, the PM, Robert Muldoon, walked a tightrope of expressing opposition but refusing to interfere with the tour. Games were played behind rolls of barbed wire, with police lining the field between the ground and the stands. Demonstrators wearing motorcycle helmets and armed with sticks and shields, fought Riot Police and pro-tour agitators outside the stadiums. New Zealand won the test series 2-1, but the country was divided. [As an epilogue; in 1995, the first post-apartheid South African President, Nelson Mandela, wore a Springbok jersey when he presented the Rugby World Cup to his team after they defeated the All Blacks in the final in Johannesburg].

When rugby went professional in 1990's its' first mega-star was New Zealand's Jonah Lomu, a 6'5" 18-stone speedster from a humble background, who made his debut as the youngest ever All Black at 19-years-old (26 days younger than Nepia). Lomu could literally run over his opponents - as England's Mike Catt found out in the 1995 World Cup - and, unlike Nepia, was paid handsomely to do so.

The All Black's last World Cup effort, in 2003, saw them stumble in the semi-finals against Australia (Australia going on to lose against England in the final) - New Zealand's coach and captain were promptly replaced.

Camping;
Matakohe Top 10 Holiday Park, Church Rd, Matakohe, Ph 09 431 6431, T$10 ◆ Pahi Beach Motor Camp, Pahi Rd, Pahi (6km from Paparoa), Ph 09 431 7322, T$10, On-site caravan$40

Hostel;
The Old Post Office Guest House, Paparoa, Ph 09 431 6444, Dorm$18, D$30 ◆ Others; Wellsford (See Wellsford Hotel & Inn)

B&B;
Matakohe House B&B, Church Rd, Matakohe, Ph 09 431 7091, S$90, D$115 ◆ Te Moemoea Retreat, Maungaturoto, Ph 09 431 8950, D$90 ◆ Wellsford Castle B&B, 1599 S.H. 1, Wellsford, Ph 09 423 8557, D$100

Motel/Hotel;
Maungaturoto Hotel, 35 Hurndel St, Maungaturoto, Ph 09 431 8006, S$20, D$35 ◆ Brynderwyn Motel, S.H. 1, Brynderwyn, Ph 09 431 8295, D$80 ◆ Best Western Gateway North Motor Lodge, S.H.1, Kaiwaka, Ph 09 431 2389, D$90 ◆ Castle Court Motel, SH 1, Wellsford, Ph 09 423 7705, S$70, D$80 ◆ Sun Valley Motor Lodge, 22 Port Albert Rd, SH 16, Wellsford, Ph 09 423 8829, D$85 ◆ Wellsford Hotel & Inn, Rodney Rd, Wellsford, Ph 09 423 8046, incl. backpackers

i;
The Albertland & Districts Museum, Port Albert Rd, Wellsford, Ph 09 423 8181, Open daily 1:00pm to 3:00pm

350 km Between Paparoa and Maungaturoto

1885 Taranaki butter maker Chew Chong exports 2 barrels of butter to England, NZ's first

Wellsford to;

Tauhoa	14km		*36 22.6, 174 27.1*
Kaukapakapa	48km	m/h	*36 36.9, 174 29.4*
Dairy Flat	66km		*36 40.2, 174 38.2*
Albany	76km	b&b, m/h, bike shop	*36 43.5, 174 41.7*
Takapuna	91km	c, b&b, m/h, i, bike shop	*36 47.4, 174 46.3*

The options for getting to Auckland from Wellsford include riding the direct, but frenetic, State Highway 1 route to Orewa and taking East Coast Rd south, or, taking the slightly longer, quieter and more scenic Highway 16, overlooking the Kaipara Harbour. This tour takes the quieter option, joining State Highway 17 near Dairy Flat and passing through Albany before connecting with East Coast Rd.

Leave State Highway 1 by going right at the service station at the south end of Wellsford's main street onto Highway 16. The road climbs gently for several kilometres before dropping and rolling through pleasant farmland. One steep climb, starting 7km after Wellsford, takes you to the top of a ridge with great views over the many inlets of the Kaipara and away to the sandy hills of South Head. Tauhoa, at the end of the descent from this lookout consists of 3 or 4 houses and a rural school.

The route continues through rolling farmland, offering glimpses of the harbour as the road rises and falls. 6km past Tauhoa the road crosses the mangrove-lined mouth of the Hoteo River and passes under electrical transmission lines that lead the way to Kaukapakapa. 3km past Hoteo River is the trailhead for the Mt Auckland walkway, a 3.5 hour walk through regenerating rimu and kauri forest to Atuanui Peak (305m).

The road continues, gently rolling, across low ridges separating streams that flow into the harbour. Farms cover the flats by the harbour with dikes to hold back highwaters. The settlements along this stretch, although named on maps, typically consist of a few loosely grouped houses with an occasional war memorial or old hall.

The route climbs to another impressive lookout then descends to Kaukapakapa. This settlement has a service station and hotel - the first shops since Wellsford. About 1km past Kaukapakapa, go left onto Kahikatea Flat Rd. This road heads east (follow the signs for Albany) and joins Highway 17 near Dairy Flat. Form here the tour passes through Albany and enters Auckland's North Shore (Takapuna is 25km from Dairy Flat, with Auckland another 7km - and a ferry ride - away).

[Note: An alternate route into Auckland from Kaukapakapa involves continuing on Highway 16, passing through Helensville and Kumeu, then entering Auckland through Henderson and the city's western suburbs. If you chose this option there is a campground and hot mineral pools at Parakai, near Helensville].

Kahikatea Flat Rd is gently rolling, with one noteworthy climb a few kilometres before Highway 17. Dairy Flat runs for a couple of kilometres along the highway with lifestyle blocks, fruit stalls, and a service station. The road south is gently rolling with a decent shoulder, but cars still rocket past at over 100km/hr. Even worse, where there are double-lane sections for passing, the shoulder narrows and cars fly by even closer to your handlebars (white crosses on some corners mark the sites of previous motor accidents and emphasize the need for caution). Just before Albany, the road crests a large hill, which, on fine days, provides good views over Auckland City.

Auckland is New Zealand's biggest suburban area and the city's sprawl has reached previously quiet, semi-rural, areas like Albany in recent years. The motorway north was extended to Albany, increasing the town's popularity considerably, and then to Orewa

1886 Kairaru, a kauri tree thought to be over 4,000 years old, is destroyed by fire

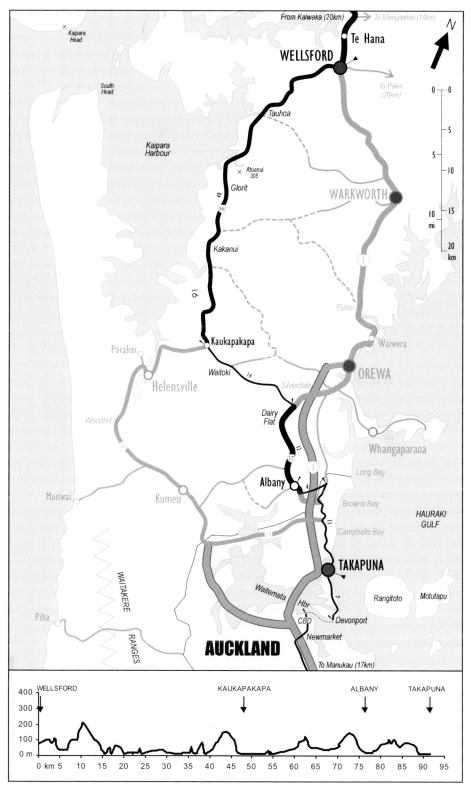

Kaipara
Head ×

From Kaiwaka (20km) — To Mangawhai (14km)

N

Te Hana
WELLSFORD

To Pakiri
(26km)

South
Head ×

Tauhoa

Kaipara
Harbour

Atuanui
305 ×
Glorit

WARKWORTH

48
(16)

Kakanui

Puhoi

16

Parakai ×

Kaukapakapa

Waiwera

OREWA

Waitoki   16
Silverdale

Helensville

Dairy
Flat

Woodhill

Whangaparaoa

17

Long Bay

Muriwai

Kumeu

Albany
4

Browns Bay

**HAURAKI
GULF**

11

Campbells Bay

WAITAKERE

TAKAPUNA

Waitemata

Rangitoto   Motutapu

Piha

Hbr

RANGES

CBD
Newmarket

Devonport

AUCKLAND

To Manukau (17km)

	0	— 0
	—	5
	5 —	10
10	—	15
mi	—	20
		km

400
300
200
100
0 m

WELLSFORD   KAUKAPAKAPA   ALBANY   TAKAPUNA

0 km 5 10 15 20 25 30 35 40 45 50 55 60 65 70 75 80 85 90 95

*1893   Richard Seddon makes NZ the first western country to give women
the vote, and appeals to the Women's Temperance movement by
introducing a law giving voters the right to refuse liquor licences*

67

in 1999, the next stage will take it to Puhoi. Unfortunately, for a country of outdoor enthusiasts, cyclists have been largely been forgotten in Auckland's expansion, and riding into downtown, through the traffic-clogged suburbs, is a stressful affair.

At Albany turn left by the football stadium onto Oteha Valley Rd. This road climbs to East Coast Rd, a ridge line road that has good views over the Hauraki Gulf with its many islands. East Coast Rd rolls along overlooking the affluent suburbs and the beaches of "The Bays", before dropping down to Milford, next to Lake Pupuke - the oldest crater in the Auckland Volcanic Field and a deep freshwater lake, a few hundred metres from the ocean. From Milford, continue on Kitchener Rd, to Hurstmere Rd (also called "The Golden Mile" due to the real estate prices), which leads into Takapuna. The campground at Takapuna is an awesome beachfront location, looking straight across to Rangitoto Island and rubbing shoulders with million dollar homes.

The Rainbow Warrior Affair

In July 1985, Greenpeace's flagship, the Rainbow Warrior, arrived in Auckland to lead a flotilla of boats to Mururoa Atoll, to protest French nuclear testing in the Pacific. On the night of July 10, the 40m ship was tied up at Marsden Wharf, at the bottom of Queen St, when a flash of blue was observed below the waterline, followed by a large explosion. As water rushed into the engine room the boat quickly sank. 11 of the 12 people on board managed to get off. Photographer Fernando Pereira, who ran below to fetch his cameras, was drowned after a second explosion rocked the ship.

It was quickly established explosive devices had been attached to the hull and Auckland Police commenced a homicide enquiry. Members of a Hobson Bay boating club reported that a man wearing scuba gear had tied up a Zodiac late that night and drove away in a blue and white van - they recorded the licence plate number. The following day forestry workers observed a suspicious meeting between people in a van and a car. Two days after the bombing a Swiss couple, Alain Turenge and his wife Sophie, tried to return the rental van and were detained. They were later identified as Major Alain Mafart and Captain Dominique Prieur, agents of the French Secret Service (the DGSE). The car that met the van was traced to a charter yacht, *The Ouvea*, which had arrived from New Caledonia, although the crew or boat could not be found.

Investigations by New Zealand Police suggested several other agents had entered the country as part of the plot, including an infiltrator in Greenpeace's Auckland office. *The Ouvea*, reportedly, had transported the explosives and was later scuttled - her crew being picked up by the French nuclear submarine *Rubis*. Mafart and Prieur, who are believed to have picked up one of the men who planted the bombs, plead "Not Guilty" to charges of conspiring to commit arson, and murder.

The bombing generated enormous publicity around the world. Initially, President Francois Mitterrand denied French involvement, however as details emerged, the French Prime Minister admitted the Secret Service had organised the attack. The Defence Minister, Charles Hernu, resigned and the head of the DGSE, Pierre Lacoste, was fired.

Back in NZ, Mafart and Prieur suddenly changed their pleas to "Guilty", on lesser charges of manslaughter and wilful damage, thus avoiding a trial. Chief Justice Ronald Davidson, sentenced each of them to 10 years jail, indicating; "People who…commit terrorist activities in this country cannot expect to have a short holiday at the expense of our Government and return home heroes". However, after the French threatened New Zealand's export trade to Europe the case went to the United Nations for mediation. France agreed to pay US$6.5 million to New Zealand, apologise for the bombing, and detain Mafart and Prieur on Hao Atoll, a French Military base in the Pacific, for 3 years.

The agents were transferred to French custody after serving 8 months of their sentences. 17 months later, Alain Mafart went to Paris for medical treatment and did not return to Hao. 5 months after this, Dominique Prieur, and her husband, who had joined her on Hao, returned to France, as she was pregnant. On their return both agents were promoted.

The Rainbow Warrior was refloated, but could not be salvaged. In 1987 the ship was sunk as an artificial reef at the Cavalli Islands, in Northland. Greenpeace launched a new Rainbow Warrior in 1987, using part of a US$8 million settlement from France.

The publicity from the bombing continued for several years, focusing world attention on France's nuclear testing programme in the South Pacific. They tested their last nuclear device at Mururoa in 1996.

Camping;
Takapuna Beach Caravan Park, 22 The Promenade, Takapuna Beach, Ph 09 489 7909, T$25, Cabin$55 ◆ North Shore Motel & Holiday Park, 52 Northcote Rd, Takapuna, Ph 09 418 2578 or 0508 909 090, T$30, Cabin$55, Motel D$100 ◆ Others; Parakai (12km E of Kaukapakapa), Auckland (p.70)

Hostel;
See Auckland (p.70)

B&B;
Albany Heights B&B, 179 Albany Heights Rd, Albany, Ph 09 415 9944, D$95 ◆ Channel View House B&B, 834 East Coast Rd, Browns Bay, Ph 09 478 1336, D$85 ◆ Others; Helensville, Albany, Milford, Auckland (p.70)

Motel/Hotel;
Kaukapakapa Hotel, S.H. 16 Kaipara Coast Highway, Kaukapakapa, Ph 09 420 5230, D$80 ◆ Albany Oak Motel, 80 Bush Rd, Albany, Ph 09 415 3131, D$115 ◆ Sea Vista Motel, 869 Beach Rd, Browns Bay, Ph 09 479 6088, D$95 City of Sails Motel, 219 Shakespere Rd, Milford, Ph 09 486 9170, D$120 ◆ Anzac Court Motel, 43 Anzac St, Takapuna, Ph 09 489 4315, D$110 ◆ Parklane Motor Inn, Cnr Lake Rd & Rewiti Ave, Takapuna, Ph 09 486 1069 or 0800 801 069, D$125 ◆ Others; Albany, Browns Bay, Milford, Takapuna, Auckland (p.70)

i;
Takapuna Visitor Information, 49 Hurstmere Rd, Ph 09 486 8670 ◆ Others; Devonport, Auckland (p.70)

Bike Shops;
Bike Albany, 6A Douglas Alexander Pde, Albany, Ph 09 443 2557 ◆ Bike Barn, 81 Barrys Pt Rd, Takapuna, Ph 09 486 2065 ◆ Hedgehog Bikes, 72 Barrys Pt Rd, Takapuna, Ph 09 489 6559 ◆ Others; Orewa, Albany, Takapuna, Auckland (p.70)

400 km Between Wellsford and Tauhoa

450 km Between Kaukapakapa and Dairy Flat

1899 Despite joking "The bigger they are, the harder they fall" Bob Fitzsimmons, NZ's only World Heavyweight Champion, loses to Jim Jeffries, who was taller, heavier, and younger than him

69

AUCKLAND

New Zealand's largest city, with a population of over a million, Auckland is located on the isthmus between the Manukau and Waitemata Harbours, with the **Waitakere Ranges** (**hiking** and dramatic **beaches**) to the west, and the **Hauraki Gulf** (**swimming**, **fishing**, and **boating**) fronting the city to the east. In between, a sea of houses on ¼-acre sections is spread out, although in-fill housing is changing this traditional pattern.

A walk, or ride, up one of Auckland's extinct basalt volcanoes (e.g. **Mt Eden**, **One Tree Hill**, or **Mt Victoria**) gives a great perspective over The City of Sails. One of the oldest volcanoes is **Lake Pupuke**, in **Takapuna**, a 140,000 year-old freshwater-filled crater popular with dinghy sailors, rowers, and canoeists. The youngest and least altered cone (several have been levelled for building material) - is **Rangitoto Island**, which erupted 10 times more magma than any of the earlier volcanoes, and is only about 600 years old. Walking up Rangitoto is a great day trip, by ferry from the city or **Devonport**.

The centre of town is **Queen St**, a thoroughfare lined with shops (including several outdoor equipment stores) and, more recently, a saturation of stores offering tourist nick-nacks. However, the waterfront at the bottom of Queen St is what gives Auckland its stunning setting, with views of the **Harbour Bridge** (guided walks over the bridge available), the **Maritime Museum**, the **Ferry Building**, and the **Viaduct Basin**. Heading east from downtown, Quay St, connects you to **Tamaki Drive**, which runs along the waterfront, past the **Parnell Baths**, **Kelly Tarlton's Underwater World**, and the fashionable café suburbs of **Mission Bay** and **St Heliers**.

Up Queen Street, **Albert Park** and the **University of Auckland** are on the left off Victoria St East. Harrah's **Sky Tower** dominates the cityscape and marks the way to their casino on Victoria St West (observation deck and **bungy-jumping** available). The city's main **Post Office** is one block west of Queen St, off Wellesley St, the **Library** and **Art Gallery** are one block east. The excellent **Auckland Museum** is in **The Domain**, about a 2km walk or ride southwest of downtown, across Grafton Gully. **The Domain** also has **Botanic Gardens**, a **Fernery**, sports fields, and great **views**.

The Link is a hop-on hop-off bus that loops around many of the city's attractions.

There is a **50km Cycle Loop** around Auckland and a **Coast to Coast Walking Route** through the city that Information Centres (see below) can give details on.

◆   ◆   ◆   ◆   ◆

Camping;
Remuera Motor Lodge & Inner City Campground, 16 Minto Rd, Remuera, Ph 09 524 5126 or 0508 244 244, T$25, Cabin$55 ◆ Others; Takapuna, Avondale

Hostel;
Auckland City YHA, Cnr City Rd & Liverpool St, Ph 09 309 2802, Dorm$23, D$66 ◆ Base Backpackers, 16 Fort St, Auckland City, Ph 09 300 9999, Dorm$24, D$68 ◆ Auckland Central Backpackers, 229 Queen St, Ph 09 358 4877 ◆ The Brown Kiwi, 7 Prosford St, Ponsonby, Dorm$18, D$46 ◆ Others; Auckland City

B&B;
Badger's of Devonport, 30 Summer St, Ph 09 445 2099, D$140 ◆ Auckland Homestay B&B, 37 Torrance St, Epsom, Ph 09 624, 3714, S$80, D$120 ◆ Others; Devonport, Auckland

Motel/Hotel;
Pacific Inn, 210 Kirkbride Rd, Mangere, Ph 09 275 1129 or 0800 504 800, S$80, D$100 ◆ Airport Gold Star Motel, 255 Kirkbride Rd, Mangere, Ph 09 275 8199 or 0800 802 090, S$75, D$95 ◆ Devonport Motel, 11 Buchanan St, Ph 09 445 1010, D$115 ◆ Parnell Inn, 320 Parnell Rd, Ph 09 358 0642, S$85, D$120 ◆ The Kiwi International Hotel, 411 Queen St, Auckland City, Ph 09 379 6487 or 0800 100 411, S$45, D$90 ◆ Others; Devonport, Parnell, Auckland City, Mangere

i;
Devonport Visitor Centre, 3 Victoria Rd, Ph 09 446 0677 ◆ Auckland Intl. Airport Visitor Centre, Intl. Terminal, Ph 09 256 8535 ◆ NZ Visitors Centre, Cnr Quay St & Hobson St, Auckland City, Ph 09 979 2333 ◆ Others; Auckland City

Bike Shops;
Velo, 80 Hobson St, Auckland City, Ph 307 0864 ◆ Adventure Cycles, Commerce St, Auckland City, Ph 309 5566 ◆ Cyco, 282 Ponsonby Rd, Ponsonby, Ph 09 376 4447 ◆ Others; Auckland

1900's Electric trams become a principal mode of transport in NZ's major cities

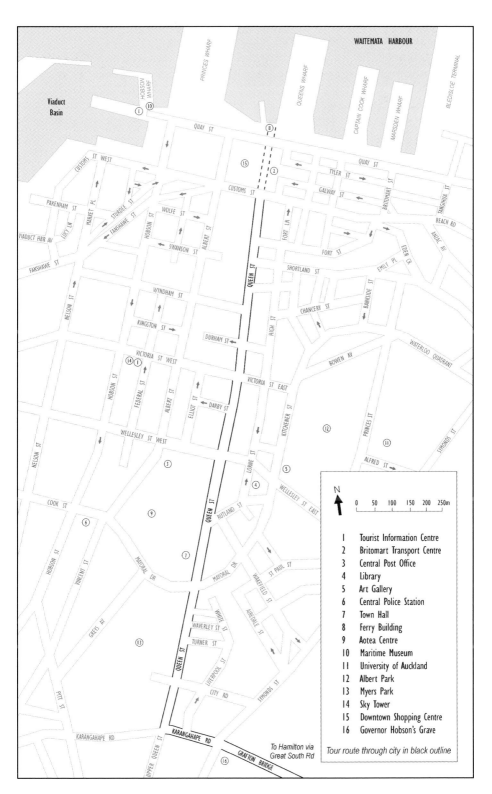

WAITEMATA HARBOUR

Viaduct
Basin

QUAY ST

CUSTOMS ST WEST

PAKENHAM ST

VIADUCT HBR AV

FANSHAWE ST

CUSTOMS ST

QUAY ST

TYLER ST

GALWAY ST

WOLFE ST

FORT ST

SWANSON ST

SHORTLAND ST

WYNDHAM ST

CHANCERY ST

KINGSTON ST

DURHAM ST

VICTORIA ST WEST

VICTORIA ST EAST

BOWEN AV

WATERLOO QUADRANT

DARBY ST

WELLESLEY ST WEST

ALFRED ST

WELLESLEY ST EAST

COOK ST

To Hamilton via
Great South Rd

KARANGAHAPE RD

GRAFTON BRIDGE

N						
0	50	100	150	200	250m	

1	Tourist Information Centre
2	Britomart Transport Centre
3	Central Post Office
4	Library
5	Art Gallery
6	Central Police Station
7	Town Hall
8	Ferry Building
9	Aotea Centre
10	Maritime Museum
11	University of Auckland
12	Albert Park
13	Myers Park
14	Sky Tower
15	Downtown Shopping Centre
16	Governor Hobson's Grave

Tour route through city in black outline

*1900 Arthur Porritt; Rhodes Scholar, third in the 100m at the Paris
Olympics, surgeon to the Queen of England, Governor-General
of NZ, and life peer, is born in Wanganui*

71

8 TAKAPUNA TO HAMILTON

Takapuna to;

Papakura	39km	m/h, bike shop	*37 03.7, 174 56.5*
Mercer	67km	m/h *(opening 2006)*, i	*37 11.5, 174 59.1*
Huntly	103km	c, m/h, i	*37 33.5, 175 09.6*
Hamilton	135km	c, h, b&b, m/h, i, bike shop	*37 47.1, 175 16.9*

Unfortunately, this stage involves riding with a considerable amount of traffic, as the tour travels between NZ's biggest and 4th biggest cities. The ride does however include very pretty stretches, following the Waikato River much of the way and passing rich farmland.

Take Lake Rd, from the end of Hurstmere Rd in the heart of Takapuna, to Devonport (a fretful piece of suburban cycling). Lake Rd ends at the foot of Mt Victoria, an 81m basalt cone. Go right, around the base of the volcano, and down to the Devonport Ferry. There are regular crossings from early till late (bikes can be wheeled on directly), and the trip has great views of the City and Harbour Bridge.

The ferry ride ends at the foot of Queen St - Auckland's main thoroughfare. This street was built in an old stream gully that, in 1840, was a muddy bog traversed by several footbridges. Today, the stream is culverted underground and modern buildings line the slopes, but the street's narrowness and overhanging verandas still have a colonial feel. Head up Queens St; past Customs St, Fort St, and Vulcan Ln. There is a plaque on Queen St marking the city's old shoreline before reclaimation, where the sea came up to about Fort St. Continue uphill to Karangahape Rd, or "K Rd" as it is locally known.

Leave downtown by going left on K Rd and crossing Grafton Bridge, a favourite suicide spot until high fences were installed. Past Auckland Hospital, Park Rd swings past the gates of Auckland Domain (the city's premier park with an excellent museum, gardens, an old pa site, and stunning views - all built in and around a volcanic crater). Go left on Khyber Pass Rd, then right onto Broadway. Continue on Broadway to the motorway overpass. Just past the overpass, veer left onto Great South Rd. This long road (the old route south, originally marked by kauri mile-posts) takes you out of the city past volcanic cones, car sales yards, industrial areas, affluent suburbs and not-so-well-off suburbs. The road crosses the Tamaki Isthmus (at 2km wide, the narrowest part of New Zealand), where Maori used to drag their canoes between harbours.

The route passes through Manukau City, technically New Zealand's largest city, although these boundaries are political only as Auckland's suburban sprawl reaches out to Papakura at least. After Papakura the houses thin, fields reappear, and the road eventually starts climbing the Bombay Hills - volcanic hills that are super productive for vegetable growing. There are several fruit and veggie shops at Bombay.

At the roundabout at Great South Rd and Mill Rd bikes can join State Highway 1 (the Waikato Expressway) which still has fast moving traffic but typically has a wide shoulder. Cross on-ramps and off-ramps with care, at the spots signposted for cyclists. After dropping off the Bombay Hills the terrain is mostly flat to gently rolling and good time can

be made if conditions are conducive, although long term earthworks to straighten Highway 1 are ongoing in places and can slow things.

The road meets the Waikato River at Mercer, a stop with basic services. From here south, the route passes through a succession of small and large river towns to Hamilton. After Meremere the route departs from the river and crosses gently rolling farmland, with the huge Whangamarino Swamp off to the east. The road rejoins the river at Rangiriri, a major battle site during the Waikato Wars.

1901 The visiting Duke of Cornwall, later George V, is gifted a huia tail feather. It is put in his hatband and the subsequent fashion craze results in this rare bird being hunted to extinction

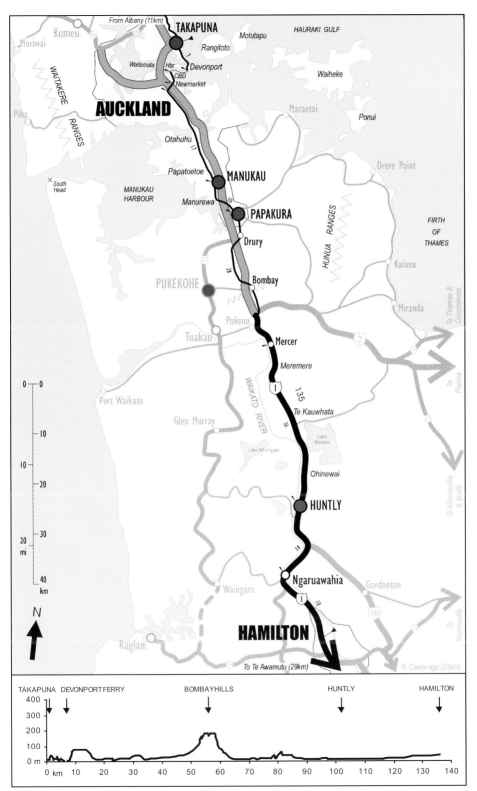

1902 or 1903 Canterbury farmer/inventor Richard Pearse reputedly takes a homemade plane on a short controlled flight. With only his sister and a farmhand watching, lack of independent evidence prevents it being recorded as the first powered flight

Huntly with a population of about 7,000, is the biggest town en-route between Papakura and Hamilton, and has a full range of services. Local coal mines fuel the power station across the river. Leaving Huntly, the road runs between the Taupiri Ranges and the river.

The route crosses the Waikato for the first time entering Ngaruawahia, at the junction of the Waikato and Waipa rivers. The town, sitting below the Hakarimata Ranges, is home to the Maori Queen. Her marae, Turangawaiwai, is visible to the left as you enter town.

In the last 19km to Hamilton the road passes the Horotiu Freezing Works and the old Te Rapa Air Force Base. State Highway 1 actually skirts Hamilton, so if you don't plan on stopping here, follow the S.H. 1 signs to S.H. 3 at the southern edge of Hamilton. To enter town, follow the City Centre signs (Route No. 4), taking Te Rapa Rd, to Ulster St, to Victoria St. Hamilton, also on the river, was called Kirikiriroa in Maori - roughly, "a long stretch of gravel". Today the city promotes its museum, art gallery, zoo and gardens.

The Waikato Wars

Governor Grey had soldiers start construction of Great South Rd (also called Grey's Rd) as a military route to protect, and advance, European interests in the Waikato.

Skirmishes with Maori since the 1840's had lead to the construction of Fencible Settlements on the outskirts of Auckland, such as Onehunga and Otahuhu, but by the 1860's tensions over land issues had resulted in full-scale war in Taranaki, and the Waikato tribes were also unhappy. Tamihana Te Rauparaha, son of the great Kapiti chief, had visited Queen Victoria and returned with the vision of a Maori King to unite the Waikato tribes and prevent further land losses. Other tribes were sceptical, however, in 1858, the old chief Te Wherowhero was crowned King and his followers in the Waikato and "King Country" gained a vision for nationhood. Grey saw this as a major threat to his plans, and Maori in turn saw Grey's Rd as a major provocation.

Queen's Redoubt, overlooking the Waikato River at Pokeno, was the forward base for the soldiers. The Maori King declared Mangatawhiri Stream a line the soldiers were not to cross. In July 1863, troops crossed the stream and war was declared. British troops, militiamen, and volunteers lead by General Duncan Cameron used Great South Rd to mobilise south, attacking Maori fortifications with support from gun boats on the Waikato. Maori, used guerrilla tactics to harry the soldiers' supply lines and defended skilfully fortified positions. Several of these battle sites are along the route of this tour.

The first and most important battle of the war began at Rangiriri, on 20 November 1863. Maori had established a hilltop defensive line. During the afternoon gunboats offloaded men and pounded the Maori's wooden parapets with cannon fire, while artillery and troops attacked from both sides. The Maoris, outnumbered 2:1, fought bravely and both sides suffered heavy losses, but with their position compromised, the Maoris retreated during the night via canoe across the small lake east of the pa. After Rangiriri, some of the Maori tribes petitioned Grey to make peace - he refused.

By the end of the year, soldiers were occupying the Maori capital, Ngaruawahia. Cameron continued his pursuit, capturing Te Awamutu and Kihikihi, and fighting another decisive battle at Orakau, in March/April 1864. The Maoris were building a large defensive fortification here, but before they could complete it, it was attacked by about 2,000 troops. 300 men, women, and children defended the pa, lead by Rewi Maniapoto, who refused to surrender. The daughter of a Taupo chief famously spoke up during truce talks, saying, if men were to die, the woman and children could die also. They held-out 3 days before breaking out and escaping to the King Country.

Cameron's advance was unstoppable, and when troops routed Gate Pa, near Tauranga, the Maori cause was effectively extinguished and they surrendered on 27 May 1865. The price of war for Maori, aside from the dead and wounded, was the confiscation of over a million acres, stretching from Port Waikato to Kihikihi.

Camping;
Manukau Top 10 Holiday Park, 902 Great South Rd, Manukau City, Ph 09 266 8016, T$10, Cabin$50 ◆ South Auckland Caravan Park, Ararimu Rd, Ramarama, Drury, Ph 09 294 8903, $T20, Cabin$30 ◆ Huntly Caravan Park, Taihua Park Ave, Huntly, Ph 07 828 8363, $T14, Cabin $25 ◆ Hamilton City Holiday Park, 14 Ruakura Rd, Hamilton, Ph 07 855 8255, $T20, Cabin $40 ◆ Others; Hamilton

Hostel;
Helen Haywood YHA, 1190 Victoria St, Hamilton, Ph 07 838 0009, Dorm$20, D$50 ◆ Others; Hamilton

B&B;
Richmond, 31 Horne St, Hamilton, Ph 07 838 2680, S$60, D$90 ◆ Others; Hamilton

Motel/Hotel;
North End Motel, S.H. 1, Huntly, Ph 07 828 8298, S$60, $D85 ◆ Beerescourt Motel, 299 Ulster St, Hamilton, Ph 07 839 3277, S$70, D$85 ◆ BJ's Budget Motor Inn, 256 Te Rapa Rd, Hamilton, Ph 07 849 5000, S$55, D$65 ◆ Others; various

i;
Franklin Info Centre, Cnr S.H. 1 & Mill Rd, Bombay, Ph 09 236 0670 ◆ Huntly Info Centre, 160 Gt Sth Rd, Ph 07 828 6406 ◆ Hamilton Visitor Centre, Anglesea St & Bryce St, Ph 07 839 3580

Bike Shops;
Cycle City, 45 Cavendish Dr, Manukau, Ph 09 262 1043 ◆ Bike Barn, Ulster St, Hamilton, Ph 07 838 0575 ◆ Others; Papatoetoe, Manurewa, Manukau, Papakura, Hamilton

500 km Between Auckland City and Manukau City

550 km Between Mercer and Meremere

600 km Between Huntly and Ngaruawahia

1905 All Black Bob Deans dives for a try against Wales but is reputedly pulled back from the line before the ref arrives, resulting in NZ's only loss of the "Originals" tour

THE NORTH ISLAND'S EAST COAST

If you have the time, and are looking for a longer route to Wellington that takes in some of the remotest settlements in New Zealand, consider touring around East Cape. Or, if you want to ride an almost complete circuit of New Zealand, you could come back this way after reaching Bluff and heading up the West Coast of the South Island! (see p.132). Suggested stages are given below and shown on the map opposite as a starting point for cyclists who may want to investigate these options further. These stages include some fairly long days, which fit cyclists would find suitable - tourers with time on their hands could shorten these with intermediate stops for a more leisurely tour.

The route shown passes through the thermal areas around Rotorua, with their geysers, boiling mud pools, and mineral baths, which have helped make this city one of New Zealand's traditional tourist towns. Highway 30 to Whakatane passes the Rotorua Lakes area, a tourist attraction in its own right.

Whakatane and Ohope look out to White Island, a steaming volcanic cone. The ride around the Cape passes beautiful bays, and small, predominantly Maori, settlements with the rugged Urewera and Raukumara Ranges as backdrops. A trip to the East Cape lighthouse involves a 21km ride (each-way) along a coastal gravel road.

The route down the southeast side of East Cape alternates between farmland and coastal villages dotted with pohutukawa trees (Te Araroa reportedly has the oldest pohutukawa in New Zealand. A huge, gnarled, and sacred tree thought to be over 600 years old). The small settlement of Whangara, between Tologa Bay and Gisborne was the setting for the popular 2003 movie *Whale Rider*.

Gisborne is where Captain Cook first landed in New Zealand, on October 9 1769, although he found the Maoris there hostile and was unable to resupply - calling the area Poverty Bay (as opposed to The Bay of Plenty, on the northwest side of East Cape, where he did get supplies).

Heading south, the route heads into the farming districts around Hawke's Bay, which were heavily affected by Cyclone Bola in 1986. Many of the hummocky hillsides visible along this stretch are the result of landslides that occurred during this storm. The regional centre of Napier is an interesting town, with many Art Deco buildings - the town was totally rebuilt following a disastrous earthquake in 1931.

The tour leaves the coast at Napier and heads inland to Dannevirke, a town established in the 1870's by immigrants from Scandinavia who broke the surrounding bush into farmland. Masterton to the south is the centre of the Wairarapa District, another farming dominated area, which holds New Zealand's "Golden Shears" shearing competition every year.

From here the final stage crosses back to the west side of the North Island, between the Tararua Ranges and Rimutaka Ranges, and enters Wellington via Upper Hutt, Lower Hutt, and Petone.

Another alternative for seeing the East Coast would be to take a bus to Whakatane (close to Ohope) and ride for 4 or 5 days around the Cape to Gisborne, a major East Coast centre where onward transport is available. Possible stages around East Cape are;

Hamilton to Rotorua (108km) ◆ Rotorua to Ohope (96km) ◆ Ohope to Te Kaha (107km) ◆ Te Kaha to Te Araroa (92km) ◆ Te Araroa to Tokomaru Bay (79km) ◆ Tokomaru Bay to Gisborne (89km) ◆ Gisbourne to Wairoa (100km) ◆ Wairoa to Napier (118km) ◆ Napier to Dannevirke (123km) ◆ Dannevirke to Masterton (109km) ◆ Masterton to Wellington (101km)

1907 The last confirmed sighting of a huia is made (a bird so unique that the sexes were initially thought to be different species - males with a short beak and females a long curved beak)

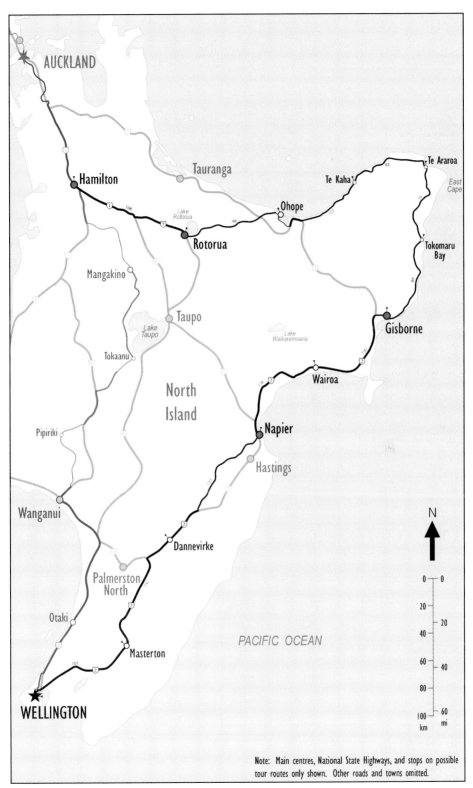

AUCKLAND

Hamilton

Tauranga

Lake
Rotorua

Te Kaha

Te Araroa

East
Cape

Ohope

Rotorua

Tokomaru
Bay

Mangakino

Taupo

Lake
Taupo

Lake
Waikaremoana

Gisborne

Tokaanu

Pipiriki

North
Island

Wairoa

Napier

Hastings

Wanganui

Dannevirke

Palmerston
North

Otaki

Masterton

PACIFIC OCEAN

WELLINGTON

N

0	0
20	
40	20
60	40
80	
100	60
km	mi

Note: Main centres, National State Highways, and stops on possible
tour routes only shown. Other roads and towns omitted.

*1907 The Plunket Society is formed by Frederic Truby King,
Superintendent of Seacliff Mental Hospital, to assist new
mothers with baby care*

9 HAMILTON TO MANGAKINO

Hamilton to;

Te Awamutu	29km	c, b&b, m/h, i, bike shop	38 00.6, 175 19.6
Kihikihi	34km	m/h	38 02.3, 175 20.7
Parawera	44km	c, h *(Owairaka Valley)*	38 04.4, 175 25.7
Arohena	70km		38 11.5, 175 36.7
Lake Waipapa	85km	c	38 17.5, 175 40.8
Mangakino	102km	h, m/h	38 22.2, 175 46.4

From Hamilton, this stage takes State Highway 3 to the small town of Kihikihi, before departing the highway for quieter country roads through farmland, plantation forest, and remnants of native bush. The ride ends at Mangakino, a timber and hydro-electric town.

At the south end of Hamilton's main street (Victoria St) turn right onto Bridge St and follow the signs for State Highway 3. Bridge St veers to the left and becomes Cobham Dr, which connects to Normandy Ave and the start of State Highway 3. The 29km to Te Awamutu are rolling and include several sections with short steep climbs.

Te Awamutu is known as the Rose Town and prides itself on its gardens. Being only 3km from the edge of the King Country Province, this was a major outpost during the Waikato Wars, with over 4,000 troops stationed here. Today, the town has a population of about 13,500 and there is a good selection of shops and accommodation.

Continue south for 5km to Kihikihi (the Maori word for cicada) and go left at the War Memorial onto Whitmore St, which becomes Arapuni Rd at the edge of town and enters gently rolling countryside. 4km from Kihikihi, a simple roadside monument amongst pretty fields, marks the Orakau battlefield site (see p.74).

There is a store and marae at Parawera, 10km past Kihikihi. The road forks here. Go right on Owairaka Valley Rd, which heads towards Waipapa Dam. The road drops into this pretty valley and gently rolls along beside Owairaka Stream before climbing past ignimbrite bluffs popular with rock climbers. At the top of this climb is a T-junction beside a rural school and hall. Go left, following Rotongata Rd and passing under the electrical lines that carry power from the Waikato hydro-electric plants. Before Rotongata, the road swings south towards Lake Waipapa, travelling through rolling countryside with occasional farmhouses and patches of native trees that have survived in the gullies of farms.

After Arohena (a location with a rural school but no services) the road starts climbing noticeably, touching the edge of Pureora State Forest Park, before dropping to Waipapa

Waipapa Dam and Lake Waipapa

Dam. The road enters dark green bush for the final few kilometres to the dam and includes a high viaduct crossing Mangawhio Stream, before reaching the Waikato River at the dam.

There are no services at Waipapa Dam but there is an unofficial campsite beside the lake, consisting of a grassy field and a toilet block. The lake has a slightly ominous look with its black water, hemmed in on both sides by dense bush, and the constant hum of the Power Station's turbines. The dam caretakers live in a small gated-community on the eastern side of the river.

From Waipapa Dam, the road follows the western shoreline briefly, crossing the

1908 The Raurimu Spiral, near National Park in the North Is, is completed - a feat of rail engineering reducing grades to 1:52 over a short distance

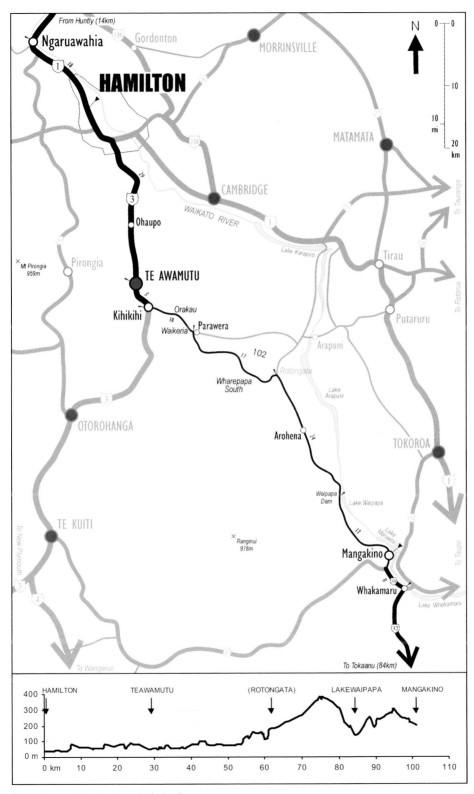

From Huntly (14km)

N

0 — 0

10

10 mi

20 km

Ngaruawahia

Gordonton

MORRINSVILLE

1 18

HAMILTON

29

13

MATAMATA

3

CAMBRIDGE

WAIKATO RIVER

1

Ohaupo

Lake Karapiro

Tirau

To Tauranga

To Rotorua

× Mt Pirongia 959m

Pirongia

TE AWAMUTU

Putaruru

5

Kihikihi

Orakau

Arapuni

10

Waikeria

Parawera

17

102

Rotongata

Wharepapa South

Lake Arapuni

3

OTOROHANGA

Arohena

24

TOKOROA

1

TE KUITI

To New Plymouth

Waipapa Dam

Lake Waipapa

× Ranginui 978m

Lake Maraetai

11

Mangakino

To Taupo

4

8

30

Whakamaru

Lake Whakamaru

32

To Wanganui

To Tokaanu (84km)

| HAMILTON | TEAWAMUTU | (ROTONGATA) | LAKEWAIPAPA | MANGAKINO |

400
300
200
100
0 m

0 km   10   20   30   40   50   60   70   80   90   100   110

1908 NZ's population is estimated to be 1 million

79

mouth of the Waipapa River and looking across the lake to white ignimbrite cliffs (formed from superhot ash flows from Taupo that cooled and cracked forming distinctive vertical fracture columns). The road climbs through exotic plantation forests that are the main industry in the area, before dropping to Mangakino.

Mangakino township, 17km past Waipapa Dam, is on a loop road slightly off the main road. The town is not a tourist destination and is usually in the news for the wrong reasons (e.g. local Police trying to ban liquor in the town centre to reduce youth drunkenness). Despite being a bit rough around the edges, the town gives a good perspective of rural New Zealand life away from more trafficked routes. The town was built in the 1960's to house workers on the Lake Maraetai Powerhouse Project (which doubled the old station's capacity). The township area was handed back to Maori when the project was finished. In 2002, the Iwi decided to sell-up, and the titles to 500 properties (about two-thirds of the town) were put up for auction by public tender. A man from Pukekohe bought the titles, and now, effectively, owns Mangakino.

Fishing on the Waikato River

The Waikato River
The Waikato is New Zealand's longest river, flowing 425km from Lake Taupo to Port Waikato (about 60km southwest of Auckland). The Waikato's watershed forms a large part of the North Island and because the river starts from New Zealand's largest active volcanic crater, Lake Taupo, the river's history has been dramatic.

The great lake of Taupo sits in a caldera that has erupted numerous times over the last 500,000 years, discharging millions of tonnes of rock, pumice, and ash over the central North Island and into the river. The river that flowed from this crater has had to change course several times as it cut through layers of ash from the latest eruption. The last major diversion occurred 20,000 years ago when the river was flowing almost directly north and discharging, via the Firth of Thames, on the east side of the North Island. A huge eruption around this time sent so much volcanic material down the river valley it dammed at a narrow spot known as the Hinuera Gap, near Matamata. When water filled the crater again it flowed north to this spot, then west via the Hamilton Basin to its present location discharging on the west coast.

For Maori, the river provided farming and fishing opportunities, hilltops above the river for fortified villages, and a means of transportation during times of war and peace.

Europeans also used the river, to access the central North Island and move troops and supplies during the Waikato Wars. After the Waikato Wars, and subsequent appropriation of the river, the settlers' thoughts turned to development. The fertile river plains and volcanic soils proved ideal dairy farming country and exotic forests were planted along the upper reaches of the river. The river's steep drop from Taupo to the sea, through numerous ignimbrite gorges, made it well suited for damming for hydro-electric power schemes, and electricity from the Waikato now lights much of the North Island. The first modern dam to be built was Arapuni, completed in 1929. Six others followed - the furthest downstream being Karapiro, completed in 1948, which flooded the old Horahora Power Station (the river's first in 1913) and created a 24km long lake, used extensively for rowing and boating. Since July 2002, Waikato River water has also been treated and piped to Auckland to supplement their drinking water supply.

Camping;
Roadrunner Motel & Holiday Park, Te Awamutu (see Motel/Hotel) ◆ Castle Rock Adventure Lodge, Owairaka Valley (see Hostel) ◆ Basic Camping, Waipapa Dam Reserve, Waipapa Dam

Hostel;
Castle Rock Adventure Lodge, 1250 Owairaka Valley Rd, Owairaka Valley, Ph 07 872 2509 or 0800 225 462, T$10pp, Woolshed $10pp, Dorm$25, D$70 ◆ Others; Mangakino (see Motel/Hotel)

B&B;
Morton B&B, 10 Brill Rd, Te Awamutu, Ph 07 871 8814, S$50, D$80

Motel/Hotel;
Roadrunner Motel & Holiday Park, 141 Bond Rd, Te Awamutu, Ph 07 871 7420, S$60, D$70 ◆ ◆ Cicada Motel, 96 Lyon St, Kihikihi, Ph, 07 871 7211, S$60, D$75 ◆ Mangakino Village Hotel & Backpackers, 55 Ranagtira Dr, Mangakino, Ph 07 882 8800, Dorm$20, S$50, D$70 ◆ Others; Te Awamutu

i;
Te Awamutu Visitor Information Centre, 1 Gorst Ave, Te Awamutu, Ph 07 871 3259

Bike Shops;
Davies Cycles, 8 Brady St, Te Awamutu, Ph: 07 870 1444 ◆ Te A Cycles, 240 Sloane St, Te Awamutu, Ph: 07 871 4816

650 km Te Awamutu

700 km Between Arohena and Waipapa Dam

*1909 The inter-island ferry The Penguin is wrecked with the loss of 72 lives.
Some think it was cursed after a passenger on a previous voyage shot
at Pelorous Jack, a dolphin that guided ships through French Pass*

81

10 MANGAKINO TO TOKAANU

Mangakino to;

Whakamaru	8km	38 25.2, 175 47.8
Kuratau	75km	38 52.9, 175 40.7
Tokaanu	92km c, m/h	38 57.8, 175 45.9

This stage travels into the volcanic heart of the North Island: the Taupo Volcanic Zone (TVZ), and into some of the last areas that Pakehas sought to settle in the late 19th Century. The countryside is mostly farmed these days but remains sparsely populated with few services available between Mangakino and Tokaanu, as most traffic travels up and down State Highway 1 on the opposite side of Lake Taupo. The terrain is undulating with some tough climbs, but the solitude is worth it and there are great lookouts over the lake and, if the weather is good, to the mountains beyond. A popular Round-the-Lake cycle ride is held annually, on the last Saturday in November, with racers and casual riders circling the Lake starting and finishing in Taupo. The fastest racers typically loop the lake in less than 4 hours.

3km after leaving Mangakino the road joins Highway 30 which takes you towards Whakamaru, another hydroelectric dam and associated community. The service station 1km before Whakamaru dam is at the junction of Routes 30 and 32. Turn right onto 32 here and head south. [Note: If you want to visit Taupo itself there is a turn-off (Poihipi Rd) 12km down Route 32 that leads into town. Taupo is about 30km from the turn-off].

The volcanic ash exposed in the road cuttings and the hummocky terrain along this stretch are a reflection of the huge 186AD eruption of Taupo, an eruption so violent it is hard to image it came from this placid blue lake. The vent for the eruption in thought to be the Horomatangi Reef area, located a few metres below the lake's surface about 5km off the western shore halfway down the lake. As magma rose, water in the lake flashed to steam and trees around the vent were blown flat - radiating like spokes from the crater. Surges of hot ash and gas flowed out across the surrounding area and ejected ash and rock rained down - deposits that can be distinguished in some of the road cuttings (the surge deposits filling valleys in the underlying topography and the air-fall ash blanketing the topography). When the eruption was over, ash had reached as far as Auckland and Antarctica, and the Waikato River's outlet was plugged with pumice. The lake refilled to about 30m above its present level before the plug at the head of the river broke down in a series of floods. The terraces from these old lake levels are visible on the far side of the lake as you ride south.

The route down Western Bay Rd involves numerous short steep climbs as the road crosses streams that drain into the lake and have cut deeply into the soft volcanic ash. The views are splendid; fantastic ignimbrite bluffs and bush clad valleys. The road criss-crosses underneath electrical pylons to Kuratau Junction where the route joins Highway 41, for 17km, to Tokaanu. From Kuratau Junction the road climbs steeply, passing the pretty little rhyolite dome of Pukekaikiore on the left. After a final lookout over the lake the road drops steeply to a lakeside junction, turn left to visit Waihi Village, 2km to the northwest, or continue straight ahead for Tokaanu, 1km down the road. The nearby town of Turangi, 6km past Tokaanu, is a slightly bigger tourist town.

Waihi Village is a historic Maori settlement at the base of steep slopes dotted with steaming fumaroles. Hot water and steam reach the surface here along the Waihi

1916 The Gallipoli campaign, part of a failed plan to capture Constantinople, ends with NZ losing over 2,700 men, with 4,700 wounded

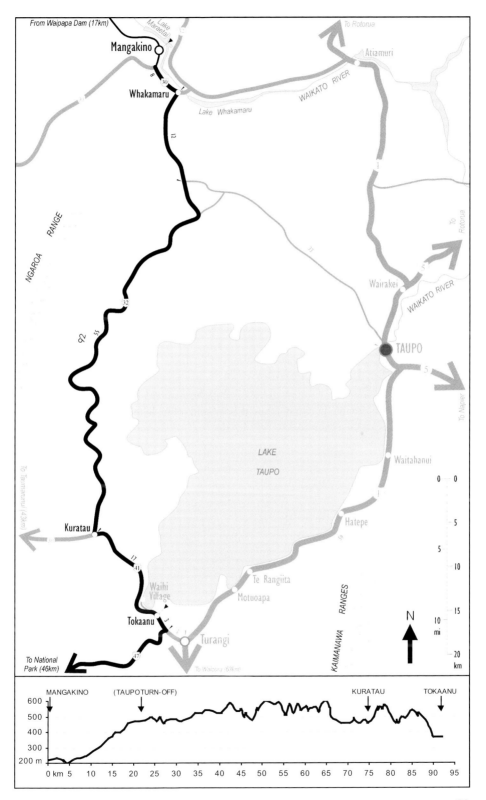

From Waipapa Dam (17km)

Lake
Maraetai

Mangakino

To Rotorua

Atiamuri

Whakamaru

WAIKATO RIVER

Lake Whakamaru

NGAROA RANGE

To Rotorua

Wairakei

WAIKATO RIVER

TAUPO

To Napier

LAKE
TAUPO

Waitahanui

To Taumarunui (43km)

Kuratau

Hatepe

Te Rangiita

Waihi
Village

Motuoapa

Tokaanu

Turangi

KAIMANAWA RANGES

To National
Park (46km)

To Waiouru (69km)

N

0 — 0

5

5

10

15

10
mi

20
km

| MANGAKINO | (TAUPO TURN-OFF) | | | | KURATAU | TOKAANU |

600
500
400
300
200 m

0 km 5   10   15   20   25   30   35   40   45   50   55   60   65   70   75   80   85   90   95

1917 Pre-eminent NZ athletics coach and developer of the
concept of jogging, Arthur Lydiard is born

Fault, which runs beneath the cliffs. Weathering of these cliffs is accelerated by the thermal activity, and a large landslide in 1846 killed 54 locals, including the father of Te Heuheu Tukino IV, the chief who gifted land for Tongariro National Park to the Crown. Another devastating landslide occurred in 1910. The 19th Century Catholic Church here is decorated with Maori carvings and has excellent stained-glass windows showing the risen Christ and the Virgin Mary as Maori.

Tokaanu also has thermal activity with public and private pools (the campground has its own pools). The town is located near the mouth of the Tongariro River - a river known internationally for trout fishing, where every stretch and bend has a designated name, such as; The Boulevard, Never Fail Pool, Breakfast Pool, and Lonely Pool.

The cone of Mt Ngaruahoe (youngest of the 3 active Tongariro Park volcanoes), and Mt Tongariro to the left

The TVZ, and The Tongariro Power Project

The Taupo Volcanic Zone (TVZ) has proved both problematic and profitable for the people of the central North Island. The dangers of living in an active volcanic region are seen in occasional natural disasters, such as the Tarawera Eruption (1886) and Tangiwai Rail Disaster (1953). The benefits of tourism, good soils for forestry and farming, and energy generating potential have been longer lasting.

TVZ volcanism is a feature of the plate boundary which runs along the Hikurangi Trench (off the south east coast of the North Island) and through the middle of the South Island. On-land, the Pacific and Indo-Australian Plates butt and slide past each other forming the Southern Alps, while in the trench the Pacific Plate is being pushed under the Indo-Australian Plate, where it is melting. The melted plate is less dense than the surrounding material and rises, causing volcanoes. This melting has moved south over the last 20 million years, leaving a trail of volcanoes down the North Island, to its current position under the TVZ, where eruptions have been occurring for the last 2 million years. Volcanic features of the TVZ include; geothermal activity, small basalt and rhyolite domes, 4 large rhyolite calderas (faulted basins sitting over huge magma chambers, such as Taupo), and the andesite-dominated volcanoes of Mt Tongariro, Mt Ngaruahoe, and Mt Ruapehu.

The different magma types are the result of different source materials melting at different depths, and the magmas being cooked differently on their way to the surface. The viscous ryholite magmas of the calderas are full of volatile gases which produce particularly explosive eruptions as the lava reaches the surface, while the magmas producing basalt and andesite volcanoes, have lower melting points, are runnier, and allow volatile gases to escape more easily.

During power shortages of the 1950's the Government's attention turned to the hydroelectric potential of the rivers that drained Mt Ruapehu, Mt Ngauruhoe, and Mt Tongariro. The Tongariro Power Project was constructed with a series of canals, tunnels, and aqueducts that tapped most of the rivers on the east and west sides of these mountains and diverted flows through Tokannu and Rangipo Power Stations. The scheme had significant technical problems to overcome, such as tunnelling through variable, active, volcanic terrain, and there was an environmental cost, as some construction inside Tongariro National Park was required to facilitate the project.

Following protests in the 1980's and 1990's the Government required minimum flows to be maintained in several rivers, including the Whanganui which had been diverted by as much as 97%.

This tour goes right past the 200-megawatt Tokaanu Power Station, which receives water from Lake Rotoaira, 200m above the station, via a 6km tunnel. Lake Rotoaira in turn receives extra water from the Whanganui and Tongariro Rivers via canals. The Tokaanu tunnel proved a difficult job for the Italian contractor - after hot geothermal water, and clay that swelled when it got wet, was encountered - a combination with enough force to buckle the steel forms that held the advancing tunnel open.

Camping;
Oasis Motel & Caravan Park, S.H. 41, Tokaanu, Ph 07 386 8569, T$10, Cabin$35, D$60 ◆ Turangi Cabins & Holiday Park, Ohuanga Rd, Turangi, Ph 07 386 8754, T$9, Cabin$16pp ◆ Others; Turangi

Hostel;
Extreme Backpackers, 26 Ngawaka Pl, Turangi, Ph 07 386 8949, Dorm$17, S$30, D$40 ◆ Others; Turangi

B&B;
Bird Cottage, 3245 Poihipi Rd, 12km S of Mangakino, Ph 07 372 8848, S$100, D$120

Motel/Hotel;
Oasis Motel & Caravan Park, Tokaanu, (see Camping) ◆ Aotearoa Thermal Resort, S.H. 41, Tokaanu, Ph 07 386 8873, D$100 ◆ Tokaanu Lodge Motel, S.H. 41, Tokaanu, Ph 07 386 8572, D$85 ◆ Creel Lodge Motel, 183 Taupahi Rd, Turangi, Ph 07 386 8081, S$55, D$80 ◆ Others; Turangi

i;
Turangi Visitor Centre, Ngawaka Place, Turangi, Ph 07 386 8999 ◆ Others; Taupo

Bike Shops;
Nearest; Taupo

750 km Between Whakamaru and Kuratau

800 km Between Kuratau and Tokaanu

11 TOKAANU TO PIPIRIKI

Tokaanu to;

National Park	49km	c, h, m/h
Raetihi	83km	c, b&b, m/h, i
Pipiriki	111km	c

39 10.6, 175 24.1
39 25.6, 175 16.8
39 28.7, 175 02.6

Tokaanu to Pipiriki is a stunning ride if the weather is okay. The first half of the stage generally climbs, as the road crosses the central plateau past the bases of Tongariro National Park's massive volcanoes. The route then drops and follows streams from Raetihi to the edge of the Whanganui River, a remote but beautiful detour off main roads.

Continue south on Highway 41. The road passes the small rhyolite dome of Manganamu on the left (a cone thought to be very young as it is not capped by ash from Taupo's 186AD eruption), and crosses the Tokaanu Power Station tailrace canal. Power at this station is generated by dropping water several hundred metres from Lake Rotoaira, which the tour soon passes. 3km from Tokannu is the junction of Highway 47. Turn south here towards National Park. A steep 6km climb starts immediately, but the bonus is great views back over the lake, then ahead to Tongariro National Park. The road undulates across Te Ponganga Saddle, where there are a couple of excellent walking tracks off to the left, including Hinemihi's Track and the Lake Rotopounamu track (the Turangi Visitor Centre can supply details). The road then drops to Lake Rotoaira.

According to popular history, the warrior-chief Te Rauparaha was on his way to Lake Rotoaira, around 1820, when his party attacked and cannibalised some Ngati Te Hou. With angry Ngati Te Hou in hot pursuit, Te Rauparaha was hidden in the bottom of a kumara pit by a friendly chief. Hiding in the dark, and waiting to be found, the cover was eventually ripped off, and, as the sun shone in, Te Rauparaha saw the hairy legs of the friendly chief. Climbing out he is said to have added new words to an old haka. The All Blacks have used the resulting chant at rugby tests since 1905; *(Approx. translation in Italics).*

Ka Mate! Ka Mate! Ka Ora! Ka Ora!	*I die! I die! I live! I live!*
Ka Mate! Ka Mate! Ka Ora! Ka Ora!	*I die! I die! I live! I live!*
Tenei te tangata puhuru huru	*Behold the hairy man*
Nana nei i tiki mai	*Who fetched the sun*
Whakawhiti te ra	*And caused it to shine again*
A upane ka upane!	*One upward step! Another upward step!*
A upane kaupane whiti te ra! Hi!	*An upward step, another…the sun shines!*

The road continues through plantation forests and enters Ruapehu District. Eivin's Lodge and shop is at the intersection of Highway's 47 and 46. Continue on Highway 47. The terrain is gently rolling with great views of the mountains, in clear weather, including the steaming Ketetahi Hot Springs on the side of Mt Tongariro. The second stream the road crosses after the Highway 47/46 intersection is the Whanganui River, which starts on the side of Mt Tongariro, near the hot springs, before going under the road here, looping north through Taumarunui, then heading south.

If you want to visit Tongariro National Park itself, take Highway 48, 40km from Tokannu, which leads 6km to Whakapapa Village where there is an excellent visitor centre, a campground and motels, and the historic (and expensive) Chateau Tongariro Hotel. Several of the Park's tramping tracks start at Whakapapa. Maori considered the summits of these mountains *tapu* (off-limits). In 1887 they were gifted to the Crown to make NZ's first National Park (the second in the world, after Yellowstone in the US) by Te Heuheu Tukino IV, chief of the Ngati Tuwharetoa to be; "a sacred place of the

1917 Kiwi Ernest Rutherford splits the atom

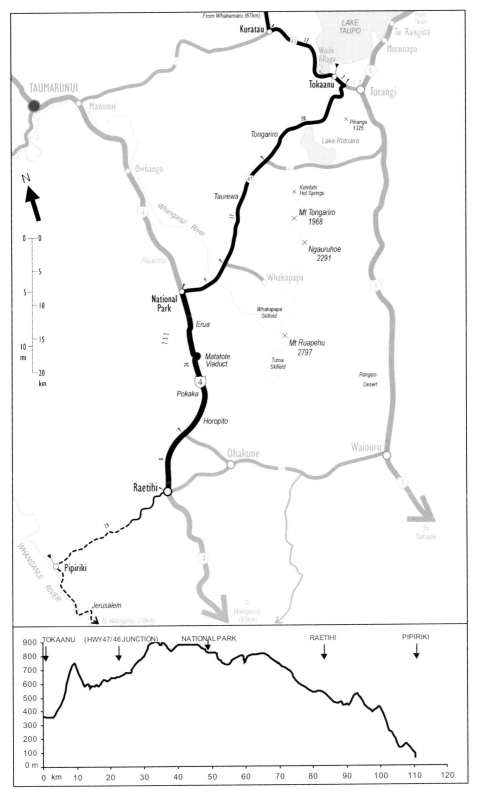

LAKE TAUPO

From Whakamaru (67km)

Kuratau

From Taupo

Te Rangita

Motuoapa

Waihi Village

Tokaanu

Turangi

TAUMARUNUI

Manunui

Pihanga 1325

Tongariro

Lake Rotoaira

Owhango

Whanganui River

Ketetahi Hot Springs

Raurimu

Taurewa

Mt Tongariro 1968

Ngauruhoe 2291

Whakapapa

National Park

Erua

Whakapapa Skifield

Matatote Viaduct

Mt Ruapehu 2797

Turoa Skifield

Pokaka

Rangipo Desert

Horopito

Ohakune

Waiouru

Raetihi

To Taihape

WHANGANUI RIVER

Pipiriki

Jerusalem

To Wanganui (78km)

To Wanganui (91km)

| | TOKAANU | (HWY 47/46 JUNCTION) | NATIONAL PARK | | RAETIHI | | PIPIRIKI |

900
800
700
600
500
400
300
200
100
0 m

0 km   10   20   30   40   50   60   70   80   90   100   110   120

1918 The Niagara docks in Auckland. It is later thought to be responsible for bringing the influenza strain that killed nearly 7,000 people in NZ, requiring the Auckland Town Hall to be used as a temporary morgue

Crown and a gift forever from me and my people". Mt Ruapehu, is the highest spot in the North Island (2797m), with skifields, permanent snow, and an acidic crater lake. If you need any reminder this volcano is active, a lahar (a boulder-laden volcanic debris flow) swept away a cafe during the 1969 ski season - luckily at night. Mt Ngauruhoe (2291m), is the classic cone often crowned with a smoking plume, and Mt Tongariro (1967m) is the lower mass to the north that includes Ketetahi Hot Springs. A track over the saddle between these last two mountains is considered "The Best One-Day Walk in the World".

At National Park, 49km from Tokannu, the route joins State Highway 4 to Raetihi and the volume of traffic increases somewhat. After National Park the route passes Waikune Prison, a few houses marking the settlement of Erua, then drops steeply to a hairpin bend over the Makatote River (the rail line goes over an impressive viaduct here). About 1km after climbing back up from the river, there is an obelisk marking the spot where, in 1908, the Prime Minister hammered in the last spike on the North Island main trunk line (a 680km Auckland to Wellington connection started in the 1870's). From here the route basically trends downhill all the way to the Whanganui River, although there are a couple of short stiff climbs on the road to Pipiriki. The road passes Tohunga Junction (the turn-off to Ohakune, a resort town with numerous accommodation options) before reaching Raetihi, a spot that caters to locals and farmers more than tourists and has not prospered quite as well as other towns from the region's boom in adventure activities. There are shops, an information centre, campground, and several accommodation options.

At Raetihi, the tour leaves S.H. 4 and heads back into remote country for the 28km to Pipiriki. As the farmland becomes more rugged, then reverts to bush, the road gets twisty and reverts to gravel - following deep valleys and traversing steep ridges.

Pipiriki, on the Whanganui River Rd, is an old Maori river settlement. The river was an important canoe route and food source in pre-European times and few Pakeha saw this area prior to 1864, when a redoubt was established after Maori Hauhau rebels moved into the area. By the 1880's Pipiriki had became quite a popular tourist stop with a riverboat service and a hotel boasting a croquet lawn. These days most of the visitors passing through are on jet-boat or kayak tours through the Whanganui National Park. The park is mostly north of Pipiriki, where the land flanking the river is so rough and remote a group of hardened WWI veterans who tried to settle the area eventually threw in the towel (a "Bridge to Nowhere" up river is one of the few traces of their settlement).

The only accommodation at Pipiriki is a basic camping area with a toilet block and water available, next to an old Maori canoe erected upright.

Te Kooti's Last Stand

Between Tokannu and National Park, 1½km past the turn-off to Highway 46, a track to the right leads to the remains of Te Porere - one of last Maori fortresses built and the site of Te Kooti's final battle in his armed struggle to expel white settlers.

Born in Poverty Bay around 1831, he had a missionary-based education that included Bible lessons in Maori. In 1865, against a backdrop of land confiscations in the Waikato, Taranaki, and Bay of Plenty, Te Kooti was actually fighting with colonial forces when he was accused of conspiring with Hauhau rebels. Followers of the Pai Marire religion, the Hauhaus believed they were a lost tribe of Israel and freedom from Pakeha would come through faith and firearms (their Pakeha nickname came from their chant "Pai Marire, Hau! Hau!" - which they believed made them immune to enemy bullets).

Te Kooti was deported to the Chatham Islands where he developed his own religious system, Ringatu, along similar lines to Pai Marire. In 1868 he escaped with

1919 A referendum on prohibition gets widespread local support, but fails after votes from overseas servicemen are included

several hundred followers, by commandeering the schooner *Rifleman*, and returned to Poverty Bay to sack Matawhero (near Gisborne), killing 70 settlers and Maori. Attacks on other settlements followed. Te Kooti proved to be an able guerrilla leader based out of the Ureweras, but as troops closed in he was forced to seek support in the central North Island, where he was pursued and eventually cornered.

On a pumice ridge overlooking the infant Whanganui River Te Kooti's followers dug their lines and erected parapets. On 4 October 1869 the Armed Constabulary and pro-Government Maori forces attacked. Te Kooti lost badly. Many of the men and woman who followed him were killed, but Te Kooti managed to escape - outrunning the law for several more years until his support finally waned. In 1889, he was pardoned and returned to the Bay of Plenty, where he died in 1893. His Ringatu Church still has a scattering of adherents.

Camping;
Eivin's Lodge & Motor Camp, Cnr S.H. 47/46, Tongariro, Ph 07 386 8062, T$11, Dorm$25 ◆ Discovery Lodge, S.H. 47, Whakapapa, Ph 07 892, 2744, $T10, D$35 (1km SW Jct. S.H's 47 & 48) ◆ Whakapapa Holiday Park, Whakapapa Village, Ph 07 892 3897, T$16, Dorm$25 ◆ Raetihi Holiday Park, 10 Parapara Rd, Raetihi, Ph 06 385 4176 ◆ Basic Camping, Pipiriki Reserve, Pipiriki ◆ Others; National Park (see Hostel)

Hostel;
Ski Haus, Carroll St, National Park, Ph 07 892 2854, T$10, Dorm$18, D$25 ◆ Others; Tongariro (see Camping), Whakapapa Village (see Camping), National Park, Ohakune

B&B;
Country Classic Lodge, 14 Amehu St, Raetihi, Ph 06 385 4151, S$50, D$100

Motel/Hotel;
The Grand Chateau, Whakapapa Village, Ph 07 892 3809, D$200 ◆ Pukenui Lodge, S.H. 4, National Park, Ph 07 892, 2882, D$30 ◆ Ruapehu Hotel & Motel, 7 Seddon St, Raetihi, Ph 06 385 4016, D$80 ◆ Others; Whakapapa Village, National Park

i;
Visitor Centre, Whakapapa Village, S.H. 48, Whakapapa, Ph 07 8922 3729 ◆ Raetihi Information Centre, 9A Seddon St, Ph 06 385 4805 ◆ DOC Pipiriki, Ph 06 385 5022 ◆ Others; Ohakune

850 km Between Tokaanu and National Park

900 km Just past Raetihi

Pipiriki to;

Jerusalem	10km	*39 33.2, 175 04.6*
Matahiwi	23km	*39 36.3, 175 09.7*
Atene Pa	41km	*39 43.4, 175 08.8*
S.H. 4 junction	63km	*39 50.8, 175 07.7*
Wanganui	78km c, h, b&b, m/h, i, bike shop	*39 55.8, 175 02.9*

This stage includes about 30km of gravel riding, following the gently rolling east bank of the Whanganui downstream until the seal starts after Koriniti Pa. Later, the road climbs a steep ridge and drops to State Highway 4 before entering Wanganui City. Apart from accommodation at a few places near Koriniti Pa, there are no services along the River Rd.

The missionary Reverend Richard Taylor travelled the Whanganui River in 1843, 12 years after the first Europeans (traders looking for shrunken heads) travelled up river and were killed. Planting poplars and willows, and establishing missions as he went, local Maori asked Taylor to rename their villages. Hence, the road south passes Jerusalem (Hiruharama), Ranana (London), Koriniti (Corinth), and Atene (Athens).

7km after Pipiriki the road doglegs over Otoutahi Stream and starts climbing for several kilometres to a great lookout over the river and a picnic area. A few kilometres further on is Jerusalem, the largest settlement along the River Rd and site of a Roman Catholic mission since 1829 (accommodation at the convent is available). 4km past Jerusalem there is a flying fox across the river, a common means of crossing the river.

Ranana is one of the larger communities along the road. There is a campground next to the river behind Ruaka Marae. In May 1864 a fierce battle was fought on Moutoa Island in front of this settlement. Hauhau rebels from Taranaki came down river and met local Maori defending the area. The Hauhaus were repulsed but over 100 Maori were killed. The hard won victory is believed to have spared Wanganui from a Hauhau attack, although they returned to besiege the mission at Pipiriki the following year.

The road, cut into the sandstone above the river, continues to the restored Kawana Flour Mill, a little over half way between Ranana and Matahiwi. The riverside Maori, who had previously planted karaka trees for berries, took up wheat growing following contact with Europeans, and by the 1850's were growing thousands of hectares of grain along the river. A short walk off the road takes you to this 1854 water-powered mill and miller's cottage. The mill ran for over 50 years - the last of many that once operated along the river.

There is a rural school and Marae at the small farming settlement of Matawhiri (the old school building was bought 46km downstream by boat).

Koriniti is another of the larger settlements on the road. Te Waiherehere meeting house at the Marae here was built in the 1920's and has impressive panelling. The community also has a church and old mission house. The cemetery at Koriniti features carved beams over entrance, showing a tui perched on a kowhai branch. The kowhai's yellow flower is New Zealand's unofficial national flower and, in season, can be seen along the river banks. Contact Koriniti Marae *(see p.93)* regarding accommodation here.

Atene consists of an old Pa site and a few houses. The location, on an abandoned loop of the river around a

The Whanganui River Valley

1920 A plane flies over Cook Strait for the first time

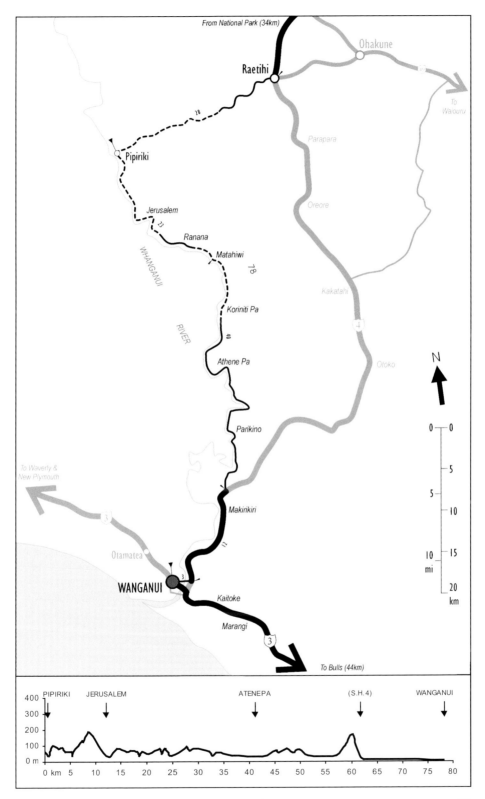

From National Park (34km)

Ohakune

Raetihi

To Waiouru

Parapara

18

Pipiriki

Oreore

Jerusalem

23

Ranana

Matahiwi

WHANGANUI

78

Kakatahi

RIVER

Koriniti Pa

4

40

Athene Pa

Otoko

N

Parikino

0 — 0

To Waverly &
New Plymouth

5

Makirikiri

5 — 10

3

12

10 — 15

Otamatea

mi

10

WANGANUI

3

Kaitoke

20

km

Marangi

3

To Bulls (44km)

400
300
200
100
0 m

PIPIRIKI   JERUSALEM   ATENEPA   (S.H.4)   WANGANUI

0 km 5   10   15   20   25   30   35   40   45   50   55   60   65   70   75   80

conical hill, is interesting. The Atene Skyline Track (6 to 8hrs, 18km) is a ridge top track along the old riverbank encircling the hill and settlement.

About 8km past Atene is Oyster Cliffs, a section of the road where giant fossilised oyster shells are visible in the bluffs by the road. These shells were laid down, along with the rest of the sandstone and mudstone beds seen along the road, within the last 10 million years (relatively young geologically) when the area was below sea level.

The road passes the tiny settlements of Parikino and Pungarehu before a tough 3km climb out of the river valley. The road drops steeply to State Highway 4, then is flat for the last 15km into Wanganui.

State Highway 4 becomes Riverbank Rd, then Anzac Parade as it enters the suburbs of Wanganui East. Go left onto Dublin St, which crosses the river and leads into the downtown area. Go left onto Victoria Ave to get to the centre of town.

A New Zealand Company schooner landed at the mouth of river in 1840 to establish a colony at Wanganui. The settlement was controversial from the start. 16,000 hectares were purchased from local Maori for blankets, tobacco, and trinkets. Friction with Maori required an armed garrison. Eventually the Crown re-negotiated the town's sale price and bought more land, at 3-pence-an-acre. Some are still unhappy about land ownership in Wanganui, and a major standoff occurred at Moutua Gardens in 1995. The Gardens is where land purchases were negotiated between Maori and Pakeha in 1840, and was renamed Moutua after the 1864 island battle upstream. Local Maori and out-of-town activists made national headlines when they occupied the Gardens for 83 days.

An interesting place to get a perspective over the city is the Durie Hill Memorial Tower and Elevator. Located at the end of Victoria Ave, opposite the Wanganui City Bridge, the tower is accessed by a pedestrian tunnel that leads to an elevator inside Durie Hill, or, a 191-step walkway up the side of the hill. There are great views over the river and city, and on fine days to Mt Egmont (Taranaki) and Mt Ruapehu. Other attractions are Queens Park (home to the Sarjeant Gallery, Wanganui Regional Museum, and Alexander Library), river cruises, and a heritage walk around the city.

Interestingly, maps show the Whanganui River, National Park, and even the town itself spelt, sometimes with and sometimes without, an "h" - a debate that the City Council here has even weighed in on. Common usage locally is; Whanganui for the river and National Park, and Wanganui for the town.

Whanganui River History

According to Maori myth the Whanganui River formed when Mt Taranaki (Egmont), who used to live in the heart of the North Island with the other volcanoes, fell in love with beautiful Mt Pihanga, the wife of Tongariro. He wooed her, but when Tongariro returned and found out, massive eruptions occurred. Taranaki lost the battle and was banished to the sea, his lonely path carving out the Whanganui River and being filled by his tears. Today, the mists that fill these remote valleys still give the river a forlorn atmosphere.

The Whanganui is the longest navigable river in New Zealand and the great explorer Kupe even paddled up its lower reaches. In pre-European times several thousand Maori lived along river, travelling up and down via canoe, planting kumara, cutting fortifications into the sandstone bluffs, and fishing for eels and lamprey.

An early European resident on the river was Mother Aubert, a Parisian who studied nursing with Florence Nightingale and piano with Franz Liszt, before ending up deep in the New Zealand bush. As a 25-year-old, Sister Aubert arrived in Auckland in 1860, inspired by a visit to France by Bishop Pompallier, who had established New Zealand's first Catholic Mission in Hokianga in 1813. After learning Maori and undertaking charity work in Auckland and Hawke's Bay she left for the Sisters of St. Joseph mission at Jerusalem in 1883. Now Mother Mary Joseph, she stocked a dispensary (often using

1923 Britain gives administrative authority of the Ross Dependency (all Antarctic land south of 60° S. and between 160° E and 150° W) to NZ

native plants based on her knowledge of Maori cures), built a church and orphanage, wrote a book entitled *A Manual on Maori Conversation*, and started the Daughters of Our Lady of Compassion convent. She left in 1899 to continue her work in Wellington and at the time of her death (1926) some said she was the greatest woman in New Zealand.

The River Road was finally opened 1934, after 30 years of construction. The last riverboat service ended in the 1950's although tourists continued to use the river for access after Bill Hamilton demonstrated the benefits of his jet boat here in 1957.

In 1969 poet James K. Baxter moved to the river after battling alcoholism and converting to Roman Catholicism. He spent the last 3 years of his life in Jerusalem, writing and seeking an alternative to what he called "chemical solutions".

In 1987 the Whanganui National Park was designated. Today, the river's easy rapids make it ideal for beginner kayakers, and jet-boat tours are popular.

Camping;
The Flying Fox, near Koriniti, Wanganui River (see B&B) ◆ 10 Holiday Park, 460 Somme Pde, Upper Aramoho, Wanganui, Ph 06 343 8402, T$10 ◆ Castlecliff Holiday Park, 1A Rangiora St, Wanganui, Ph 06 344 2227, T$10

Hostel;
Dorm beds at Koriniti Marae, Koriniti Pa, Wanganui River (see Motel/Hotel) ◆ Wanganui Riverside Inn, 2 Plymouth St, Wanganui, Ph 03 347 2529, $20

B&B;
The Flying Fox, near Koriniti Pa, Whanganui River, Ph 06 342 8160, $100pp, cabin & camping also available (access across river via flying fox or water taxi)

Motel/Hotel;
Koriniti Marae accommodation, Whanganui River Rd, Whanganui River, Ph: 06 342 8198, $25pp ◆ Kohu Cottage (1 Bedroom rental cottage), near Koriniti, Whanganui River, Ph 06 342 8178, D$70 ◆ Riverside Motel, 30 Somme Pde, Wanganui, Ph 06 345 2448, S$80, D$100 ◆ Kings Court Motel, 60 Plymouth St, Wanganui, Ph 06 345 8586, S$85, D$105 ◆ Others; Wanganui

i;
i-Site, 101 Guyton St, Wanganui, Ph 06 345 3286

Bike Shops;
Cycle Centre, 199 Victoria Ave, Wanganui, Ph 06 345 3715 ◆ Gonville Cycles, 106 Alma Rd, Wanganui, Ph 06 344 4238 ◆ Others; Wanganui

950 km Between Matahiwi and Makirikiri

1000 km Entering Wanganui

13 WANGANUI TO OTAKI

Wanganui to;

Turakina	23km		40 02.8, 175 12.9
Bulls	44km	c, m/h	40 10.5, 175 23.1
Sanson	50km	c, h	40 13.2, 175 25.5
Foxton	81km	c, m/h, bike shop	40 28.3, 175 17.1
Levin	100km	c, h, m/h, i, bike shop	40 37.3, 175 17.2
Otaki	120km	c, h, b&b, m/h	40 45.7, 175 09.4

The penultimate North Island leg has mostly gentle grades. With favourable conditions this stage can be easy cycling, but the roads do get busier as the route nears Wellington.

Leave Wanganui by continuing southeast down Victoria Ave, crossing Wanganui City Bridge, and joining State Highway 3 to Bulls. The road enters pretty farm country almost immediately and gradually climbs for 5km before becoming rolling. About 16km from Wanganui the road drops to cross the Whangaehu River, also known as Sulphur Creek, which has its headwaters on the east side of Mt Ruapehu and discharges to the sea several miles west of here. A debris flow down came down the

Whangaehu on Christmas Eve 1953, after an ash blockage in the ice tunnel draining Ruapehu's Crater Lake breached. The resulting lahar severely damaged the rail bridge on the main trunk line. When the Auckland overnight express crossed the bridge it collapsed, sending the train into the floodwaters and killing 151 people in New Zealand's worst rail accident. Recently, a similar condition has developed at the Crater Lake and the

Crater Lake, Mt Ruapehu, source of the Tangiwhai Rail Disaster floodwaters

Government commissioned a report into possible ways to lower the level of Crater Lake. After looking at ways to artificially drain the lake, it was decided to install a better lahar alarm system on the Whangaehu, which would give adequate warning downstream.

The road crosses the Turakina River and flood plain and continues across a flat to gently rolling plateau before descending to Bulls, a town with a population of about 1,800 that supports the surrounding farmland and has most basic services.

Continue on State Highway 3 for 6km, crossing the Rangitikei River and passing Ohakea Air Force Base, to Sanson where the route joins State Highway 1 towards Wellington. The road is flat, with a hint of downhill, for the next 31km to Foxton, passing productive farmland with the Tararua Ranges away in the distance.

Foxton, one of the of the first towns settled in the area, was a major commercial centre in the district in the late 19th Century - a stage post on the Wanganui-Wellington road, a stop on the main trunk rail line, and a busy port where local flax was exported. The town's dominance shrunk after the main trunk rail line bypassed Foxton for Palmerston North. Larger ships eventually found the port uneconomic and it was closed in 1951, then, in 1973, flax production ceased after synthetic ropes rose in popularity.

3km after Foxton the road crosses the Moutoa Floodway (a channel with floodgates upstream on the Manawatu River designed to prevent flooding), then the Manawatu itself.

Levin is the largest town between Wanganui and Otaki, with a population of 19,000. There are plenty of accommodation options here and Lake Horowhenua, a couple of

1925 American Zane Grey catches a 438kg black marlin in the Bay of Islands, a world record unbroken for 27 years

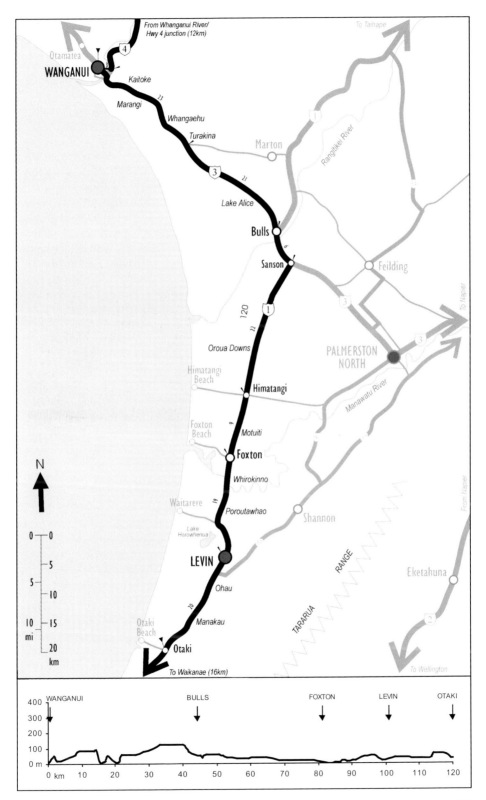

From Whanganui River/
Hwy 4 junction (12km)

To Taihape

Otamatea

WANGANUI

Kaitoke

Marangi

23

Whangaehu

Turakina

Marton

Rangitikei River

3

21

Lake Alice

Bulls

Feilding

6

Sanson

To Napier

120

1

22

Oroua Downs

PALMERSTON NORTH

Himatangi
Beach

Himatangi

3

Manawatu River

Foxton
Beach

Motuiti

9

Foxton

Whirokinno

3

Waitarere

19

Poroutawhao

Shannon

From Napier

Lake
Horowhenua

LEVIN

RANGE

Eketahuna

Ohau

20

Manakau

TARARUA

2

Otaki
Beach

Otaki

To Wellington

To Waikanae (16km)

N

0 — 0

5

5 — 10

10 — 15
mi
— 20
km

	WANGANUI		BULLS		FOXTON	LEVIN	OTAKI
400							
300							
200							
100							
0 m							

0 km   10   20   30   40   50   60   70   80   90   100   110   120

kilometres west of town, is a popular recreation area.

The last 20km to Otaki are flat to gently rolling and follow the main trunk rail line along the foot of the Tararua Ranges.

Otaki is a town with a rich Maori heritage. Rangiatea Church, built here in 1849 for Te Rauparaha, was an impressive structure until it burnt down in 1995. There is camping and other accommodation at Otaki, and the seaside community of Otaki Beach.

Te Rauparaha

The warrior-chief Te Rauparaha of the Ngati Toa died in Otaki, on 27 November 1849. Born before Cook arrived in New Zealand, he died aged about 81, of natural causes, after a life that witnessed some of the worst intertribal warfare in Maori history and colonisation by white men who took advantage of these hostilities to purchase land.

Not a chief by birthright, Te Rauparaha established himself over the Ngati Toa in Kawhia (east of Hamilton) by his reputation in battle and in business, and by his adherence to the concept of *tika* - anything that increased the mana of the tribe was acceptable. He was involved in numerous conflicts to the north and south, involving bravery, treachery, treaties and feigned treaties *(see p.86)*. His early dealings with whalers and flax traders convinced him of the potential for conquest using firearms.

When Ngati Toa became hemmed in by stronger Waikato tribes, who also wanted to deal with the traders, Te Rauparaha did not want to negotiate, rather he antagonised them further by slaughtering several hundred Ngati Toas after a perceived slight against his youngest wife, Marore. Worse was to follow, when Marore herself was killed while attending a Waikato funeral. Te Rauparaha had a Waikato chief killed and Nagti Toa came under siege. Eventually, in 1821, Te Rauparaha made the strategic decision to migrate south to Otaki where there were better trading opportunities. As the tribe slowly moved down the coast Nagti Toa fought, using muskets, against Waikato and Taranaki tribes. In Horowhenua, the Muaupoko tribe invited Te Rauparaha to a feast. It was a trap and several of his children were killed - resulting in numerous brutal campaigns against the Muaupoko. During this time, Kapati Island was taken from Muaupoko and Te Rauparaha used the island as a secure base for raids elsewhere.

By 1823, Te Rauparaha was using slave labour on Kapiti to scrape flax, which he could sell to traders in return for muskets (the New Zealand flax fibres being stronger than the European varieties previously used in Royal Navy ropes). He also allowed white men to operate a whaling station from the island. With the advantage of muskets Te Rauparaha decimated tribes near and far, defeating attackers, and forming tribal-alliances where necessary. Te Rauparaha also had an eye on the South Island greenstone trade and successfully attacked tribes in the north of the South Island. In 1830 the brig *Elizabeth* arrived at Kapiti for cargo. Te Rauparaha convinced the unscrupulous Captain, in return for a load of flax, to transport him and a group of warriors to Akaroa Harbour for a raid. Te Rauparaha captured the Akaroa chief, whom he took back to Kapiti, along with baskets of human flesh (some reputedly cooked in the ship's galley), for a cannibal feast.

By the 1830's Ngati Toa controlled most of the southwest of the North Island and the north of the South Island and Te Rauparaha's ambitions in the deep south were only thwarted when Otago tribes obtained muskets of their own. In 1839, New Zealand Company representative William Wakefield visited Kapiti, on the ship *Tory*, and although Te Rauparaha was generally against land sales, a land-for-muskets deal was negotiated. In 1840, Te Rauparaha signed a copy of the Treaty of Waitangi, in the hopes it would cement his ownership of the vast areas he had conquered and not yet sold. Ironically, the great chief's clearing out and weakening of his neighbours aided The New Zealand Company's desire for land and Te Rauparaha was present at Wairau when tensions over supposed Ngati Toa land sales erupted into a massacre *(see p.124)*.

By the 1840's almost all the tribes had muskets and an uneasy stalemate brought the era of great intertribal raiding in New Zealand to an end. At the same time, Maori/Settler problems were increasing. In 1846, when Te Rauparaha's allies attacked a Hutt Valley garrison and there were rumours of a planned attack on Wellington, Governor Grey had the chief arrested at Porirua. He was held without trial for 18 months before his son negotiated his release (an agreement on the sale of the disputed Wairau lands, was one of the conditions). Te Rauparaha returned to Otaki.

When "The Old Serpent", or "Satan", as the early traders referred to him, passed away he was buried near Rangiatea Church in Otaki, although his body is believed to have been posthumously removed to Kapiti Island.

Camping;
Bridge Motor Lodge & Caravan Park, 2 Bridge St, Bulls, Ph 06 322 0894 or 0800 274 343, T$10, Cabin $30, S$70, D$85 ◆ Brooklyne Motels & Caravan Park, 32 Dundas Rd, Sanson, Ph 06 329 3412 or 0800 117 201, T$10, Cabin$15, S$60, D$80 ◆ Foxton Beach Motor Camp, Holben Pde, Ph 06 363 8211 ◆ Playford Park Motor Camp, 38 Parker Ave, Levin, Ph 06 368 3549, T$10, Cabin $25 ◆ Tatum Park, SH1 (10 km S of Levin), Ph 0800 11 3080 or 06 362 6799 ◆ Byron's Resort Motel & Camping, 20 Tasman Rd, Otaki Beach, Ph 06 364 8121 or 0800 800 122, T$17, S$75, D$95 ◆ Bridge Lodge, Otaki (see Hostel) ◆ Others; Himitangi Beach, Waitarere Beach

Hostel;
Woodland Lodge, S.H 1, Sanson, Ph 06 329 3456, $13pp ◆ Amble Inn Backpackers, Levin, Ph 06 368 3115 ◆ Otaki Oasis, 33 Rahui Rd, Otaki, Ph 06 364 6860, Dorm$19, D$50 ◆ Bridge Lodge, Gorge Rd, Otaki, Ph 06 364 5405, T$9, Dorm$20

Motel/Hotel;
Castletown Motel, Cnr S.H. 1 & Norbiton Rd, Foxton, Ph 06 363 8863, S$65, D$72 ◆ Panorama Motel, S.H. 1, Levin, Ph 0800 660 220, S$60, D$70 ◆ Welcome Inn Motel, 353A Oxford St, S.H. 1, Levin, Ph 06 368 3834, S$70, D$80 ◆ Otaki Motel, 260 Main Hwy, Otaki, Ph 06 364 8469, S$65, D$70 ◆ Others; Bulls, Levin, Otaki

i;
Horowhenua Visitor Information, 93 Oxford St, Levin, Ph 06 367 8440

Bike Shops;
Dustins Cycles & Mowers, Hall St, Foxton, Ph 06 363 7401 ◆ Southend Pro Cycles, 155 Oxford St, Levin, Ph 06 368 5459

1050 km Between Bulls and Sanson

1100 km Between Foxton and Levin

1931 NZ's worst earthquake disaster occurs when a quake kills 255 in Hawkes Bay. The town is rebuilt in Art Deco style

97

14 OTAKI TO WELLINGTON

Otaki to;

Waikanae	16km	m/h	*40 52.6, 175 03.9*
Paraparaumu	23km	c, h, b&b, m/h, i, bike shop	*40 55.0, 175 00.4*
Paekakariki	33km	c, h, m/h	*40 59.2, 174 57.3*
Porirua	54km	c, m/h, i	*41 07.9, 174 50.7*
Wellington	73km	c, h, b&b, m/h, i, bike shop	*41 15.9, 174 47.2*

The ride into New Zealand's capital city is a pretty one, but busy. State Highway 1 continues south across the plain at the foot of the Tararua Ranges, hitting the coast at Paekakariki, then climbing out of Pukerua Bay, before dropping to Porirua Harbour. More climbing takes you through Tawa and Johnsonville, before descending to Wellington Harbour. An alternative some cyclists may prefer is to take the train from Porirua, or one of the other towns on this stage, to avoid riding in the city traffic.

From Otaki, head south over the Otaki River and continue past farms and market gardens. The road nears the bush clad Tararua Ranges near Waikanae, a sizeable town 15km from Otaki that backs onto the rugged Hemi Matenga Memorial Park.

As the road leads south you get better views of Kapiti Island (the route from Otaki to Paekakariki is referred to as the Kapiti Coast). Following Te Raupharaha's use of the island in the 1820's as a base for Ngati Toa, flax trading, and whaling, it is now a bird sanctuary. Boat trips to the island are available where you can hear, and possibly see, tui, saddleback, stitchbird, kaka, kakariki, and bellbird amongst others.

Paraparaumu (Maori for "scraps from an earth oven"), and the nearby coastal communities of Paraparaumu Beach and Raumati, have a good range of services. South of Paraparaumu the sandy coastal plain narrows and the road and rail line hug the base of the foothills. Paekakariki has a steam rail museum and an attraction called Fly By Wire - a typically kiwi adrenaline-boosting invention - involving a one-man wingless plane hanging on a wire, which complete novices fly around at high-speed.

The coastal plain ends south of Paekakariki, with the mountains dropping straight into the sea and the road built behind a sea wall. From Pukerua Bay the road climbs over Paekakariki Hill to Porirua Harbour. A lookout at the top has great views back to the Kapiti Coast, out to Cook Strait and, on good days, the peaks of the Kaikoura Ranges.

Entering Porirua from the north, the highway follows the east side of Porirua Harbour, almost on top of the Owhariu Fault - one of a handful of major, parallel, faults that trend northeast across the Wellington region. These faults have the potential to shake the capital with a significant earthquake. The last really big earthquake, in 1855 when Wellington was just a town, resulted in over 10m of displacement on one of these faults and a good chunk of seafloor on the harbour front was lifted above water.

Bicycles are not permitted on the motorway into Wellington. At Porirua take the Parumoana St off-ramp over Porirua Stream and go left on Parumoana St. After a few hundred metres turn left on Lyttleton Ave and continue for about ¾km (crossing Tetahi Bay Rd) until the road intersects Kenepuru Dr. Go left on Kenepuru Dr, which becomes Main Rd after a couple more kilometres. Continue on Main Rd through Linden and Tawa.

About 7km from Porirua turn left onto Willowbank Rd, which becomes Middleton Rd. After about 5½km go left onto Moorefield Rd at the edge of Johnsonville. Moorefield Rd becomes Burma Rd after 1km. Continue straight ahead for about 2km before going left onto Station Rd, continuing straight onto Cashmere Rd in the suburb of Khandallah. Cashmere Rd drops and becomes Onslow Rd, winding down to Hutt Rd on the harbour. This road takes you to the Ferry and into the City via Aotea and Waterloo Quays.

1931 NZ is in the midst of the Great Depression after world commodity prices drop

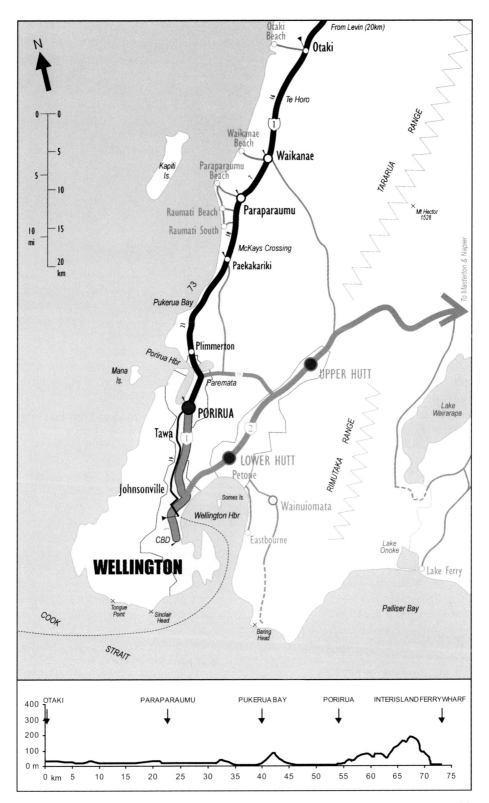

Inter-Island Ferries to Picton

If you plan on connecting with the ferry to Picton, and not staying in Wellington, the Ferry terminals are located before downtown. The options are; one of the Interislander ferries, or the Bluebridge ferry. The Interislanders depart from Aotea Quay, with standard fares at ~$50 adult, $10 bike, one way, for the 3hr crossing. This service is a New Zealand institution, providing transport for generations of Kiwi families on vacation. The Bluebridge ferry departs from Waterloo Quay, near Wellington Train Station, and costs $45 adult, $10 bike, one way, for the 3hr 20min crossing.

Discount fares are also available, but need to be pre-booked. Bikes are wheeled into the ferries via the car-loading ramps, and should be secured against the railings in the vehicle area (the trip can get rough). Take your panniers, or at least any valuables, upstairs with you.

The trip across Cook Strait can be a windy affair, with the ferry sometimes on a permanent lean during the crossing, but the views are

Travelling south on the Cook Strait ferry

stunning, especially when you enter the more sheltered Tory Channel and Queen Charlotte Sound at the top of the South Island. The ferry service has been an economic boom to Picton, although the owners recently looked into making Clifford Bay (near Cape Campbell) the southern port, to make the trip shorter and avoid speed restrictions on their ferries in the Marlborough Sounds (due to coastal damage from wakes). Picton however is a beautiful spot and worth visiting in its own right. The town is flushed with visitors at each docking, and on the busiest tourist days all beds are sometimes booked. Campsites are less likely to be sold-out.

The Wahine Disaster

Wellington's Perfect Storm happened on 10 April 1968, when Cyclone Giselle rolled in from the Pacific and was met by a cold front coming up the West Coast. The storms collided over the city to produce Wellington's worst weather in recorded history. Roofs were ripped off houses, landslides blocked roads, and people were injured by flying debris. On the coast, waves over 5m pounded the beaches.

As the full force of the storm hit, the inter-island ferry *Wahine* was trying to enter Wellington Harbour. With winds gusting 160km/hr and the ship's radar knocked out, Captain Hector Robertson was having trouble controlling the ferry. In the low visibility conditions a huge wave pushed the ship off course, towards Barrett Reef. With hurricane force winds and large swells impeding steering, and the ship's position not clearly known, the Captain decided to turn the ship around and head out of the harbour. After battling the seas for 25 minutes the ferry finally went aground on the reef at 6:40am, although many of the passengers did not even feel this due to the hammering the boat was already taking from the waves. The anchors were dropped and watertight bulkheads closed, but, as the wind continued, the anchors dragged and the ferry scrapped along, then off, the reef. With the starboard propeller missing and the port engine out the Captain had no steering and the *Wahine* was blown into the harbour.

A tug was sent out to tow the ferry, but the line snapped. As she started taking on water and listing to starboard, a siren was sounded and the order was given to abandon ship. The passengers, who had earlier been told everything was okay, were now panicky, and in some cases, screaming.

Sliding down the sloping deck, some made their way to the 4 starboard lifeboats that were the only ones that could be lowered. A huge crash was heard below deck as

1933 Tame Horomona Rehe, also known as Tommy Solomon and the last full-blooded member of the Chatham Is. Moriori, dies of heart failure

cars and trucks on the vehicle level slid across the boat. Other passengers got into inflatable lifeboats thrown over the side, or jumped into the water and clung to debris or the sides of lifeboats. Survivors reached the shore on both sides of the harbour, but had to contend with heavy surf and in some places rocks. In the bitterly cold and stormy conditions, 51 people perished. The *Wahine* could not be salvaged and was battered to pieces by subsequent storms.

A Court of Inquiry found that human error had contributed to the disaster, but the main cause was the freak storm, which had winds of 145km/hr, gusting to over 187km/hr.

Camping;
Lindale Motor Park, S.H.1, Paraparaumu North, Ph 04 298 8046, T$10 ◆ Paekakariki Holiday Park, Wellington Rd, Paekakariki, Ph 04 292 8292, T$10 ◆ Camp Elsdon Inc., 18 Raiha St, Porirua, Ph 04 292 8292 ◆ Hutt Park Holiday Village & Motel, 95 Hutt Park Rd, Lower Hutt, Ph 04 568 5913, T$30 (2 people)

Hostel;
Barnacles Seaside Inn, 3 Marine Pde, Paraparaumu Beach, Ph 04 298 6106, Dorm$20, S$35, D$50 ◆ Paekakariki Backpackers, Paekakariki, Ph 04 292 8749 ◆ Wellington YHA, Cnr Cambridge Tce & Wakefield St, Wellington, Ph 04 801 7280, D$64 ◆ Downtown Wellington Backpackers, (opposite Railway Stn), Ph 04 473 8482, S$23, D$7095 ◆ Others; Wellington

B&B;
Tinakori Lodge, 182 Tinakouri Rd, Thorndon, Wellington, Ph 04 473 3478, S$70, D$95 ◆ Others; Te Horo, Paraparaumu, Plimmerton, etc

Motel/Hotel;
Kapiti Gateway Motel, Cnr S.H. 1 & Martin St, Waikanae, Ph 04 902 5876 or 0800 429 360, S$75, D$95 ◆ Paraparaumu Motel, 65 Amohia St, S.H. 1, Paraparaumu, Ph 04 298 4476 or 0800 746 000, S$65, D$75 ◆ Belvedere Motel, S.H. 1, Paekakariki, Ph 04 292 8478 or 0800 780 781, S$65, D$75 ◆ Jade Court Motel, 44 Huanui St SH1, Porirua, Ph 04 237 5255, S$80, D$90 ◆ Cambridge Hotel, 28 Cambridge Tce, Wellington, Ph 04 385 8829, S$60, D$80, Budget$25 ◆ Others; Levin, Waikanae, Paraparaumu, Paraparaumu Beach, Porirua, Wellington

i;
Visitor Information Centre, 101 Wakefield St, Wellington, Ph 04 801 4000 ◆ Others; Porirua

Bike Shops;
Penny Farthing Cycles, 89 Courtenay Pl, Wellington, Ph 04 385 2279 ◆ Others; Paraparaumu, Johnsonville, Wellington

1150 km Paraparaumu

1200 km Wellington

1934 An internal airmail service starts. Regular overseas airmail starts 5 years later

101

WELLINGTON

The city was named in honour of Arthur Wellesley, Duke of Wellington, 12 years before his death, for his services to England at Waterloo, and for his support of the New Zealand Company's settlement schemes. Wellington has been New Zealand's capital since 1865, when the seat of power was moved from Auckland to a more central location. The city has a reputation of strong wind, good **restaurants**, and the **arts**.

The city sits in a natural amphitheatre around **Port Nicholson** with most of the downtown area constructed on reclaimed land or land uplifted during a massive earthquake in 1855. A reminder the city is built across major fault lines.

Wellington's premier tourist attraction is New Zealand's national museum, **Te Papa Tongarewa**, located on the harbour near the CBD. The museum opened in 1998 to excellent reviews. There is also the **Museum of Wellington City and Sea** nearby.

Other sites are located around the Civic Square and the Parliament Buildings areas. Near Civic Square are the **Town Hall**, **Art Gallery**, **State Opera House** and **Michael Fowler Centre**. Near **Parliament Buildings** is the distinctive **Beehive** building with the offices of the Prime Minister and Cabinet, the **National** and **Alexander Turnbull Libraries**, and the **National Archives** which houses the Treaty of Waitangi - essentially New Zealand's founding document - drawn up by Governor Hobson in 1840.

Good overviews of the city can be obtained from the **Mt Victoria Lookout** in the southwest, and from the top of the **Cable Car**, a 100-year-old Wellington tradition, which can be taken from Lambton Quay up to the **Botanic Gardens** and **Carter Observatory**, and nearby, **Victoria University**.

Cricket and rugby tests are played at **Westpac Stadium**. A reasonably good train system connects Wellington with outlying suburbs along State Highway 1 and the Hutt Valley. A ferry leaves Queens Wharf for picturesque **Somes Island**, once a POW camp, and **Days Bay**, a pretty beachside community on the east side of the harbour.

Marine Drive is a good ride to the southern shores of the harbour. It is mostly flat and passes through **Oriental Bay**, past Wellington's dramatically located airport, to **Lyall Bay** (a good surf spot in the right conditions) and the beaches of **Houghton**, **Island Bay** and **Owhiro Bay**, where the Kaikoura Ranges can be seen across Cook Strait in good weather. Information Centres have details on this ride and the return options.

View from Wellington's Cable Car

1935 Barry Crump, author of the folk classic "A Good Keen Man", is born in Papatoetoe

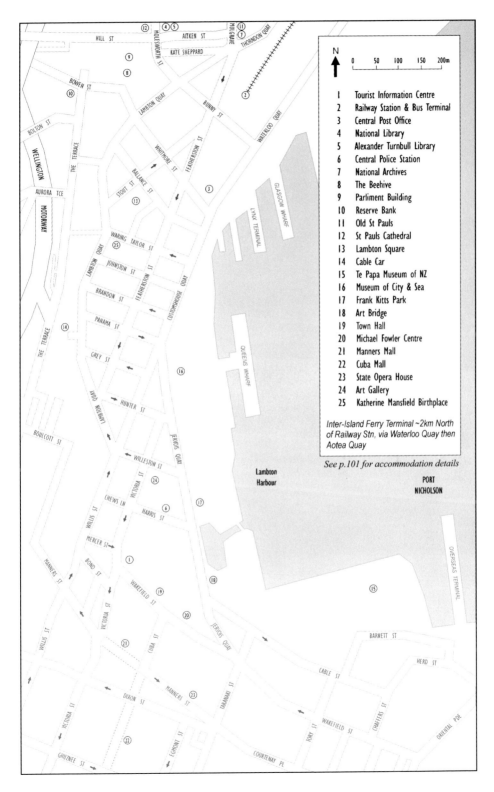

N

| | 0 | 50 | 100 | 150 | 200m |

1 Tourist Information Centre
2 Railway Station & Bus Terminal
3 Central Post Office
4 National Library
5 Alexander Turnbull Library
6 Central Police Station
7 National Archives
8 The Beehive
9 Parliment Building
10 Reserve Bank
11 Old St Pauls
12 St Pauls Cathedral
13 Lambton Square
14 Cable Car
15 Te Papa Museum of NZ
16 Museum of City & Sea
17 Frank Kitts Park
18 Art Bridge
19 Town Hall
20 Michael Fowler Centre
21 Manners Mall
22 Cuba Mall
23 State Opera House
24 Art Gallery
25 Katherine Mansfield Birthplace

Inter-Island Ferry Terminal ~2km North of Railway Stn, via Waterloo Quay then Aotea Quay

See p.101 for accommodation details

Lambton
Harbour

PORT
NICHOLSON

Marker for The Long Pathway

Road safety warning

Cyclists at traffic lights

Cape Reinga

Cape Reinga Signpost

Maori war canoe mural

Northland farmland

Pohutukawa flowers

Mangamuka Ranges summit

Hokianga Hbr. Bar

Bike lane sign

Joseph Coates memorial, Brynderwyn

Kaukapakapa Library

Possum roadkill

Hokianga Harbour

Moko tattoo

Old Ford Cortina

Auckland housing

Jackson's Museum, Devonport

Sign on Highway 16

1936 A bridge over the Whanganui River, deep in the present day
      National Park, is completed for a new subdivision. Today it is
      known as "The Bridge to Nowhere"

1936 Aviation adventurer Jean Batten is the first to fly solo direct from England to NZ

William Hobson's grave, Karangahape Rd, Auckland

Queen St, Auckland

Auckland apartment boom

ANZAC Day Dawn Parade, Auckland Domain

Auckland City

Viaduct Basin, Auckland

One Tree Hill

Auckland Ferry Building

Roadside crosses, State Highway 1

Mr 4 Square

South Auckland mural

Hamilton Art Gallery

Old Mangere Bridge

Waitakere Ranges

Road sign, State Highway 1

Rangiriri sign

Green Vauxhall, Ngaruawahia

Rangiriri Redoubt remnants

Mercer War Memorial

Manganamu rhyolite dome, Tokaanu Canal and Lake Taupo

Te Awamutu countryside

Sheep muster

End of the seal, road to Pipiriki

Leaving the Whanganui River Valley

Governor George Grey

Silver Fern

Last Spike Monument, near National Pk.

New Zealand farmland

Marae, Whanganui River

Whanganui River Rd

Ohakea Air Museum

Flax

Flax

State Highway 1 and the Tararua Ranges, near Wellington

NZ Airforce insignia

Te Wherowhero, First Maori King

Kapiti Coast

The Beehive, Wellington

1938 Bill Gallagher starts a company to market his concept of electric fences to contain livestock

1939 NZ-born plastic surgeon Archibald McIndoe sets up a burns clinic for disfigured WWII pilots in Queen Victoria Hospital, London. He is later knighted for his work

109

*1940's The Buzzy Bee, a wooden pull-along toy that almost every
kiwi kid knows, is introduced*

1940 TEAL the predecessor to Air NZ, initiates a service between
Auckland and Sydney using the flying boat Aotearoa

*1943 Skellerup, which makes Red Band gumboots - an icon
on NZ farms - makes its first pair of gumboots*

Picton

Trig

Road and rail bridge, Seddon

State Highway 1, south of Kaikoura

Awatere Plains, south of Blenheim

Kaikoura

Coast south of Seddon

Wairau Incident Memorial, Tuamarina

Seaward Kaikoura Ranges

Titoki tree, Tuamarina

Kaikoura fish & chips

Lyttelton Harbour from the Port Hills

Christchurch

Kiwi

Christchurch Catherdral

Sign of the Kiwi, Port Hills

Vintage car

1944   *The Battle of Manners St, a 3-hour brawl between NZ and US servicemen in Wellington, reportedly starts after Southern US soldiers racially insult Maori*

113

Orari River bridge

Burke Pass summit

Kiwifruit

State Highway 8 sign, Fairlie

Moa sculpture

Lake Pukaki

Church of the Good Shepherd, Lake Tekapo

Meat pie

Pipeline from canal to Lake Pukaki

Lindis Pass, travelling towards Cromwell

Lindis Pass, view back to Longslip Creek

Flying cow letterbox

Road worker

Mr Whippy ice-cream van

Electric fence

Cycle tourer

Relocated building, Old-town Cromwell

1944 Marmite is introduced into NZ by the Sanitarium Health Food Company

*1945 Picton and Bluff are linked by rail, following the
completion of the South Island Main Trunk line*

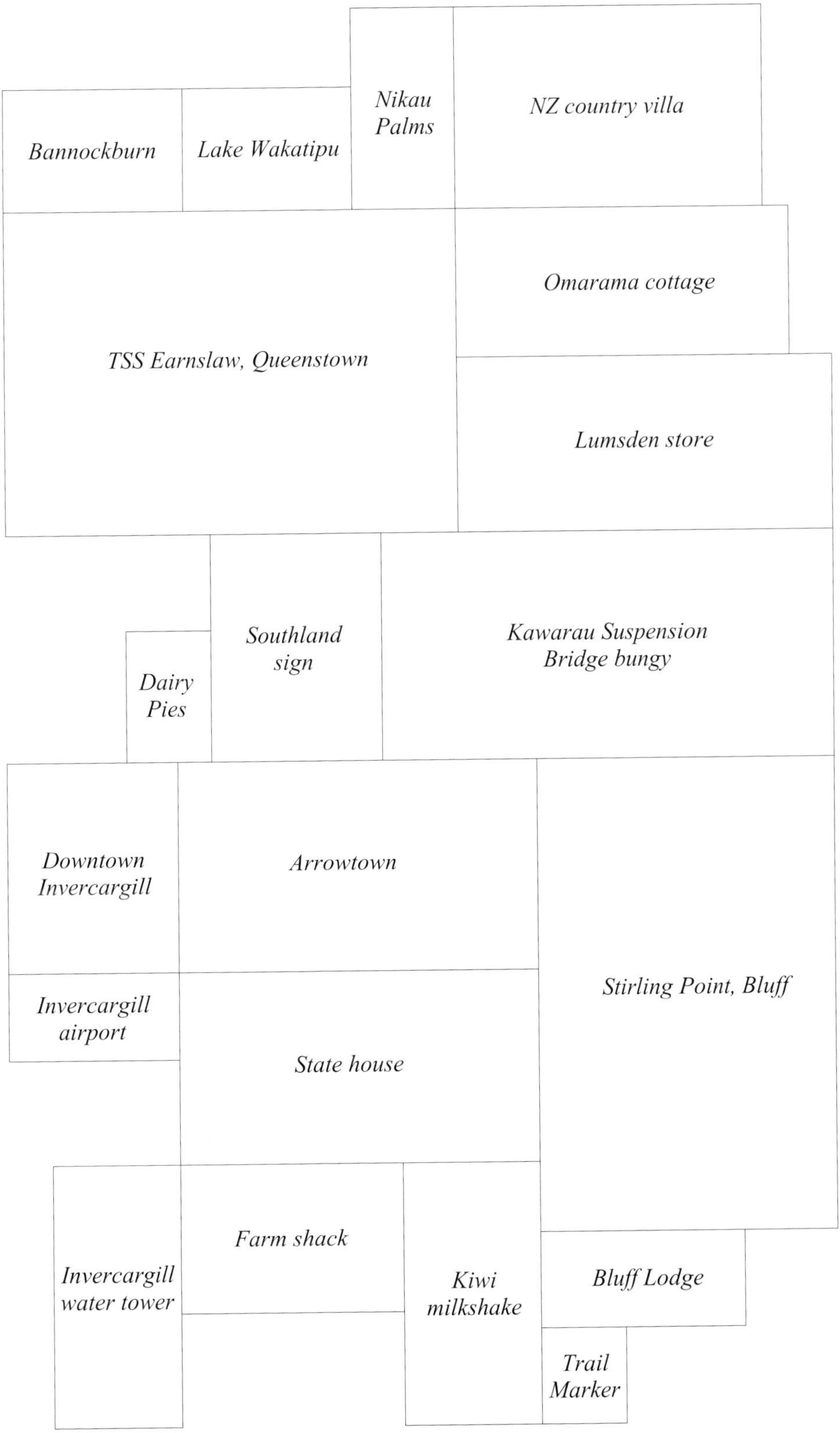

Bannockburn

Lake Wakatipu

Nikau Palms

NZ country villa

TSS Earnslaw, Queenstown

Omarama cottage

Lumsden store

Dairy Pies

Southland sign

Kawarau Suspension Bridge bungy

Downtown Invercargill

Arrowtown

Invercargill airport

State house

Stirling Point, Bluff

Invercargill water tower

Farm shack

Kiwi milkshake

Bluff Lodge

Trail Marker

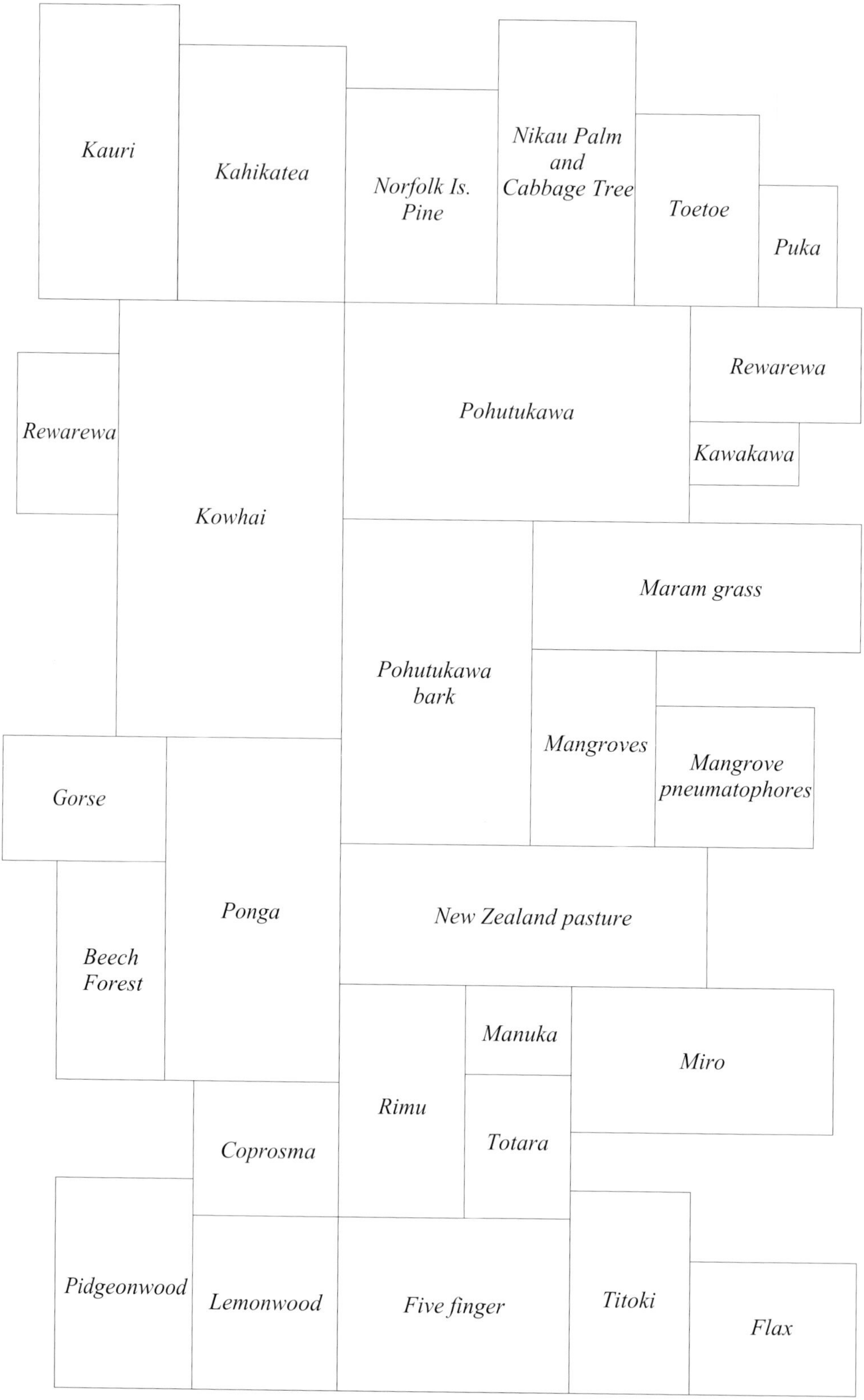
Kauri
Kahikatea
Norfolk Is. Pine
Nikau Palm and Cabbage Tree
Toetoe
Puka
Rewarewa
Kowhai
Pohutukawa
Rewarewa
Kawakawa
Maram grass
Pohutukawa bark
Mangroves
Mangrove pneumatophores
Gorse
Ponga
Beech Forest
New Zealand pasture
Manuka
Miro
Rimu
Totara
Coprosma
Pidgeonwood
Lemonwood
Five finger
Titoki
Flax

1950's For the first time, more New Zealanders travel on holiday by car rather than train

120

1951 A book of Janet Frame's short stories is published. It wins NZ's top
prize for a first fiction book, leading to her release from Seacliff
Mental Hospital. She becomes one of NZ's most distinguished authors

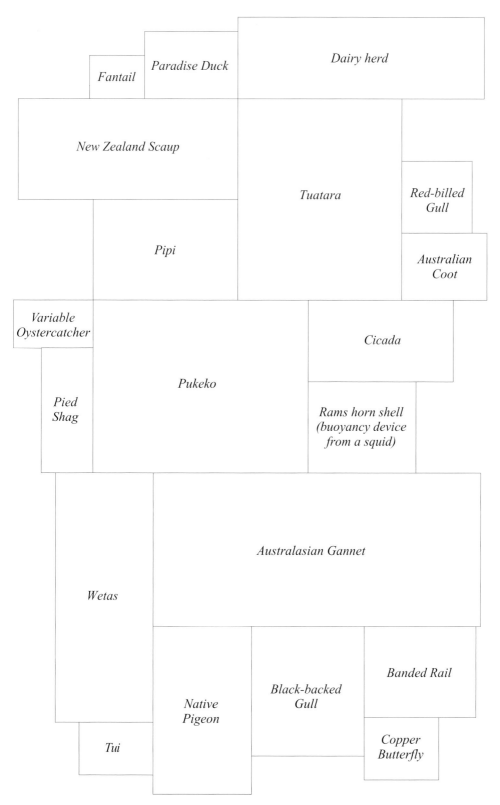

Fantail

Paradise Duck

Dairy herd

New Zealand Scaup

Tuatara

Red-billed Gull

Pipi

Australian Coot

Variable Oystercatcher

Cicada

Pukeko

Pied Shag

Rams horn shell (buoyancy device from a squid)

Australasian Gannet

Wetas

Banded Rail

Native Pigeon

Black-backed Gull

Tui

Copper Butterfly

15 PICTON TO SEDDON

Picton to;

Koromiko	8km	b&b	*41 17.3, 174 00.3*
Tuamarina	20km		*41 20.5, 173 57.7*
Blenheim	29km	c, h, b&b, m/h, i, bike shop	*41 25.6, 173 57.6*
Seddon	53km	c, h	*41 30.8, 173 57.4*

This stage is short enough to ride if you get a morning ferry from Wellington to Picton. It involves a climb out of Picton, then flat to gently rolling riding along the Tuamarina River to the Wairau River and Blenheim. The route does include a significant climb, to Weld Pass, before dropping to the Awatere River and Seddon.

Leave Picton and head south on State Highway 1. 3½km from town, the road climbs briefly before dropping to the Tuamarina River Valley. The small settlement of Koromiko has a school founded in 1873, a petrol station and a motel. The surrounding countryside includes deer farms behind tall fences, pine plantations on the surrounding hills, and the river - which is swampy and home to an interesting range of birdlife.

At Tuamarina a signpost next to a titoki tree marks the spot where the Wairau Incident, a significant event in early Maori/Pakeha relations, occurred (see p.124). These days, Tuamarina is famous for its award winning cheeses.

The road crosses the Wairau River, which starts deep inland near Nelson Lakes National Park. Spring Creek has a turn-off to Nelson, motels, and a campground. Grovetown, with a hotel and taxidermist shop, is a little further down the road. The flats around Blenheim are a good introduction to the river plains of the South Island that can make for great cycling with a tail wind, or near-impossible cycling with a strong headwind.

Blenheim, on the Wairau Plains, is the commercial centre of the Marlborough District, and bills itself as New Zealand's Sunniest Town (although Nelson disputes this title). The town started as a centre for large-scale sheep farming, and grew with the discovery of gold in the region in the 1860's. The area is renowned for its wine production. Blenheim has a good range of services, including a bike shop.

Leave town by following the signs to Christchurch (312km) and Kaikoura (128km). The road follows the Opawa River to Riverlands, 5km from town, where there is a restored 1859 cobb cottage, showing the type of accommodations early pastoralists set up when they moved into the area. After the cobb cottage the road passes a winery before starting the 5½ km climb up the brown, gravely, Wither Hills. After 2km, the road crosses Pukapuka Stream and the climb gets steeper. This can be a tough ride in summer, with the road snaking up river terraces cut into the brown hills, the sun beating down, and hawks circling above. There is a 4½km descent on the other side of Weld Pass, to the Awatere River Plain, followed by flat to gently rolling country to Seddon.

Just before Seddon, the road and rail line join on an interesting over/under bridge across the Awatere. Seddon has a campground, a hostel (phone to confirm bookings), pub, and store.

In 1847, Flaxbourne Run, the first big pastoral station in the South Island, was established in the area. 3,000 sheep were brought from Sydney and Port Underwood, and the wool from these sheep made a select few very wealthy, while tying up land and restricting settlement options for smaller farm operators. The Labour Prime Minister Richard Seddon set about breaking these estates up for subdivision in the 1890's. Thankful locals named the new town that grew after Seddon.

1953 Radio show, and eventual TV game show, "It's In The Bag" debuts with Selwyn Toogood. Contestants choose between "The Money or the Bag?" - with some losing guaranteed cash for booby prizes

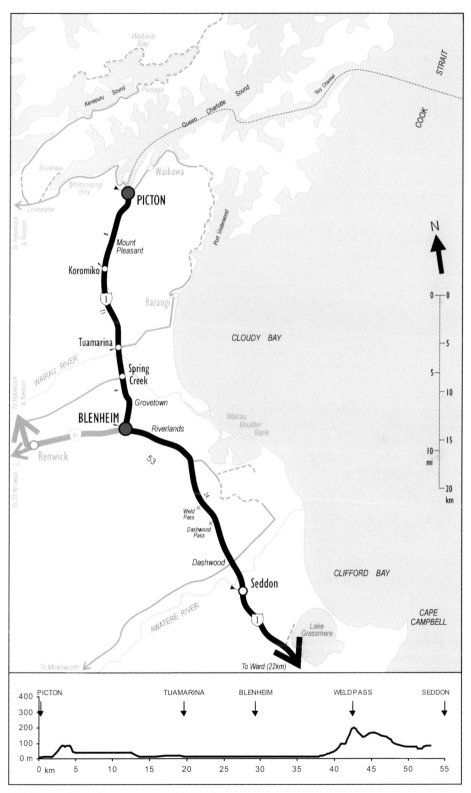

COOK STRAIT

Waitaria Bay

Kenepuru Sound   Portage

Queen Charlotte Sound

Tory Channel

Anakiwa

Momorangi Bay

Waikawa

Linkwater

To Havelock & Nelson

PICTON

Mount Pleasant

Koromiko

Rarangi

Port Underwood

CLOUDY BAY

N

0 — 0

5

5 — 10

15

10 — 20
mi   km

Tuamarina

WAIRAU RIVER

Spring Creek

To Havelock & Nelson

Grovetown

BLENHEIM

Riverlands

Wairau Boulder Bank

Renwick

To St Arnaud

53

Weld Pass ✕

Dashwood Pass ✕

Dashwood

CLIFFORD BAY

Seddon

CAPE CAMPBELL

AWATERE RIVER

Lake Grassmere

To Molesworth

To Ward (22km)

PICTON   TUAMARINA   BLENHEIM   WELD PASS   SEDDON

400
300
200
100
0 m

0 km   5   10   15   20   25   30   35   40   45   50   55

1953 Elizabeth II is the first reigning monarch to tour NZ

The Wairau Incident

Tension between European settlers in Nelson and Marlborough, and Maori chiefs who controlled the lower North Island and upper South Island, boiled over at Tuamarina Stream on 17 June 1843, leaving 22 white men, and 4 Maori dead.

Trouble had been brewing in the area for several years prior, with New Zealand Company settlers arriving in Wellington and Nelson anticipating cheap land but finding it in short supply. In addition, the recently signed Treaty of Waitangi prohibited their direct negotiation with Maori for more land. The Treaty was meant to stop the kind of fraud practised by whaler John Blinkinsopp, who had seen the potential of the Wairau Plains when he visited in 1839 to pick up timber and water. He sailed through Cook Strait to Kapiti Island and offered the warrior chief Te Rauparaha, who had acquired the Wairau by conquest, a six-pound cannon for the timber and water he had collected. The receipt he had the Ngati Toa chiefs (who could not read) sign was actually a deed of sale for the Wairau Plains - of course they tore their copy up as soon as they were made aware of this.

Blinkinsopp died at sea before he could capitalise on his trickery, but the New Zealand Company managed to acquire the deed from his estate. In early 1843, a party of surveyors set off to mark out the land for future development. Maori frustrations at the time were fanned by reports of grave-robbers digging for Maori ornaments, and the acquittal of a man on charges of raping and murdering a local woman despite evidence pointing to the contrary and a later confession. With Maori already feeling "Queen Wickitoria's" justice was biased, they set out for Wellington to talk to the Land Commissioner - who said he could not hear their case for several weeks. Te Rauparaha, and his nephew Te Rangihaeata (who had plainly said the Wairau would not pass from Maori hands in his lifetime without bloodshed), continued on to the Wairau with dozens of armed warriors to deal with the problem themselves.

The surveyors were rounded up, without violence (although survey pegs were pulled and a makeshift hut destroyed), and sent back to Nelson. This immediately raised the ire of Captain Arthur Wakefield, the leader of the New Zealand Company settlement at Nelson. A warrant was issued, on the charge of destroying the surveyors' hut, and a posse of men including Wakefield, the local magistrate, several surveyors, and some labourers from a road-making crew, headed out to arrest Te Raupararaha (the most dominant warrior chief in New Zealand) and his nephew.

The two parties met beside the Tuamarina Stream, near its junction with the Wairau River - a signpost by the highway 20km from Picton marks the spot. A Maori canoe was tied to a titoki tree as a bridge and Wakefield, the magistrate, and several men crossed to talk with Te Raupararaha, who had 100 warriors with him - some visible, some concealed in the ferns. Handcuffs were produced, threats of force were made, and Te Rangihaeata appeared shouting insults. The delicate negotiations deteriorated and the magistrate called on his men to advance.

From somewhere, a shot rang out. Both sides started firing and the Maoris advanced. The settlers retreated to the hill overlooking the stream but were overrun and had to surrender. Several white men escaped during the melee, and one prisoner managed to sneak off into the undergrowth after the surrender - only to hear the dreadful outcome. There was some debate as to what to do next, although this was short-lived since Te Rangihaeata's wife had been shot dead and, in warrior tradition, revenge was required. The prisoners were hacked to death and their bodies mutilated.

As news of the massacre spread, the settlers armed themselves and Maori massed in Otaki to support their leaders. The Land Commissioner was sent to calm both sides, promising Maori that revenge would not be taken and Governor FitzRoy would judge the case, and obtaining a commitment from the tribes that they would not escalate the situation. In the end, FitzRoy found the settlers were largely to blame for the incident (a judgement not well received by the New Zealand Company), but denounced the Maoris for killing unarmed prisoners. In London, reports of the Wairau Incident caused many backers to lose confidence in the New Zealand Company's plans.

There is memorial and cemetery on Massacre Hill, across the road from the titoki tree, and Blinkinsopp's cannon sits in Alfred St, Blenheim. The Wairau Plains were officially purchased by Governor Grey in 1847.

Camping;
Alexanders, Canterbury St, Picton, Ph 03 573 6378, T$18, C$35 ◆ Blue Anchor, 70 Waikawa Rd, Picton, Ph 03 573 7212, T$12, Cabin$40 ◆ Blenheim Grove Bridge Park, 78 Grove Rd, S.H.1, Blenheim, Ph 03 578 3667, T$14, Cabin $45 ◆ Awatere Motor Camp, Seymour St, Seddon, Ph 03 575 7187 or 027 252 7187 T$10 ◆ Others: Picton, Spring Creek, Blenheim

Hostel;
The Villa, 34 Auckland St, Picton, Ph 03 573 6598, Dorm$20, D$54 ◆ Wedgewood House YHA, 10 Dublin St, Picton, Ph 03 573 7797, Dorm$20, D$50 ◆ Blenheim Backpackers, 29 Park Tce, Blenheim, Ph 03 578 6062 ◆ Leeways, 33 Landsdowne St, Blenheim, Ph 03 578 2213, Dorm$18 ◆ Stoneyacres, Seddon, Ph 03 575 7940 (Phone to confirm) ◆ Others: Picton, Spring Creek, Blenheim

B&B
Admiral's Lodge, 22 Waikawa Rd, Picton, Ph 03 573 6590, Fax 03 573 8318, S$55, D$85 ◆ McCormick House B&B, 21 Leicester St, Picton, Ph 03 573 5253,

S$90, D$370 ◆ Others: Picton, Koromiko, Blenheim

Motel/Hotel
Americano Motor Inn, 32 High St, Picton, Ph 03 573 6398 or 0800 104 104, S$90 ◆ Bell Bird Motel, 96 Waikawa Rd, Picton, Ph 03 573 6912, S$65, D$85 ◆ Cherylea Motor Lodge, 73 Nelson St, Blenheim, Ph 03 578 6319 or 0800 358 835, D$85 ◆ Aston Court Motel, 72 Main St S.H.1, Blenheim, Ph 03 577 7407 or 0800 163 165, D$90 ◆ Middle Park Motel, 138 Middle Renwick Rd, Blenheim, Ph 03 578 3329 ◆ Others: Picton, Spring Creek, Blenheim

i;
Visitor Info Centre, Foreshore, Picton, Ph 03 520 3113 ◆ Visitor Info Centre, Railway Stn, Sinclair St, Blenheim, Ph 03 577 8080

Bike Shops;
Spokesman Cycles, 61 Queen St, Blenheim, Ph 03 578 0433 ◆ Reidie Cycles, 82 Cleghorn St, Blenheim, Ph 03 577 7202 ◆ Others: Blenheim

1200 km Picton

1250 km   Between Dashwood Pass and Seddon

16 SEDDON TO KAIKOURA

Seddon to;

Ward	22km	m/h	*41 49.6, 174 08.0*
Kekerengu	46km	b&b	*42 00.2, 174 00.6*
Clarence	65km		*42 09.3, 173 55.6*
Waipapa Bay	74km	c	*42 12.7, 173 52.3*
Kaikoura	105km	c, h, b&b, m/h, i	*42 24.0, 173 40.8*

Continue south on State Highway 1. The route to Kaikoura is gently rolling to rolling until it hits the ocean near Wharanui. From here, the ride to Kaikoura is basically flat as the road follows a beautiful, unpopulated, stretch of coast.

After a few short steep hills the road passes the white mounds of Dominion Salt Ltd's Lake Grassmere saltworks, 10km after Seddon, where evaporation in shallow ponds on the lagoon produces enough salt for all New Zealand's commercial and household requirements. The 1800 hectares of ponds take on a pink hue in summer due to the presence of red brine shrimp (the same animal that gives the Red Sea its colour). Tours of the saltworks facilities are available Tuesday and Friday afternoons (Ph 03 575 7021).

There is accommodation, a service station, and tearooms (with fine cappuccinos) at Ward, a settlement named after Sir Joseph Ward - the PM that followed Richard Seddon into office and continued Seddon's policy of breaking up large scale pastoral leases to allow smaller farmers access to land. The main settlement is on a loop road just east of State Highway 1. If you want some gravel road riding, Ward Beach is a splendidly isolated spot with a seal colony (ask the locals for directions).

State Highway 1 continues rolling along, including a final 1½km climb, after which the road drops and a beautiful seascape comes into view. The snow capped Inland Kaikoura Ranges are visible in the distance and the road and rail line run along the base of coastal foothills dotted with flax and cabbage trees. The highway crosses several fords along this section. The fords are usually dry but have bridges next to them for when the streambeds start flowing. Inland, the hills are rugged enough to include two Mt Horribles, a Mt Misery, and a Devil's Backbone.

There are tearooms at Kekerengu, although at one stage signs outside warned that bikes were not allowed near the tables, and only food purchased at the store could be eaten - making for a less than friendly welcome. Stopping on a log on the beach nearby is just as rewarding, and offers the possibility of spotting sea lions on the sand.

Clarence is a tiny settlement near the mouth of the Clarence River, a 209km long river that originates near Nelson Lakes National Park and flows south then northeast down the valley between the Inland and Seaward Kaikoura Ranges. A large early Maori settlement (present before the big canoe migrations of the 15th Century) lived around this river mouth, where food sources were plentiful. In the 19th Century this river was an obstacle to travellers coming down the coast, who had to wait till the river was safe to cross by ferry. These days, the river provides a challenge for whitewater kayakers. The area offshore from the river mouth is treacherous too. In 1886 the *Taiaroa* hit rocks here and thirty-four people where drowned. The graves of some of the victims are in the local churchyard, others, presumably those who got washed further up the coast, are buried at Kekerengu,. The wreck got widespread publicity because of rumours that the Captain was below decks at the time privately entertaining the leading lady of an opera company that was on-board. He apparently survived the wreck but high tailed it inland up the Clarence Valley.

1955 Pilot Henry Wigley devises an undercarriage with skis and retractable wheels, allowing planes to land on the glaciers of the Southern Alps (a tourist attraction that continues today)

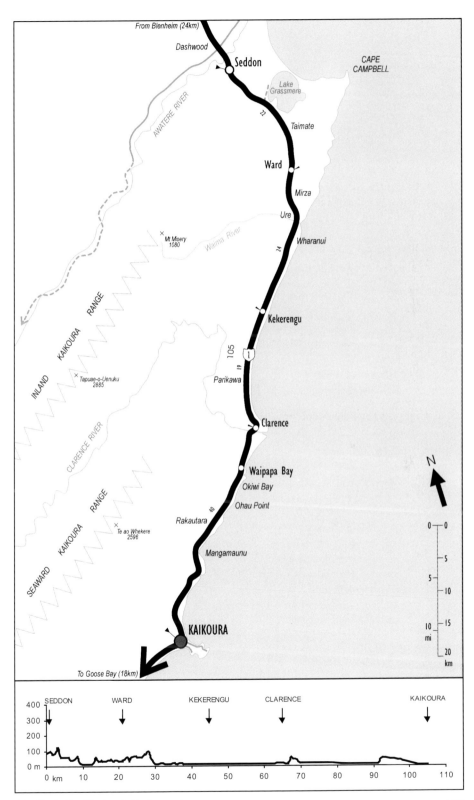

From Blenheim (24km)

Dashwood

Seddon

CAPE
CAMPBELL

Lake
Grassmere

AWATERE RIVER

22

Taimate

Ward

Mirza

Ure

24

Wharanui

Waima River

Mt Misery
1080

KAIKOURA RANGE

Kekerengu

INLAND

Tapuae-o-Uenuku
2885

105

19

1

Parikawa

CLARENCE RIVER

Clarence

Waipapa Bay

Okiwi Bay

Ohau Point

40

Rakautara

Te ao Whekere
2596

KAIKOURA RANGE

Mangamaunu

SEAWARD

N

0 — 0

5

5 — 10

10 — 15
mi
20
km

KAIKOURA

To Goose Bay (18km)

| | SEDDON | WARD | KEKERENGU | CLARENCE | | KAIKOURA |

400
300
200
100
0 m

0 km   10   20   30   40   50   60   70   80   90   100   110

Takeaways Kaikoura style

The road continues to be flat to gently rolling, passing a caravan park at Waipapa Bay and, 6km past this, a seal colony at Ohau Point.

The final 26km into Kaikoura passes more rocky coves and beautiful bays, including Mangamaunu - a right hand point break that is one of the South Island's best surf spots.

Kaikoura has grown into a premier tourist destination over the last decade or so, partly due to the marketing of its whale-watching tours. The town is in a stunning location below the Seaward Kaikouras and there is an excellent walkway around the end of the Peninsula. Because of the fertile land and bountiful marine life, the Kaikoura Peninsula has a long history of Maori settlement (Kaikoura translates to "Meals of Crayfish"). Maoris paddled out to see Captain Cook when he visited the area in 1770 and European settlement started when Robert Fyffe established a whaling station here in the 1840's.

Whales and Whaling

Whale-watching has become a multi-million dollar industry in Kaikoura since the 1990's - a complete turn around from the early days, where whales were hunted from the beachfront for over 80 years, until 1922.

Whales are attracted to the area by a cold southerly current, which hits the continental shelf off Kaikoura and lifts plankton to the surface - allowing whales to congregate and feast. Species in the area include the sperm, southern right, humpback, and minke. Before the utilisation of petroleum based oils for lubrication and lighting these whales were hunted heavily for the oil that could be rendered from boiling their blubber.

Robert Fyffe's station was established at Kaikoura in 1842. Known as "bay whaling", stations such as Fyffe's benefited from the regular migration of whales, such as the southern right, to the area where they would come into shallower water to calve. This allowed small boats to be used from shore stations (as opposed to whaling ships hunting at sea for sperm whales, for example). These small boats consisted of a headman (Captain), harpooner, and common hands to man the oars. Considering the size of the boats used versus the size of the whale, the job was risky, and boats could get towed for miles, at speed, by harpooned whales (a "Nantucket sleigh ride"), or simply get smashed by a huge tail.

Once a dead whale had been towed back to the beach, processing usually consisted of lifting the whale up on a scaffold to make stripping the blubber easier. The blubber was placed in steel pots, known as trypots, which were put into a furnace for rendering. The resulting oil was then transferred into wooden barrels until a passing ship could make a pick up. The process stunk and was gruesome - leaving a blood soaked beach with piles of bones.

These types of whaling stations were often the first white settlements in their area and were typically wild and rough, with rum being the main distraction from the pervasive stink of whale oil. The whalers indiscriminate practice of killing the calve then the mother made the industry self-limiting and even early observers such as Dr Ernst Dieffenbach, who arrived on the New Zealand Company's ship *Tory* in 1839, could see the whalers had "felled the tree to obtain the fruit". From about 1840, catch numbers started dropping and by 1860 many stations had closed, although the rich waters off Kaikoura extended the industry here.

Fyffe House, on Avoca St, was built by George Fyffe (Robert's cousin) in 1860, on a foundation of whale vertebrae, and painted with a mix of paint and whale oil. It is the only surviving building from Kaikoura's early whaling days and is open most days. Also from the early day's are the whalebone ribs forming arches in the town's Garden of Memories. New Zealand's last whaling station, in Cook Strait, closed in the 1960's.

Camping;
Waipapa Bay Campground, S.H. 1, Waipapa Bay, Ph 03 319 6340, T$8 ◆ Kaikoura Top 10 Holiday Park, 34 Beach Rd, Kaikoura, Ph 03 319 5362 or 0800 36 36 38, T$13, Cabin$45 ◆ 69 Beach Rd Holiday Park, 69 Beach Rd, Kaikoura, Ph 03 319 6275 or 0800 69 23 22, T$20, Cabin$45 ◆ Others; Kaikoura

Hostel;
Maui YHA, 270 Esplinade, Kaikoura, Ph 03 319 5931, Dorm$24, D$52 ◆ Sunrise Lodge, 74 Beach Rd, Kaikoura, Ph 03 319 7444, Dorm$20, D$50 ◆ The Lazy Shag, 37 Beach Road, Kaikoura, Ph 319 6662, Dorm$18, S$35 ◆ Others; Kaikoura

B&B;
Kulnine, 5 Kekerengu Valley Rd, Kekerengu, Ph 03 575 8911, D$320 ◆ The Old Convent, Cnr Mill Rd and Mt Fyffe Rd, Kaikoura, Ph 03 319 6603 or 0800 365 603, S$85, D$120 ◆ Adara, 233 Schoolhouse Rd, Kaikoura, Ph 03 319 5736 S$100, D$120 ◆ Others; Kaikoura

Hotel/Motel;
A1 Ward Motel, S.H. 1, Ward, Ph 03 575 6891 or 0800 421 9273, S$75, D$120 ◆ East Coast Inn, S.H. 1, Ward, Ph 03 575 6414, D$60 ◆ Colonial Court Motel, 205 Beach Rd, Kaikoura, Ph 03 319 6037 or 0800 743 537, S$75, D$95 ◆ Panorama Motel, 266 The Esplanade, Kaikoura, Ph 03 319 5053 or 0800 288 299, S$90, D$110 ◆ White Morph Motor Inn, 92 The Esplanade, Kaikoura, Ph 03 319 5014 or 0800 803 666, S$120, D$150 ◆ Others; Kaikoura

i;
i-Site Kaikoura, West End, Kaikoura, Ph 03 319 5641

1300 km Between Kekerengu and Parikawa

1350 km Between Mangamaunu and Clarence

17 KAIKOURA TO CHEVIOT

Kaikoura to;

Goose Bay	18km	c	*42 28.8, 173 31.7*
Oaro	23km	b&b	*42 30.7, 173 30.4*
Parnassus	59km		*42 42.6, 173 17.6*
Cheviot	72km	c, m/h	*42 48.8, 173 16.4*

Leaving Kaikoura, State Highway 1 makes a short climb to the top of the Peninsula, before dropping to the flat coastal plain of the Kowhai and Kahutara Rivers. The road follows the coast and stays flat until Oaro, where it turns inland and the terrain becomes gently rolling, or rolling, to Cheviot.

There is a campground at Peketa, just before the Kahutara River, 8½km from Kaikoura. After Peketa the plain ends and the road passes Rileys Hill and becomes

hemmed between the mountains and the sea. The scenery is beautiful - rocky coves dotted with cray pots, basking seals, and New Zealanders taking their caravan and camping holidays. There are several coastal campsites that can be booked along this stretch *(see the Kaikoura information centre for details)*. The road passes through Parititahi Tunnel and Raramai Tunnels before Goose Bay, where there is a commercial campground and a seal colony on the rocks.

At Oaro, which has a service station and campground with cabins, the road heads inland into hills that are sunburnt brown in summer. After a couple of kilometres a 3km climb starts, followed by a very steep descent with a number of tight

Seal colony at Goose Bay   hairpins. Several more short steep climbs and descents follow as the route crosses minor streams before dropping to Hundalee, where the road parallels the Conway River for several kilometres before crossing Siberia Ford and climbing a minor hill to Hawkswood - an old staging post with a campground and cabins. From here, the road crosses the old Hawkeswood Bridge and settles into gently rolling to rolling countryside with a wide-open feel.

At Parnassus, on the northern bank of the Waiau River, there is a 3-room school and a service station. The Waiau is a major river, flowing from deep inland between Hanmer and Sumner Forest Parks, and is popular with white water rafters and fishermen. The road crosses the braided river to a scattering of houses called Spotswood, continuing on flat to gently rolling roads, before cresting a final hill with Cheviot's reservoir on top, overlooking the little town of 400 below.

State Highway 1 south of Kaikoura

1960 Peter Snell wins the 800m Olympic gold in 1 min 46.3 sec, an Olympic record

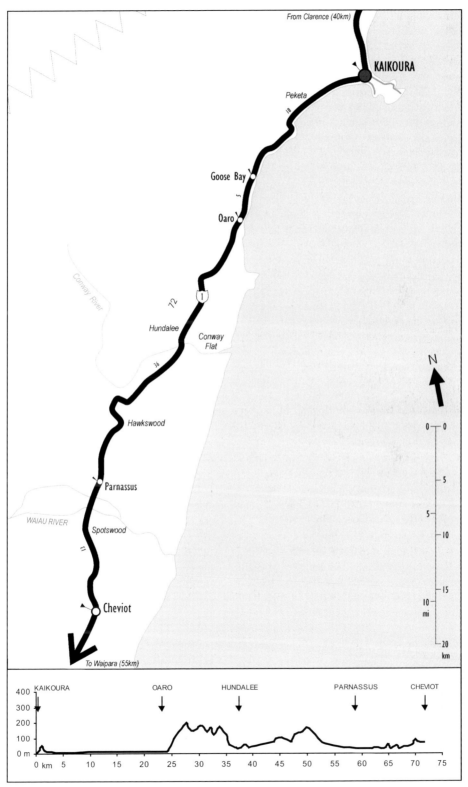

From Clarence (40km)

KAIKOURA

Peketa

18

Goose Bay

5

Oaro

1

72

Hundalee

Conway Flat

36

Conway River

Hawkswood

Parnassus

WAIAU RIVER

Spotswood

13

Cheviot

To Waipara (55km)

N

	0 — 0
	5
5 —	10
	15
10 mi	20 km

| | KAIKOURA | OARO | HUNDALEE | PARNASSUS | CHEVIOT |

400
300
200
100
0 m

0 km   5   10   15   20   25   30   35   40   45   50   55   60   65   70   75

Cheviot is a pleasant place to stop in North Canterbury during the heat of summer. It has a couple of campgrounds and motels, an information centre, and several stores, but more importantly if it's hot - a school with a swimming pool on the main street. Keys to the pool are available from the local hotel.

In 1848 John Caverhill established a massive sheep station in the Cheviot area, a 340,000ha estate he called the "The Retreat". During the early 1890's John McKenzie, the Minister of Lands, made a concerted effort to break up The Retreat into smaller holdings that new settlers could realistically afford. He finally succeeded in 1893. McKenzie worked tirelessly to support the new landholders and his policies contributed to New Zealand's tradition of small, vibrant, farming communities rather than land locked-up in huge estates. There is a monument to him in the main street and the town was renamed after him, although it eventually reverted to the name in common usage - Cheviot.

Charles Upham, one New Zealand's most respected WWII heroes, lived a quiet farming life at Conway Flat, about half way between Cheviot and Kaikoura, until his death in 1994.

Charles Upham

A few miles down the Conway River from Hundalee is Conway Flat. Charles Upham farmed here for 47 years, after becoming New Zealand's most distinguished WWII combatant. In the 1950's the shy farmer reluctantly agreed to collaborate on an biography with Kenneth Sandford and in 1963 Sandford's *Mark of the Lion, The Story of Charles Upham V.C. and Bar* was published, providing insight into this modest, determined, man. The book has been reprinted several times since.

Upham was born in 1908, in Christchurch, where he attended Christ's College. In his twenties he roamed the North Canterbury countryside as a musterer and shepherd, and later as a land appraiser with the Government Valuation Department. He was 30 years old when Britain declared war on Germany, on 3 September 1939.

His strong opinions on German fascism lead him to immediately volunteer for the New Zealand Army (despite being engaged at the time) and he was assigned as an enlisted man to the 20th Battalion of the New Zealand Expeditionary Force. Three months later he sailed for Egypt.

By May 1941 he had seen active service in Greece and was in Crete, leading a platoon after being promoted to Second Lieutenant for his leadership qualities. With the island under heavy attack by German paratroopers and infantry, Upham's men were on the back foot. Over a 9-day period at the end of May, Upham lead his men in brutal close-quarter combat. In counter-attacks on heavily defended positions Upham got close enough to several machine-gun posts to destroy them with grenades. When men were wounded or trapped behind enemy lines it was Upham who returned alone to retrieve them. Badly wounded by mortar shells and wracked with dysentery he refused treatment and continued to fight with his arm in a sling, holding off a fierce attack on an Allied position by felling 22 attackers with deadly aim until he was wounded again and reluctantly evacuated. His heroic deeds earned him the Victoria Cross, a plain bronze cross that is the Army's highest award for bravery - although Upham was embarrassed by the attention and felt there were others just as worthy.

In June 1942 Upham was in North Africa under another heavy attacked by the German Army and nearly surrounded. In open country he moved around and organised a breakout that included attacks on fortified positions and a truckload of German soldiers. On the night of 14 July his men launched an attack on Ruweisat

Ridge, overlooking El Alamein battlefield, in Egypt. The armoured support scheduled to arrive never came and Upham was left to hold the line, which he planned to do by counter-attacking. He personally destroyed a German tank, several military vehicles, and several machine-gun outposts. During this fighting he was badly wounded in the elbow. After having his wounds dressed Upham rejoined his men and helped defend their position in a vicious firefight that wounded him again. Only 6 of Upham's platoon survived the attack and when German tanks overran them they were all taken prisoner.

Upham proved a problematic P.O.W, and after repeated escape attempts he was sent to the castle fortress Colditz - the only New Zealand combat officer to go there. When the war ended Upham married his fiancée in England and returned to Canterbury where he found out he had been awarded the extremely rare distinction of a second Victoria Cross (presented as a Bar).

Charles Upham and his wife had 4 daughters. He lived on his Conway Flat farm until 1994, when he moved to a home in Christchurch. He died later that year, aged 86. Thousands turned out for his funeral at Christchurch Cathedral.

As a soldier, Upham displayed a mix of fearlessness, concern for the men under his command, and the ability to assess the lay of the land and use it to his advantage, making him perhaps New Zealand's ultimate digger. The Prime Minister posthumously unveiled a bronze sculpture of Upham, in 1997, in front of the District Council Building in Amberley.

Camping;
Goose Bay Campground, S.H. 1, Goose Bay, Ph 03 319 5348, $T10 ◆ The Staging Post, S.H. 1, Hawkswood, Ph 03 319 2898, T$9 ◆ Cheviot Motel and Holiday Park, 44 Ward Rd, Cheviot, Ph 03 319 8607 or 0800 424 384, T$20, Cabin$35 ◆ Cheviot Trust Caravan Park, S.H. 1, Cheviot (behind Cheviot Motor Lodge) Ph 03 319 8616

Hostel;
The Staging Post, S.H. 1, Hawkswood, Ph 03 319 2898

B&B;
Greystones Exclusive Homestay B&B, S.H. 1, Oaro, Ph 03 319 5299, S$567, D$845 ◆ Elliotts Garden, 257 Cathedral Road, Gore Bay, (10km E of Cheviot), Ph 03 3198139, S$80, D$100

Motel/Hotel;
Broadview Motels, Main Highway, Cheviot, Ph 03 319 8594, S$70, D$85 ◆ Cheviot Motel and Holiday Park, 44 Ward Rd, Cheviot, Ph 0800 424 384 or 03 319 8607, S$62, D$80 ◆ Cheviot Motor Lodge, 43 Hall St, Cheviot, Ph 03 319 8616, S$45, D$95

1400 km Between Hundalee and Hawkswood

1964 The Beehive is designed by Sir Basil Spence

18 CHEVIOT TO CHRISTCHURCH

Cheviot to;

Greta Valley	35km		*42 57.8, 172 58.1*
Waipara	55km	c, h	*43 03.3, 172 45.8*
Amberley	66km	c, b&b, m/h	*43 09.3, 172 43.8*
Kaiapoi	93km	c, b&b, m/h, bike shop	*43 23.0, 172 39.4*
Christchurch	113km	c, h, b&b, m/h, i, bike shop	*43 31.9, 172 38.2*

After climbing into, then out of, Greta Valley the route drops onto the Canterbury Plains - a huge alluvial fan created by the region's numerous rivers running off the Southern Alps. During summer this section can be baking hot, even by early morning, and if the wind is not co-operating it can be hard going.

Leaving Cheviot the road is gently rolling to Domett, a tiny spot named after New Zealand's fifth Prime Minister. From here the route follows the Hurunui River Valley to a one-way bridge, 20km from Cheviot, where you may need to wait for a break to cross. The road then follows the Greta River, a tributary to the Hurunui, and after a series of small hills reaches Greta Valley, a productive sheep farming area where there is a caravan park, store, and service station. During most summers, the countryside around here is a scorched brown.

The small settlement of Waipara is a short detour off the main highway. There are few services here but the area is a growing wine producing area. A couple of kilometres further on, before the road crosses the Waipara River, there is a service station.

After Amberley, which has campground and motel accommodation, the countryside starts getting more populated. There is a campground on the beach at Waikuku and shops at Woodend. 2½km after Woodend, at Pineacres, cyclists are required to exit State Highway 1, which becomes a motorway. Turn left at the service station and take the route sign-posted "Alt. Route South", also called Main North Road. Unfortunately, this is a narrow and quite busy road. The road goes through the large town of Kaiapoi, before crossing the braided Waimakariri River, passing market gardens, light industry, and run-down homes on the outskirts of town, and entering Christchurch's suburbs.

To get to downtown, continue on "Alt Route South" (Main North Rd), which becomes Marshland Rd and continues straight, through a roundabout, into the suburb of Shirley. Turn right, at Palms Plaza, onto Shirley Rd and continue for about 1km. Turn left onto Hills Road (on a good day the Sugarloaf Antenna should be visible on the hills to the south) and continue for about 1½km (Hills Rd becomes Whitmore St at to the south). Turn right off Whitmore St onto Bealey Ave and continue for about ¾km. Turn left onto Manchester St, which leads into the heart of the city and passes a YHA hostel. To get to Cathedral Square go right off Manchester St onto Gloucester St then left on Columbo St.

134

1964 Peter Snell wins his second 800m Olympic gold, setting a new Olympic record; 1 min 45.1 sec. He also wins the 1,500m, in 3 min 38.1 secretary.

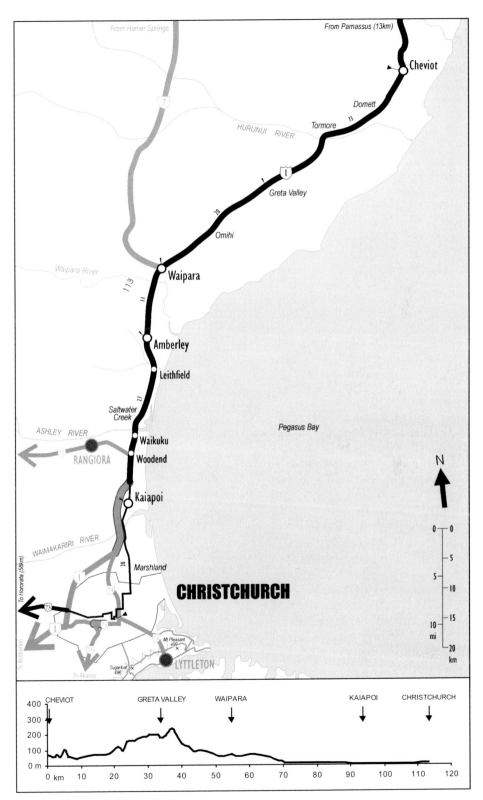

From Hamer Springs

From Parnassus (13km)

Cheviot

Domett

Tormore

35

HURUNUI RIVER

1

Greta Valley

20

Omihi

Waipara River

113

11

Waipara

Amberley

Leithfield

27

Saltwater Creek

ASHLEY RIVER

Waikuku

Woodend

RANGIORA

Pegasus Bay

Kaiapoi

N

WAIMAKARIRI RIVER

To Hororata (58km)

20

Marshland

CHRISTCHURCH

To Akaroa

Mt Pleasant
499

Sugarloaf
495

LYTTLETON

0 — 0

5

5 — 10

15

10 — mi

20
km

CHEVIOT   GRETA VALLEY   WAIPARA   KAIAPOI   CHRISTCHURCH

400
300
200
100
0 m

0 km 10   20   30   40   50   60   70   80   90   100   110   120

Edward Wakefield and The Canterbury Association

Christchurch was the last settlement founded under the guidance of Edward Gibbon Wakefield, a proponent of colonisation who, from England, influenced emigration schemes in Western Australia, South Australia, and New Zealand.

From a privileged background, Wakefield's early life included expulsion from Edinburgh High School, elopement with a well-to-do woman at age 20, and a stint in prison for kidnapping and tricking his second wife into marriage - a school-aged heiress to a textile fortune. While doing time, he published articles outlining his theories on financing and running successful colonies. These were based around the idea that land prices should be high enough to prevent poor settlers gaining large holdings that would disperse the labour force, with the profits of the land sales used to subsidise farm workers (rather than using convict labour). He advocated private enterprise developing self-sufficient colonies, with less government involvement.

Wakefield's track record in Australia was mixed. In 1836 the South Australia Company settled Adelaide, using Wakefield's principals, but by 1840 the colony had not become self-sufficient, and was burdened by administrative problems. With London haemorrhaging cash to support the settlement, George Grey *(see p.109)* was dispatched to sort out the mess. In 1841, backers of settlement in Western Australia also adopted Wakefield's doctrines for a settlement called "Australind", although in the tough environment of WA the settlement failed - partly due to insufficient labour (one of Wakefield's key requirements). By 1849 WA had became a penal colony.

In New Zealand, Wakefield was more successful. He was influential in forming The New Zealand Association, which later became The New Zealand Company. Wakefield's brother William sailed to New Zealand on the *Tory*, to purchase land and in 1840 settlers headed for Wellington. Ships later left for Wanganui, Nelson, and New Plymouth. All the settlements had their problems but eventually succeeded.

Wakefield, however, became disillusioned with The New Zealand Company and set his sights on other schemes. In 1848 he supported George Rennie's vision of a utopian Free Presbyterian settlement with The Otago Association, and a year later supported the Church of England's plans for a Anglican colony - which eventually became Christchurch.

The Christchurch Association included some seriously influential backers, including the Archbishop of Canterbury, bishops, MP's, and financiers. John Robert Godley was CEO, a personal friend of Wakefield, and a driving force behind the project. 1,000,000 acres were allotted by Governor Grey and in 1850 3,247 settlers arrived on 8 ships. The first arrivals, from the *Charlotte Jane*, climbed The Bridle Track over the Port Hills and looked down on the Canterbury Plain; miles of tussock, sandhills, swamp, and the Avon River (named by the Deans brothers who had been farming the Riccarton area since 1843). With drainage and hard work a town named after Godley's Oxford college was laid out with a large square left for a future cathedral.

Wakefield arrived himself, in 1853, after the Constitution Act establishing representative Government in New Zealand and the Provinces system had been passed in 1852. He was elected to the House of Representatives and Wellington Provincial Council. He lived to see all the land in Canterbury eagerly taken up, and died in Wellington in 1862 - the year Christchurch was incorporated as a city. Today Christchurch is considered by many to be the most English city outside England.

Edward Gibbon Wakefield's 4 younger brothers also had roles in the early European settlement of New Zealand; William, was purchaser of Wellington and executive agent of The New Zealand Company in New Zealand. Arthur, was leader of the Nelson settlement and was, unfortunately, killed in the Wairau Incident *(see p.124)*.

1965 Cinema attendance continues to drop as the number of licenced TV's reaches 500,000

Daniel, was a Judge in Wellington, and Felix, the youngest, was a horticulturist and engineer in the South Island. Wakefield's own son, Edward Jerningham, was also a prominent Canterbury settler.

Despite some shortcomings, Wakefield's vision directly impacted the course of New Zealand settlement and influenced Britain's decision to annex the country.

Camping;
Waipara Sleepers, 12 Glenmark Dr, Waipara, Ph 03 314 6003, T$10 ◆ Delhaven Motels & Holiday Park, 124 Carters Rd, S.H. 1, Amberley, Ph 03 314 8550, T$18, Cabins$45 ◆ Leithfield Beach Motor Camp, 18 Lucas Drive, Leithfield Beach, Ph 03 314 8518, T$16 ◆ Pineacres Motels & Holiday Park, 740 Main North Rd, Kaiapoi, Ph 03 327 5022, T$11, Cabin $35 ◆ Others; Rangiora, Kaiapoi

Hostel;
Waipara Sleepers, 12 Glenmark Dr, Waipara, Ph 03 314 6003, Dorm$18, S$25

B&B;
Awen Lodge, 480 Cramptons Bush Rd, Amberley, Ph 03 314 9244, S$90 ◆ Fairway View B&B, 465 Williams St, Kaiapoi, Ph 03 327 5688, S$95, D$135 ◆ Cam River Lodge, 208 Williams St, Kaiapoi, Ph 03 327 9550, S$85, D$120

Hotel/Motel;
Delhaven Motels & Holiday Park, 124 Carters Rd, S.H. 1, Amberley, Ph 03 314 8550, D$80 ◆ Rangiora Lodge

Motel, 436 High St, Rangiora, Ph 03 313 8796, S$75, D$90 ◆ Others; Rangiora, Kaiapoi

Bike Shops;
Push Bikes Ltd, Gables Arcade, 96 High St, Rangiora, Ph 03 313 5298

See p.131 for Christchurch details

1450 km Between Tormore and Greta Valley

1500 km Between Amberley and Leithfield

1966 Classic kiwi farming show "Country Calendar" starts. It's still going

CHRISTCHURCH

Christchurch has an English feel to it, with an orderly layout around **Cathedral Square** and the Anglican **Cathedral** (1881) and punts cruising the **Avon River**, which winds through **Hagley Park** and the centre of town. The effect was deliberate on the part of the early European colonisers who wanted a reminder of their old home after arriving in **Lyttleton Harbour** and climbing the **Port Hills** to look out over a huge plain backed by the Southern Alps. Only a few hundred years earlier, kahikatea forest had covered the plain and large flightless moa were roaming the area (the forest was burnt off after Polynesians arrived and the resulting loss of habitat, and hunting, caused the moa's extinction). The **Canterbury Museum** on Rolleston Ave has reconstructed moa skeletons and good pre-European and Antarctic displays.

Starting at Cathedral Square there is a **Visitor Centre**, and a **tram** that runs in a loop around several city blocks, with stops near the museum, **Arts Centre**, **Canterbury University**, **Christ's College** School, and **Hagley Park**. The main **Post Office** is on Hereford St. The central city has a lively **restaurant** and **café** scene.

Colombo Rd heads south and connects with Dyers Pass Rd, a tough 300m ride up to **Summit Rd** which runs along the Port Hills and has great views (in good weather) over the city, Pacific Ocean, Lyttleton and Banks Peninsula, and away to the Alps. The **Sign of the Kiwi** at the top of Dyers Pass Rd is one of a string of old rest-stops on Summit Rd. A good loop ride is to head east, past the antenna on **The Sugarloaf**, pass **The Tors Scenic Reserve**, and head down **Evan's Pass** to the seaside suburb of **Sumner**. **Taylor's Mistake**, the next bay south of Sumner, is a pretty spot with good surfing. The road back into town skirts the estuary of the Avon and Heathcote Rivers

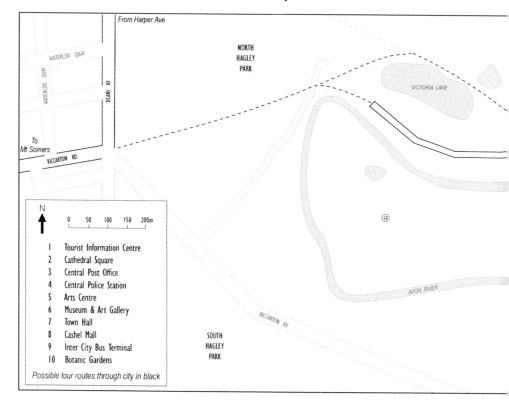

From Harper Ave

WATERLOO QUAY

WATERLOO QUAY

DEANS AV

NORTH
HAGLEY
PARK

VICTORIA LAKE

To
Mt Somers

RICCARTON RD

N

0   50   100   150   200m

1   Tourist Information Centre
2   Cathedral Square
3   Central Post Office
4   Central Police Station
5   Arts Centre
6   Museum & Art Gallery
7   Town Hall
8   Cashel Mall
9   Inter City Bus Terminal
10   Botanic Gardens

Possible tour routes through city in black

RICCARTON AV

SOUTH
HAGLEY
PARK

AVON RIVER

138

passing an important **archaeological cave site** and an 1863 **sod cottage**. [Note: a **gondola** also runs to the top of the Port Hills, near the original **Bridle Path**, or you can take a **balloon ride** from near downtown to get an view over the city.

Christchurch has had a long association with Antarctic exploration, with both Scott and Shackleton stopping here to stock-up for their ill-fated expeditions (the Canterbury Museum also has one of Roald Amundsen's dog sleds). The **International Antarctic Centre**, next to Christchurch Airport, houses support staff for the current NZ, US, and Italian missions to Antarctica and exhibits there have won several tourism awards.

The old volcanic headland of Banks Peninsula, with the French influenced town of **Akaroa**, also make for excellent, albeit hilly, cycle touring.

◆　　◆　　◆　　◆　　◆

Camping;
North South Holiday Park, 530 Sawyers Arms Rd, Christchurch, Ph 03 359 5993, T$21, Cabin$40 ◆ Riccarton Holiday Park, 19 Main South Rd, Christchurch, Ph 03 348 5690, T$20, Cabin$40 ◆ Others; Christchurch

Hostel;
Christchurch City Central YHA, 273 Manchester St, Christchurch, Ph 03 379 9535, Fax 03 379 9537, $26, D$65 ◆ Around the World Backpackers, 314 Barbadoes St, Christchurch, Ph 03 365 4363, Dorm$20, D$50 ◆ Chester Street Backpackers, 148 Chester St East, Christchurch, Ph 03 377 1897, Dorm$20, D$46 ◆ Others; Christchurch

B&B;
Windsor Hotel, 52 Armagh St, Christchurch, Ph 03 366 1503, S$85 ◆ The Ambassador, 19 Manchester St, Christchurch, Ph 03 366 7808, S$60 Single, D$85 ◆ Others; Christchurch

Hotel/Motel;
Admiral Motel, 168 Bealey Ave, Christchurch, Ph 03 379 3554, S$85, D$105 ◆ Cherry Tree Lodge, 12 Riccarton Rd, Christchurch, Ph 03 343 1133, D$100 ◆ Others; Christchurch

i;
i-Site, Cathedral Sq, Christchurch, Ph 03 379 9629

Bike Shops;
John Bulls, Cnr Tuam/Colombo Sts, Christchurch Ph 03 377 2058 ◆ Others; Christchurch

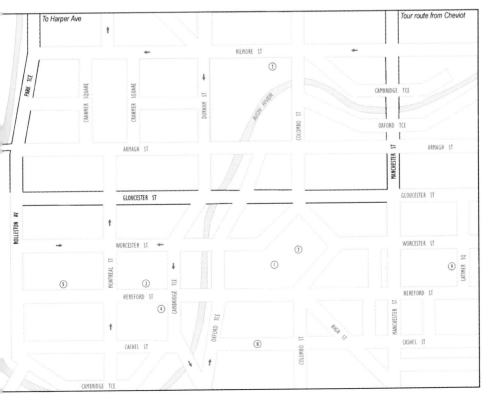

THE SOUTH ISLAND'S WEST COAST

Like the North Island's East Coast, the West Coast of the South Island is the less populated side of the island, making it an attractive alternative for cycle tourers. The Southern Alps form a significant barrier between the east and west sides of the island, resulting in considerably more rain on this side, from prevailing weather systems.

Consider doing this route, after some additional research, if you are independent minded and fit, as there are fewer facilities (especially bike shops) outside of the main towns along the West Coast, and fewer options for intermediate stops. The route is best done in summer, late spring, or early autumn, when better weather is more likely - although you can strike miserable weather anytime of year on the West Coast.

The route follows the Marlborough Sounds to Havelock, then skirts the northern end of the Richmond Range into Nelson - a fast growing city with a reputation for sunshine. The town is technically the geographical centre of New Zealand and sits further north than Wellington. A long climb over the Hope Saddle to Murchison follows. The road down to the West Coast hugs the Buller River, passing through the Buller Gorge and old coal-mining settlements to Westport, which (along with Greymouth) is a major town on the West Coast. The road south along the coast borders Paparoa National Park and passes the Pancake Rocks at Punakaiki - limestone formations with interesting erosional features.

Greymouth to Hokatika is another coastal stretch, with Shantytown (a replica gold mining town) a short detour to the east. The last part of the leg to Ross runs inland. New Zealand's largest gold nugget was found in Ross in 1907, weighing 3.1kg it was nicknamed "The Honourable Roddy" after the Minister of Mines at the time (a cast of the nugget is in Ross' small museum).

The route south passes several lakes and numerous rivers that drain the western slopes of the Southern Alps. Franz Josef Glacier and Fox Glacier have long been popular tourist destinations on the West Coast and walking tours onto, and even inside, the glaciers are offered, along with scenic flights over Westland National Park and Mount Cook National Park, which is immediately adjacent. The glaciers have been retreating over the last 200 years and it is interesting to observe the vegetation in various stages of recovery as the ice moves back.

The road heads southeast and inland from Haast, climbing over Haast Pass via an old Maori route, into Otago. The road from Makarora hugs Lake Wanaka and Lake Hawea before reaching Wanaka itself. This town is second only to Queenstown as an adventure tourist destination and is another beautiful location.

The Cardrona road to Queenstown is a tough ride (on gravel in places), following the Cardrona River then crossing the Crown Range. The road is steep and winding in sections, making it off-limits to cars towing caravans. As the highest State Highway in New Zealand snow sometimes blocks this road. Cardrona itself was once a booming gold-town of several thousand. Today, there are only a handful of residents, with the town centred around the historic Cardrona Hotel.

Possible stages for a north-south trip down the West Coast are listed below. These stages could be reversed and added to the main route down the island described in this guide to make an almost complete loop of the South Island.

Picton to Nelson (111km) ◆ Nelson to Murchison (112km) ◆ Murchison to Westport (98km) ◆ Westport to Greymouth (101km) ◆ Greymouth to Ross (70km) ◆ Ross to Franz Josef (109km) ◆ Franz Josef to Lake Moeraki (110km) ◆ Lake Moeraki to Makarora (96km) ◆ Makarora to Wanaka (64km) ◆ Wanaka to Queenstown (71km)

1969 Construction of the Bluff aluminium smelter starts

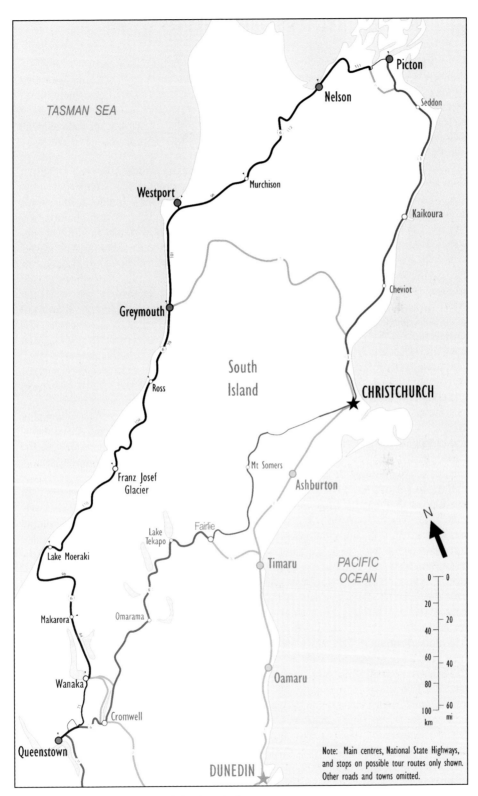

TASMAN SEA

Picton

Nelson

Seddon

Westport

Murchison

Kaikoura

Greymouth

Cheviot

Ross

South
Island

CHRISTCHURCH

Franz Josef
Glacier

Mt Somers

Ashburton

Fairlie

Lake
Tekapo

Timaru

PACIFIC
OCEAN

Lake Moeraki

Makarora

Omarama

N

Wanaka

Oamaru

0	0
20	
40	20
60	40
80	
100	60
km	mi

Cromwell

Queenstown

DUNEDIN

Note: Main centres, National State Highways,
and stops on possible tour routes only shown.
Other roads and towns omitted.

*1970 Kiwi Bruce McLaren, founder of the Formula 1
Championship racing team McLaren, dies*

19 CHRISTCHURCH TO MT SOMERS

Christchurch to;

Charing Cross	42km		*43 32.6, 172 09.4*
Hororata	58km		*43 32.3, 171 57.3*
Rakaia Gorge	86km	b&b, m/h	*43 31.1, 171 39.4*
Alford Forest	104km		*43 36.7, 171 30.3*
Mt Somers	119km	c, b&b	*43 42.2, 171 23.9*

If the wind is from the northeast the quickest way south is via State Highway 1, getting blown across the tabular Canterbury Plains, although the route is heavy with traffic and not as picturesque as heading to Mt Hutt and connecting with the Inland Scenic Route 72, as described here.

Leave Christchurch via Hagley Park, which is to the west of Cathedral Square (see p.138). Take Gloucester, Worcester, or Hereford Streets from the Square to Rolleston Ave, at the edge of the Park, and turn right (north). To take a direct route through the Park, go left at the intersection of Rolleston Ave and Armagh St. A road and paved trails lead to Victoria Lake, after which you should veer left and aim for Deans Ave on the far west side of the Park. The trail leaves the Park near a roundabout on Deans Ave from which Riccarton Rd heads west. [Alternatively, to stay on main roads and not go on the Hagley Park trails; continue north on Rolleston Ave past the Armagh St intersection (Rolleston Ave becomes Park Tce going north). Go left at the roundabout at the northeast corner of the Park onto Harper Ave, crossing the Avon River. Harper Ave goes through North Hagley Park to Deans Ave. Turn left and continue south to the roundabout for Riccarton Rd].

Continue on Riccarton Rd for several kilometres to Yaldhurst Rd, which veers off to the right. As in many New Zealand cities, an electric tram used to run down Riccarton Rd as a main source of transport, until buses and personal cars took precedent in the 1960's. Yaldhurst Rd (Highway 73) takes you past Riccarton Racecourse and out of Christchurch's suburbs.

Highway 73 is a series of long, seemingly flat, straights, which imperceptibly gain elevation as the road heads up the Canterbury Plains alluvial fan towards the mountains. The countryside is a grid of paddocks and fields separated by planted windbreaks. With the addition of fertilizers these plains have become super-productive for sheep farming and cereal production.

Continue to West Melton, passing the turn-off to Paparua Prison, then to Aylesbury where the road meets the West Coast-Christchurch rail-line. Here the tour leaves Highway 73 (which continues on over Arthur's Pass) and veers left towards Charing Cross and Hororata. Charing Cross is a location only - marked by a signpost (which is a necessity as eight roads meet at this one spot). Follow the "Hororata 16km" sign pointing straight ahead.

Hororata has a service station and pub. Go left at the roundabout here and continue for 4km. Veer right at the sawmill onto Leachs Rd, towards the Rakaia Gorge and Mt Hutt. 18km from this intersection the road connects to Highway 77. After 2km on Highway 77 the road drops for 4km to the Rakaia River which runs

*1971 Kiri Te Kanawa debuts at Covent Garden as The
Countess in Le nozze di Figaro*

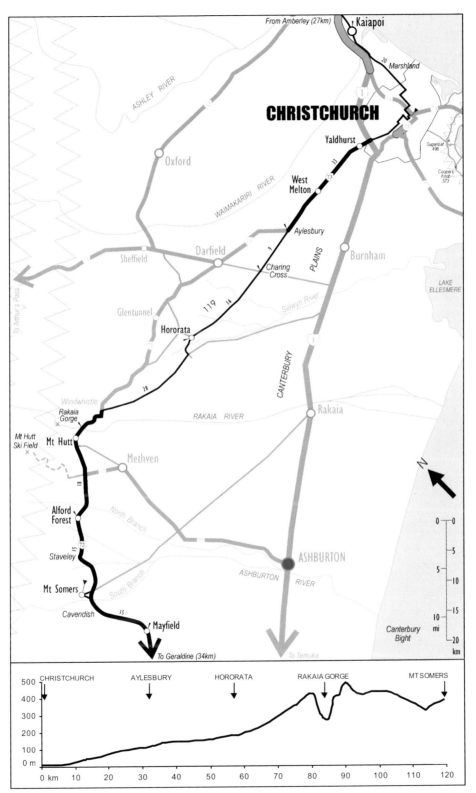

From Amberley (27km)

Kaiapoi

20 Marshland

CHRISTCHURCH

Yaldhurst

Oxford

33

West
Melton

73

ASHLEY RIVER

WAIMAKARIRI RIVER

Aylesbury

Sugarloaf
496

Coopers
Knob
573

Darfield

Sheffield

9

Charing
Cross

Burnham

PLAINS

LAKE
ELLESMERE

To Arthur's Pass

Glentunnel

119

18

Selwyn River

Hororata

28

CANTERBURY

Rakaia

Windwhistle

Rakaia
Gorge

RAKAIA RIVER

Mt Hutt
Ski Field

Mt Hutt

Methven

18

N

Alford
Forest

North Branch

15

72

Staveley

Mt Somers

South Branch

ASHBURTON

ASHBURTON RIVER

Cavendish

15

Mayfield

To Geraldine (34km)

To Temuka

0 — 0

5

5 — 10

15

10 — 15

Canterbury   mi
Bight

20
km

CHRISTCHURCH   AYLESBURY   HORORATA   RAKAIA GORGE   MT SOMERS

500
400
300
200
100
0 m

0 km   10   20   30   40   50   60   70   80   90   100   110   120

1972 The 90th baby to survive an in-vitro blood transfusion (a
technique pioneered by kiwi Sir William Liley) is born at
National Women's Hospital in Auckland

143

fast and milky brown. Until the 1880's a punt was used to transport travellers and sheep across the river. A couple of bridges now cross the river here; one is an historic 1882 wooden bridge, supported with an interesting truss design. A plaque marks the bridge as an important part of New Zealand's engineering history. There are jet-boat tours available up the gorge and the Rakaia Gorge Walkway starts nearby (the Christchurch Visitors Information Centre can supply details).

A steep 1.5km climb starts on the opposite side of the river, followed by ½km of more gradual climbing, until the road flattens out again and heads towards Mt Hutt station. On a clear day the views to the mountains along this stretch are brilliant. Mt Hutt Station is a privately owned 8,000-acre deer farm (there is a B&B at the station).

A few kilometres past Rakaia River, Mt Hutt Stn Rd, heads south to Methven (a medium-sized town with a campground). 10km past the river another intersection leads to Methven to the left, and the Mt Hutt skifield to the right. Continuing straight ahead as Route 72, the road crosses the shingly expanse of the North Branch of the Ashburton River. From here to Mt Somers the road heads down the alluvial fan, dropping about 50m elevation in a faint downhill towards Mt Somers, located near the South Branch of the Ashburton River. The town village itself is a short signposted detour off the highway.

Mt Somers has a motor camp with cabins, pub, and service station.

New Zealand Film

The huge success of Kiwi Director Peter Jackson's *Lord of the Rings* trilogy, and favourable exchange rates, have focused moviemakers attention on New Zealand as a film location. However, long before mega-movie production houses thought about coming, New Zealand had its own movie-making community, turning out distinctly kiwi-flavoured feature films.

The first films made in New Zealand were news reels shot in 1898, 2 years after imported films had been screened in Christchurch. The kiwi versions featured such topics as Lord Ranfurly opening the Auckland Exhibition, and the running of the Auckland Cup. The first feature film shot in New Zealand was Frenchman, Gaston Melies' 1912 *Hinemoa, Loved by a Maori Chieftess* - shot with an all-Maori cast. Local George Tarr's 1914 version of *Hinemoa* was the first New Zealand made feature.

Other early films also featured Maori legend and history, such as *The Birth of New Zealand* (1920), *The Lady of the Cave* (1922), and *The Te Kooti Trail* (1927).

In 1929, Edwin Coubray used recording equipment he had made himself to shoot the first local film with sound, *Under Southern Skies*. One of the most famous early New Zealand movies was Rudall Hayward's 1939 remake of a movie he had made silent in 1925; *Rewi's Last Stand* - the story of the Orakau battle (see p.74) during the Waikato Wars and starring "Genuine Maori Screen Star" Ramai Te Miha. Unfortunately many of these early New Zealand films have been lost or deteriorated irreparably in their reel canisters.

After the war there were only 4 feature length films made in New Zealand, until the watershed year of 1977 when grants from The QEII Arts Council allowed 3 films to be made, including Roger Donaldson's *Sleeping Dogs* a thriller featuring Sam Neil fighting an authoritarian government regime.

The 1980's and 1990's saw a bunch of original New Zealand films. Geoff Murphy's 1981 *Goodbye Pork Pie*, featuring a stolen yellow Mini on a jaunt from Auckland to Invercargill, was a local hit that competed strongly against *Star Wars*. Other memorable movies include; *Smash Palace* 1982, *Footrot Flats* 1986, *Bad Taste* 1988, *The Navigator* 1988, *The Piano* 1993, and *Once Were Warriors* 1994.

1973 NZ's population is estimated to be 3 million

Camping;
Pudding Hill Lodge, Hwy 72 (5km S of <u>Mt Hutt</u>), Ph 03 302 9627 or 0800 783 445, T$12, Cabins ◆ Mt Somers Holiday Park, Hoods Rd, <u>Mt Somers</u>, Ph 03 303 9719, T$10 Cabin$39 ◆ Others; <u>Glentunnel</u>

Hostel;
Pudding Hill Lodge, backpacker accommodation, <u>Mt Hutt</u> (see camping)

B&B;
Benlea Cottage, Terrace Downs, <u>Rakaia Gorge</u>, Ph 03 318 6545, S$75 ◆ Ross Cottage, <u>Staveley</u>, Ph 03 303 0880, S$70 ◆ Stronechrubie Resturant & Chalets, Cnr Hwy 72 & Hoods Rd, <u>Mt Somers</u>, Ph 03 303 9814, D$160 ◆ Others; <u>Darfield</u>, near <u>Rakaia Gorge</u>

Motel Hotel;
Rakaia Gorge Mount Hutt Lodge, Zig Zag Road, Whindwhistle, <u>Rakaia Gorge</u>, Ph 03 318 6898, D$130 ◆ Others; <u>Darfield</u>, <u>Methvern</u>

1550 km Riccarton Road, Christchurch

1600 km Between Charing Cross and Hororata

1650 km Between Alford Forest and Staveley

1975   A Land March from Wellington to near Cape Reinga emphasises Maori land grievances. The Government forms the Waitangi Tribunal to hear Maori claims

145

MT SOMERS TO FAIRLIE

Mt Somers to;

Mayfield	15km		*43 49.3, 171 25.3*
Geraldine	49km	c, h, b&b, m/h, i	*44 05.5, 171 14.6*
Fairlie	95km	c, h, b&b, m/h	*44 05.9, 170 49.7*

From Mt Somers, return to Route 72 via Hood Rd and cross the South Branch of the Ashburton River. The route is essentially flat, or slightly downhill, all the way to Geraldine, before leaving the Canterbury Plains and climbing into the rolling foothills of the Southern Alps.

At Mayfield there is a service station, pub, and store. After Mayfield, a totally straight 14km section takes you to the edge of the Rangitata River flood plain. The Rangitata is a major South Canterbury river, over 120km long, and a popular fishing river. The small village of Arundel is off the Highway, on the south bank of the river.

For a detour, a road north from Arundel leads 8km to Peel Forest, where there is a campground and hiking trails through a stand of original Canterbury forest. A gravel road continues on from here, deep into the foothills, where novelist Samuel Butler owned a station he called Mesopotamia. From Arundel, the tour continues through productive sheep farming country around the Orari River to Geraldine.

Geraldine is a mid-sized country town, with a population of 2,200 and a good range of facilities, although, like many rural towns, there is ongoing pressure to centralize government-funded services in larger regional centres. Still, the town has grown a long way from its 1854 start, when a sheep farmer established a bark hut here. The town was not named after the settler's wife or girlfriend, but got its name via James Fitzgerald, one-time head of The Canterbury Association, who came from Geraldine in County Limerick, Ireland. Geraldine is noteworthy for its elderberry wine, made from an introduced plant that other areas consider a nuisance weed.

Leaving Geraldine on Highway 79, the road is flat for 6km across the Hae Hae Te Moana River flood plain, then, gently rolling to rolling as it trends upward to Fairlie. The highway passes Gapes Valley and briefly climbs through Kakahu State Forest - a plantation forest with Kakahu Hill visible on the left - before entering Beautiful Valley. At the western end of the valley the road crosses the Opuha River and a sign indicates you are entering Mackenzie Country (although the Mackenzie Basin does not start until after Burke Pass, on the next stage). More rolling terrain follows, with some short steep climbs, then a tough 3km climb to a hill with a roadside café and great views. The final 7km into Fairlie are mostly downhill.

Fairlie is a small town, with about 750 residents, beside the Opihi River. The campground is next to the river, with good camping spots and large trees for shade. There are several motels, a service station, pub, shops, and like many small towns, a museum documenting local history. On Easter Monday the town holds it's A&P (Agricultural & Pastoral) Show, and in December - The Mackenzie Shears shearing competition.

25km down the Opihi River from Fairlie is Pleasant Point, where in 1902 or 1903 (no one is sure which) reclusive farmer and inventor Richard Pearse is thought to have taken his homemade aeroplane on a brief flight. His plane, made out of bamboo, canvas, and scrap metal, was ahead of its time - sporting a lightweight 2-cyclinder engine he built himself and using ailerons to steer. Lacking any hills to launch down, his plane had to taxi itself, which it apparently did, before lurching into the air and flying briefly, until the engine quit and he was dumped in a gorse bush. Without independent observers, his feat was never publicised or authenticated and it was left to

1975 The All Blacks start doing the pre-match Haka at home games as well as away games

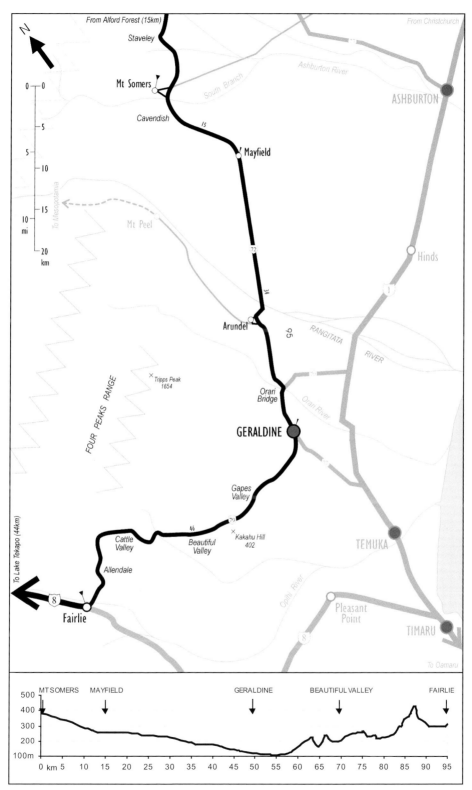

From Alford Forest (15km)

Staveley

Mt Somers

Cavendish

15

Mayfield

72

34

Arundel

95

RANGITATA

RIVER

Orari Bridge

GERALDINE

Gapes Valley

46

70

Cattle Valley

Beautiful Valley

× Kakahu Hill 402

Allendale

Fairlie

8

To Lake Tekapo (44km)

× Tripps Peak 1654

FOUR PEAKS RANGE

Mt Peel

To Mesopotamia

South Branch

Ashburton River

From Christchurch

ASHBURTON

Hinds

1

TEMUKA

Opihi River

Pleasant Point

8

TIMARU

To Oamaru

N

0 — 0

— 5

5 —

— 10

— 15

10 —

mi

— 20

km

Elevation profile:

MT SOMERS   MAYFIELD   GERALDINE   BEAUTIFUL VALLEY   FAIRLIE

500
400
300
200
100m

0 km 5 10 15 20 25 30 35 40 45 50 55 60 65 70 75 80 85 90 95

1975   John Walker is the first person to run a mile in under
3 min 50 sec

147

the Wright Brothers, in December 1903, to claim the first heavier-than-air controlled flight after launching off the dunes of Kitty Hawk. Pearse died, forgotten, in a psychiatric hospital in Christchurch in 1953. Today, a monument marks his runway near Pleasant Point and the Timaru Museum has a reconstruction of his plane. One of his later planes is on display at Auckland's Museum of Transport and Technology.

Samuel Butler

North of Arundel, on the west bank of the Rangitata River, is Peel Forest, and a little further upstream; Mt Peel Station, the first hill-country run in South Canterbury. About 40km past Mt Peel Station, via a gravel road even deeper into this remote valley, is Mesopotamia Station - the home of English author Samuel Butler for 4 years. Butler's writings, based on his pioneering life, provide a vivid picture of early settler life.

He had arrived in Lyttleton, in January 1860, aged 24, with money from his father and plans to become a sheep farmer in The New Zealand Company's last sponsored settlement - Canterbury. He differed from most immigrants in that he was a Cambridge scholar, a musician and painter, and had only emigrated after he was unable to agree on a career with his father, the Rev. Thomas Butler of Nottinghamshire.

Unfortunately, by the time Butler arrived the whole of the Canterbury Plains and the surrounding hill country had already been taken up, after The New Zealand Company's agent had started offering land at the peppercorn rental of a few farthings an acre.

Rather than pay the going rate to lease occupied land (100 times the unsettled rate of £1 per 1,000 acres), Butler bought a horse and set off in search of suitable sheep country in unexplored areas. His expeditions up the snow-fed braided rivers of Canterbury included a trip up the Waimakariri River, where he was the first white man to see Arthur's Pass - 4 years before it was crossed by explorer Arthur Dobson. He didn't find promising land until a trip up the Rangitata River and its tributary, Forest Creek. When Butler climbed the Two Thumb Range at the head of Forest Creek, leaving behind lands that had already been claimed, he came upon a stunning sight. "Suddenly, as my eyes got on a level with the top, so that I could see over, I was struck almost breathless by the wonderful mountain that burst on my sight…If a person says he thinks he has seen Mount Cook, you may be quite sure that he has not seen it. The moment it comes into sight the exclamation is, "That is Mount Cook!'…". More importantly for Butler, he also got a view of 10,000 unoccupied acres in the Bush Stream watershed (the next tributary to the Rangitata upstream of Forest Creek) which had never been seen before by Europeans, as the lower reaches were impassable.

Although the area was so high up sheep could not winter there - they had to be taken over a saddle to Forest Creek before the snow set it - this land formed the nucleus of Mesopotamia Station, in Greek "the land between the rivers".

Butler found additional land in the Forest Creek area, acquired it from the Waste Land Board, and purchased the holdings of several neighbours, to turn Mesopotamia into a viable year-round sheep station. He spent his first winter 8 miles up Forest Creek, in a 8 x 12 foot "V-hut" with a dirt floor and a stone for a seat - literally a world away from his Cambridge life. The following spring he decided to build a homestead overlooking the Rangitata 5 miles upstream from Forest Creek, but found a neighbour had already built there. Both parties realised the boundary dispute would only be settled with the outright purchase of the 20-acre block in question. Butler won a horseback race to Christchurch for the title and returned to build a sod hut. A more substantial cob cottage followed, with bricks made from a mixture of clay and cut-up tussock, and a snow-grass thatched roof.

With his homestead established and an overseer running his profitable holdings,

Butler was freed to continue his explorations, play the piano that he had brought up by bullock dray, paint, write, and make visits to Mount Peel and Mount Somers.

While at Mesopotamia, Butler wrote a series of articles for a magazine published by his old Cambridge College, and submitted several articles to the Christchurch *Press*. His family edited his letters home and other pieces, to compile the book *A First Year in Canterbury Settlement*, which was published in 1863, although Butler expressed a low opinion of the few pages he bothered reading after it was sent out to him.

In June 1864 Butler sensed it was time to sell. He returned to England, having turned his father's £4,400 into £8,000, to live the life of a painter and writer. He is most well known for the novel *Erewhon* (a rearrangement of "nowhere") (1872) and the semi-autobiographical *The Way of All Flesh* (1903).

Camping;
Geraldine Motor Camp & Caravan Park, Cnr Cox (S.H. 79) & Hislop St, Geraldine, Ph 03 693 8147, T$20 ◆ Gateway Top 10 Holiday Park, 10 Allendale Rd, S.H. 79, Fairlie, Ph 03 685 8375, T$10, Cabin$30

Hostel;
Rawhiti Backpackers, 27 Hewlings St, Geraldine, Ph 03 693 8252, Dorm$20, S$26 ◆ Tallyho Lodge and Backpackers, 7 School Rd, Farlie, Ph 03 685 8723 ◆ Gladstone Grand Hotel, 43 Main St Fairlie, Ph 3 685 8140, S$25

B&B;
Victoria Villa, 55 Cox St, Geraldine, Ph 03 693 8605 or 0800 537 533, S$90, D$100 ◆ Forest View, 128 Talbot St, Geraldine, Ph 03 693 9928 , S$75, D$110 ◆

Fontmell, Nixons Rd, 3km W of Fairlie, Ph 03 85 8379, S$65, D$100 ◆ Others; Geraldine

Hotel/Motel;
4 Peaks Motel, 28 McKenzie St, Geraldine, Ph 03 693 8339, D$80 ◆ Andorra Motel, 16 McKenzie St, Geraldine, Ph 03 693 8622, S$70, D$85 ◆ Farlie Lodge, 16 School Rd, Fairlie, Ph 03 685 8452 ◆ Aorangi Motel, 26 Denmark St, Fairlie, Ph 03 685 8340, D$75 ◆ Pinewood Motels, 25 Mt Cook Rd, Fairlie, Ph 03 685 8599, S$75, D$90

i;
i-Site, Cnr Talbot & Cox St, Geraldine, Ph 03 693 1006

1700 km Between Arundel and Geraldine

1750 km Between Geraldine and Fairlie

21 FAIRLIE TO LAKE TEKAPO

Fairlie to;

Burke Pass Village	22km	b&b	*44 05.4, 170 39.2*
Burke Pass	26km		*44 05.4, 170 36.0*
Lake Tekapo	44km	c, h, b&b, m/h	*44 00.3, 170 28.7*

This is a short stage, through one of New Zealand's most picturesque areas, so it is worth spending some time enjoying the scenery. The road climbs into the mountains bordering the Southern Alps along a route, *Te Kopi Ophi*, first used by Maori to reach Otago, rediscovered by Michael Burke in 1855, and now called Highway 8. The terrain along the stage changes dramatically as the tour enters the vast, tussock covered Mackenzie Basin, with Mt Cook - New Zealand's highest mountain - as a backdrop.

The road is flat for several kilometres to Kimbell then gradually rises and becomes gently rolling as the route climbs between the Two Thumb and Rollesby Ranges. Burke Pass village, 3½ km before the Pass itself, has a motel and store with an old stone watering trough. The church here dates from 1871 and the graveyard tells the sorry story of pioneer life in the harsh countryside; deaths from drownings, farm accidents, and avalanches. From Burke Pass village the road keeps climbing, the last kilometre or so being moderately steep.

A monument at the top recognises Burke, the first farmer at Raincliff Station near Fairlie, as the discoverer of this Pass into the Mackenzie Basin. Most people however, associate the area with James (Jock) McKenzie, the legendary sheep rustler who gave his name (incorrectly spelt) to the Mackenzie Basin. In a story that has taken on mythical status, McKenzie was using his own pass, 12km south, to access the Basin for years before Burke found a way in. McKenzie would graze his flocks here (sheep stolen from the rich wool barons of the plains) until he could drive them south over Lindis Pass, a route this tour also takes, to sale yards in Otago and Southland. His companion in this connivance was a collie, Friday, who was said to possess magical powers over sheep and who has also become a legend. McKenzie was finally apprehended at the foot of his pass on 4th March 1855, driving 1,000 sheep stolen from The Levels Estate near Timaru - although he managed to escape the same night. Friday however was caught. McKenzie was tracked down to Lyttelton and put on trail in

Tribute statue to border collies, Tekapo

Christchurch, where he refused to plead until Friday was bought into court. When he did plead it was "Not Guilty". He was convicted and sentenced to 5 years jail (although the wealthy pastoralists he had fleeced for years wanted him hung). He is said to have begged to be allowed to keep Friday with him but she was sent south, where she supposedly mothered much-in-demand working dogs, or in another more gruesome version, was hung as a witch.

After several escapes and recaptures McKenzie was released on condition he leave the country, which he did, heading for Australia never to be heard from again.

The run out of Burke Pass into the Mackenzie Basin is stunning, a near treeless expanse of golden snowgrass and tussock that bakes in summer and lies under snow in winter, surrounded by low rolling hills and the massive Southern Alps as a backdrop. A roadside monument along this stretch pays tribute to the old border kennel dogs, border collies like McKenzie's Friday, who were put at the edge of stations before they were fenced to turn back sheep.

1976 Joe Hawke leads a 506-day Maori occupation of Bastion Point in Auckland over ownership of a section of prime Auckland real estate

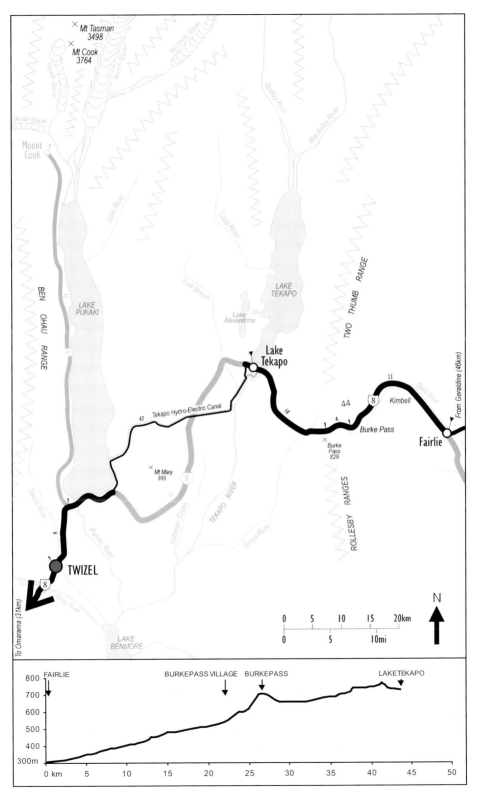

1978 In the general election, National wins fewer votes than Labour but more electorates, and remains in power. The same thing happens at the next election

Lake Tekapo is in another beautiful setting. The lake's milky blue-green colour is due to suspended rock flour - fine sediment milled by glacial action in the Alps and washed downstream. New Zealand's highest peaks are to the north, and the Mackenzie Basin stretches away to the south. A dam at the southern edge of Lake Tekapo is part of the Tekapo Hydro-electric Canal System and forms a bridge into the village, which is nestled amongst mountain pines.

Lake Tekapo caters to large numbers of tourists who usually stop here, briefly, on bus tours to Mt Cook. There is a good campground by the lake and the YHA hostel, also in a superb location, offers a few camp sites in addition to dormitory and twin rooms. The town is looked down on from the west by Mt John, which is capped by an observatory and a controversial US satellite tracking station.

Possibly the best known church in New Zealand is on the lake here. The Church of the Good Shepherd is a small, simple, stone and oak building with an altar consisting of a cross in front of a large window looking out to the lake and mountains. Next to the church is a bronze statue of a sheep dog, in tribute to the dogs that local shepherds still use in mustering. It is not, as some think, a statue of James McKenzie's dog Friday.

The Hamilton Jet Boat

One of New Zealand's great innovators, Bill Hamilton, is buried in the small cemetery at Burke Pass before the final climb to Lake Tekapo and the Mackenzie Basin. In a life full of invention, it is the successful development of the Hamilton Waterjet, used around the world for boat propulsion, that he is most remembered.

Charles (Bill) Hamilton was born in 1899, on a 45,000-acre sheep station just north of Fairlie, which his father managed. At a time when the world was rapidly becoming mechanised, farm life gave young Bill plenty of opportunity for design-and-build projects that took his fancy. After a stint as a border at Christ's College, Christchurch, Bill was called back to work on the farm during WWI. When he was 22, he purchased Irishman Creek Station, a 25,000-acre run in the Mackenzie Basin, for £16,000. Soon after, during a trip to England, he met his wife and they headed back to start life together on the station. Hamilton's creative space was his station workshop. There he tinkered with farm machinery and cars, including a 1914 Sunbeam that he managed to increase in horsepower in to the point where he became the first person in Australasia to official drive over 100 miles per hour.

His need for electricity on the station proved to be a defining challenge. In order to build a 5-acre dam for personal hydro-electric generation, he designed and built an excavator. The machine proved such a success he used it to undertake several construction projects around the country, and several more machines were made for sale in New Zealand and overseas. His workforce grew and during WWII the Irishman Creek workshop was contributing to the war effort by producing munitions as well as excavators, bulldozers, and earth scrapers. As business grew, a small workshop was opened in Bath St, Christchurch, which was soon vacated for a 25-acre site in the suburb of Middleton. With the machinery side of his business based in Christchurch, Hamilton went back to the workshop in the 1950's with the germ of an idea to develop a boat that could navigate Canterbury's shallow braided rivers against the flow.

With his dam and the Mackenzie Basin rivers as a test area Hamilton tried various propeller, air-jet, and water screw propulsion systems without success. His assessment of the American Hanley Hydro-Jet system, which sucked in water and used a centrifugal pump to fire it out a steerable nozzle below the boat, looked more promising, although the technology only worked well for low-speed, deep draught, boats. Hamilton's big contribution was developing a jet that discharged just above the

1979 During the Iranian Revolution, most NZ motorists are forced to pick a "carless day" - a coloured sticker on their car indicating which day they won't drive - and weekend sales of gasoline are banned

waterline and could be used to power planing hulls at speed with great manoeuvrability. With the help of a design team, versions of his Waterjet, using a 2-stage axial flow pump system, were developed which provided great power with very shallow displacement, allowing boats to travel previously unnavigable sections of river.

Modern jet boat jet unit

Hamilton amazed the world in 1960 when his boats made the first traverse up the Grand Canyon in the US. Expeditions up the Amazon and Ganges followed. The business blossomed and although the machinery side of Hamilton's company eventually closed in the 1980's, the Hamilton Waterjets are still being produced in Christchurch, and around the world under licence. Today the system developed by a high country farmer in the Mackenzie Basin is being used all over the world in pleasure, passenger, commercial, and search and rescue craft, up to 60m in length.

One of Queenstown's biggest attractions is the Shotover Jet, which uses the speed and manoeuvrability of the Waterjet to dazzle passengers on a high-speed canyon-hugging trip up the Shotover River. Bill Hamilton was knighted in 1974 for his services to manufacturing. He died, near Fairlie, in 1978.

Camping;
Lake Tekapo Motels and Holiday Park, Lakeside Drive, Lake Tekapo, Ph 03 680 6825, T$12, Cabin$45, Motel$120

Hostel;
Tailor-made-Tekapo Backpackers, 9-11 Aorangi Cres, Lake Tekapo, Ph 03 680 6700, Dorm$18, D$46 ◆ Lake Tekapo YHA, Simpson Ln, Lake Tekapo, Ph 03 680 6857 Dorm$23, D$50 ◆ Lakefront Backpackers Lodge, Lakeside Dr, Lake Tekapo, Ph 680 6955 or 0800 853 853, Dorm$22, D$56

B&B;
Rivendell Lodge, 15 Stanton Rd, Kimbell, Ph 03 685 8833, S$75, D$110 ◆ Dobson Lodge, 1km from Burkes Pass, Ph 03 685 8316, S$90, D$150 ◆ Creel House, 36 Murray Pl, Lake Tekapo, Ph 03 680 6516, S$75, D$140 ◆ Alpine Vista B&B, 12 Hamilton Dr, Lake Tekapo, Ph 03 680 6702, D$120 ◆ Others; Lake Tekapo

Motel/Hotel;
Lake Tekapo Scenic Resort, Lakeside Drive, Lake Tekapo, Ph 03 680 6808, D$120 ◆ The Chalet Motel, 14 Pioneer Dr, Lake Tekapo, Ph 03 680 6774, D$120 ◆ The Godley Resort Hotel, S.H. 8, Lake Tekapo, Ph 03 680 6848, S$90, D$120 ◆ Lake Tekapo Motor Camp (see camping)

1800 km Between Burke Pass and Lake Tekapo

22 LAKE TEKAPO TO OMARAMA

Lake Tekapo to;

Mt Cook turn-off	47km	c	*44 11.3, 170 07.5*
Twizel	56km	c, h, b&b, m/h	*44 15.5, 170 06.0*
Omarama	87km	c, h, b&b, m/h	*44 29.2, 169 58.0*

In the heat of summer the high altitude, sun baked, Mackenzie Basin can make for harsh cycling - even the cans by the roadside are roasted back to bare aluminium. But the bonuses are easy grades and superb scenery under a wide-open sky. Options for getting to Lake Pukaki include continuing on Highway 8, or taking the quieter Tekapo-Pukaki Canal Tourist Drive. The canal route, described here, has the additional benefit of being at the same smooth grade as the canal, which enables water to flow from Lake Tekapo to Lake Pukaki as part of the Upper Waitaki Valley Hydro-electric Power Scheme.

Leave Lake Tekapo and continue west on Highway 8 for a couple of kilometres (this includes a small climb out of town) before turning left onto Canal Tourist Drive, which is also called Bullock Wagon Trail. This road drops 1km to a powerhouse, then is flat, running beside the canal, until it drops to Lake Pukaki 30km distant. The turquoise canal flows above the braided, and now reduced, Tekapo River for 7km before bending west towards Pukaki. The canal and road cross Highway 8, 16km from Lake Tekapo, and immediately cross an embankment over Irishman Creek - a stream made famous by the perfector of the jet-boat, Bill Hamilton. Another elevated section, known as the Maryborn Fill, includes signs indicating "Beware Of Strong Winds" - presumably a warning about getting blown down the embankment.

27km from Lake Tekapo the canal road passes a salmon farm right in the middle of the canal, where they will net a fresh fish for paying customers. 4km past the salmon farm the road reaches a lookout over Lake Pukaki, with Mt Cook visible at the end of

Highway 80 to Mt Cook

the lake on fine days. The canal drops to the lake via two huge pipes and the road drops nearly as steeply. From here, the road gently rolls along the lake edge lined by purple lupins, to a camping area near the Pukaki Spillway. A couple of kilometres past the spillway is the turnoff to Highway 80 and Mt Cook.

If you have the time, a detour to Mt Cook village is well worth the ride. The road follows the edge of Lake Pukaki, then the braided expanse of the Tasman River, 55km to the village. There is a campground at Glentanner Park, about halfway up Highway 80, and at Mt Cook village there is a YHA Youth Hostel, and motel and hotel accommodation. Basic DOC camp sites are available on a first come first served basis about 2km away from the village. There is also a store and pub. The rewards for riding to Mt Cook include great views, bush walks near the village where keas (a precocious native parrot) abound, and longer walks - such as the 4-hour return trip up the Hooker Valley to the terminus of the Hooker Glacier. If you have deep pockets you can even take a plane or helicopter flight over the mountains, including landing and walking around on a glacier.

From the Mt Cook turn-off, continue south on Highway 8 to Twizel. On the way the road crosses the Pukaki Canal (which drains to Lake Ruataniwha) and Pukaki

1979 Arthur Allan Thomas receives a royal pardon and compensation for wrongful convictions for murder

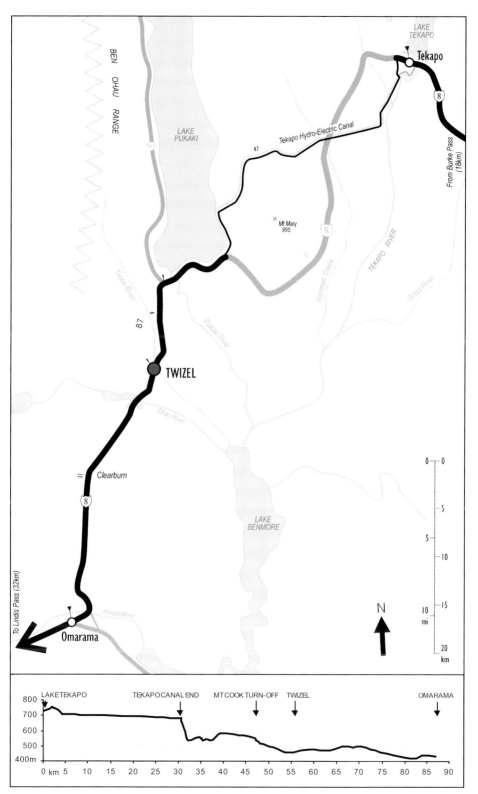

LAKE
TEKAPO

Tekapo

BEN
OHAU
RANGE

LAKE
PUKAKI

Tekapo Hydro-Electric Canal

47

From Burke Pass (18km)

8

× Mt Mary
995

8

TEKAPO RIVER

Irishman Creek

Grays River

Twizel River

87 9

Pukaki River

TWIZEL

Ohau River

31 Clearburn

8

LAKE
BENMORE

To Lindis Pass (32km)

Ahuriri River

Omarama

N

0 — 0
5
5 — 10
10 — 15
mi
20
km

800
700
600
500
400m

LAKE TEKAPO   TEKAPO CANAL END   MT COOK TURN-OFF   TWIZEL   OMARAMA

0 km 5   10   15   20   25   30   35   40   45   50   55   60   65   70   75   80   85   90

1980's   Treks or Nomads? (shoes by Clarks) is the fashion decision
faced by most NZ High School students

155

Aerodrome - where sightseeing flights are offered.

Twizel is a town specifically built in 1968 to house workers on the Upper Waitaki hydroelectric scheme. In Maori, Waitaki means "weeping waters", fitting for a watershed, second only in size to the Clutha catchment and fed by most of the rivers and lakes of the Mackenzie Basin, that has been dammed and canalled into producing 12,000 gigawatts of power. The hydro scheme includes 8 power stations, sending power across the South Island and into the North Island via a Cook Strait cable.

Omarama is a basically flat 32km ride from Twizel, crossing the Lake Ruataniwha Dam spillway and passing through classic Mackenzie Basin farmland. The Basin's thermal up-draughts make Omarama a popular gliding centre and the 1995 World Gliding Championships were held here. In 2003 American adventurer Steve Fossett attempted to break the world glider altitude record from here, reaching

Tribute to Merino sheep, Omarama

9km before abandoning his attempt to reach 15km. Omarama which translates to "Place of Light", is a tiny town of a few hundred residents but it does have a campground and several motels.

The Black Stilt (Kaki)

A couple of kilometres south of Twizel, on the left side of State Highway 8, the route passes several low buildings with aviaries next to them. This is the Department of Conservation's Black Stilt Hide and Captive Breeding Centre, which aims to increase numbers of the world's rarest wading bird.

Before Europeans arrived, these beautiful all-black birds with their long, red, stick-legs were found throughout the lower North Island and much of the South Island and were considered by Maori a taonga (living treasure). These days, if you see a kaki in the wild while riding through the Mackenzie Basin, count yourself exceedingly fortunate as there are only about 60 adults in the wild, even fewer in captivity, and the Basin is their only remaining breeding area.

Although hardier than the more common pied stilt (poaka), which leaves the Mackenzie Country during winter, the kaki has suffered predation from introduced species such as weasels, ferrets, stoats, rats, cats and dogs. Predatory birds, such as the black-backed gull, harrier, and falcon have also taken their toll. Other factors have been the dramatic alteration of the birds habitat by the construction of hydro-electric dams and canals, agricultural expansion, the

BLACK STILT HIDE AND CAPTIVE BREEDING CENTRE

growth of exotic plants along waterways, and by man himself - boating, camping, and driving where kaki live. The Mackenzie Basin's farmers battle against rabbits, another introduced species, has probably even hurt the kaki, with predators looking for other food sources as rabbit numbers drop. Against this, the kaki's only defence when their chicks are in danger is to run away while feigning a broken wing, in the hopes that the predator will be distracted by the prospect of an easy meal.

By 1981 there were only 23 adults left alive, despite the fact that females typically laid 3 or 4 eggs at a time in up to five clutches per season. From the early 1980's

1980 A merger between Fletchers, Challenge Corp, and Tasman Pulp & Paper forms Fletcher Challenge, NZ's largest Co. with interests in forestry, property, manufacturing, and energy

serious efforts were being made to start a captive breeding programme and to better understand the kaki.

In the wild, kaki nest on the edge of braided rivers and wetlands, where they fossick for insects and snails at the water's edge with their long beaks. They mate for life and both parents care for the chicks, which are patchy black and white until 1½ years old. When their chicks are still at a young age, the parents actively encourage them to leave the nest and the young kaki have to fend for themselves.

These days, eggs from captive birds and some wild breeding pairs are removed for artificial incubation. A discovery that the addition of a small amount of iodine into the kaki's diet can significantly increase a chick's chances of survival has improved breeding success, although once released back into the wild, at 3 to 9 months, mortality is still high. DOC has a 10-year Kaki Recovery Program, which includes electric fences and traps around kaki habitat, and the Department is optimistic the wild population can increase, despite a current shortage of female birds that has caused some males to mate with pied stilts - producing hybrid chicks. It would be sad irony if the critically endangered kaki, which was once an emblem for New Zealand's Royal Forest and Bird Protection Society, finally disappeared from the wild.

Guided tours of the Kaki Visitor Hide at DOC's Captive Breeding Centre allow visitors to see kaki close-up. Tours leave from the Twizel Information Centre (Market Place, Twizel, Ph 03 435 3124) at 9:30am and 4:30pm during spring and summer.

Camping;

Lake Pukaki, basic camp site, E side of Pukaki Dam ◆ Parklands Alpine Tourist Park, 122 Mackenzie Dr, Twizel, Ph 03 435 0507, T$20, Cabin$40 ◆ Ruataniwha Holiday Park, S.H. 8, Lake Ruataniwha (4km S of Twizel), Ph 03 435 0613, T$11, Cabin$40 ◆ Omarama Holiday Park & Motels, Junction S.H. 8 & S.H. 83, Omarama, Ph 03 438 9875, T$24, Cabin$40, Motel $70 ◆ Ahuriri Motel, Omarama (see motel/hotel) ◆ Others; Glentanner Park, Ph 03 435 1855 (59km NE of intersection S.H. 8 & S.H. 80)

Hostel;

Mountain Chalet Motels Backpackers Lodge, Wairepo rd, Twizel, Ph 03 435 0785 or 0800 629 999, Dorm$18 ◆ High Country Holiday Lodge, Twizel (see motel/hotel) ◆ Buscot Station, S.H. 8 (10km N of Omarama), Ph 03 438 9646, Dorm$18, S$40 ◆ Merino Backpackers, Broken Hut Rd, Omarama. Mobile 027 406 9522, Ph 03 438 9820, Dorm$15,

D$40 ◆ Ahuriri Motel, Omarama (see motel/hotel) ◆ Others; Mt Cook

B&B;

Pukaki Homestay, Lake Pukaki, S.H. 80 (3.5km N of intersection S.H. 8 & S.H. 80), Ph 3 435 3240 ◆ Aoraki Lodge, 32 Mackenzie Dr, Twizel, Ph 03 435 0300, S$100, D$150 ◆ Omarama Station, 1 km S of Omarama, Ph (03) 438 9821, S$60, D$110 ◆ Others; Twizel

Motel/Hotel;

High Country Holiday Lodge & Motels, 23 Mackenzie Dr, Twizel, Ph 03 435 0671, Dorm$20, S$40, D$55 ◆ Best Western Aspen Court Motel, 10 Mackenzie Dr, Twizel, Ph 03 435 0274, D$110 ◆ Sierra Motels, Omarama Ave, S.H. 8, Omarama, Ph 03 438 9785, D$85 ◆ Ahuriri Motel, S.H. 83 Omarama, Dorm$25, D$85 ◆ Others; Mt Cook, Twizel, Omarama

1850 km Between Lake Pukaki and Twizel

1981 Brian McKechnie throws his cricket bat in disgust and walks off after Australian Trevor Chappell bowls an underarm delivery to ensure NZ does not win a one-day match

157

23 OMARAMA TO CROMWELL

Omarama to;

Lindis Pass	32km		*44 35.3, 169 38.6*
Tarras	78km		*44 50.2, 169 24.7*
Cromwell	109km	c, h, b&b, m/h, i, bike shop	*45 02.6, 169 11.4*

Highway 8 leads out of Omarama, over Lindis Pass, and into Otago, where it follows the edge of Lake Dunstan to Cromwell (this 26km² lake came into existence with the construction of the Clyde Dam, 22km downstream of Cromwell). The climb to Lindis Pass and a long descent dominate this stage, followed by gently rolling then essentially flat terrain to Cromwell.

The road west of Omarama follows the Ahuriri River, a major tributary to the Waitaki, upstream. 19km from Omarama the road turns left at Longslip Junction and follows Longslip Creek up towards Lindis Pass. A few kilometres after this turn-off the road starts climbing more noticeably, gently rolling upward through tussock-covered hills. 29km after leaving Omarama the road gets steep for a final 2½ km to the top of the Pass. There is a turnout near the top to rest and admire the view back down the valley. A significant change in the geology becomes apparent as you head over the Pass with the surficial clays and gravels of the Mackenzie Basin giving way to hard shiny schist exposures that dominate throughout much of Otago.

From the top of Lindis Pass a great 12km freewheel starts, taking you down to the Lindis River, which runs along the base of a set of stair-step river terraces. In 1858, Otago's Chief Surveyor, J.T. Thomson, found a hint of gold in the Lindis River, but nothing to suggest the bounty that would later be discovered in Otago. In March 1861, roadworkers in Lindis Pass found more gold, and several miners were reportedly digging about an ounce a day from the river gravels, although the real rush to Otago did not start until Gabriel Read's discovery on the Tuapeka River in South Otago (see p.160). The terrain continues flat to gently rolling after the road meets the river although there is a 2km hill to climb before Tarras.

The first store and service station on the stage are 78km from Omarama at Tarras. The café here serves a great almond and apricot cake. The road crosses the Lindis River just upstream of its junction with the Clutha River and soon after reaches the shore of the northern end of Lake Dunstan.

The Clutha is the largest river in New Zealand in terms of volume (the Waikato is the longest). It flows from Lake Wanaka and discharges water at about 650 cubic metres per second into the South Pacific, 15km southeast of Balclutha (between Dunedin and Invercargill). The river is dammed in 2 places and produces 750 megawatts of electricity. The latest, and largest, of these dams was the Clyde Dam, completed in the 1990's.

10km past Tarras is the turn-off to Bendigo and nearby Logantown. A ghost town now, Bendigo was a rough and ready gold town from the 1860's to 1920's. The loop road leads to the old town site and gold workings that started in alluvial deposits before turning to hard-rock mining in a search for the source of the gold - quartz veins in the schist containing disseminated gold. If you visit Bendigo be careful walking around, as there are numerous old shafts.

From the Bendigo turn-off the road continues along the lake edge for 18km to the Cromwell turn-off. Turn left here onto Highway 8B to reach Cromwell.

Cromwell sits at the junction of the Kawarau and Clutha Rivers, above the original town location, which was flooded by Lake Dunstan. As part of the deal to build the

1981 Kiwi's embrace a 24-hour telethon that raises over $5 million for the disabled

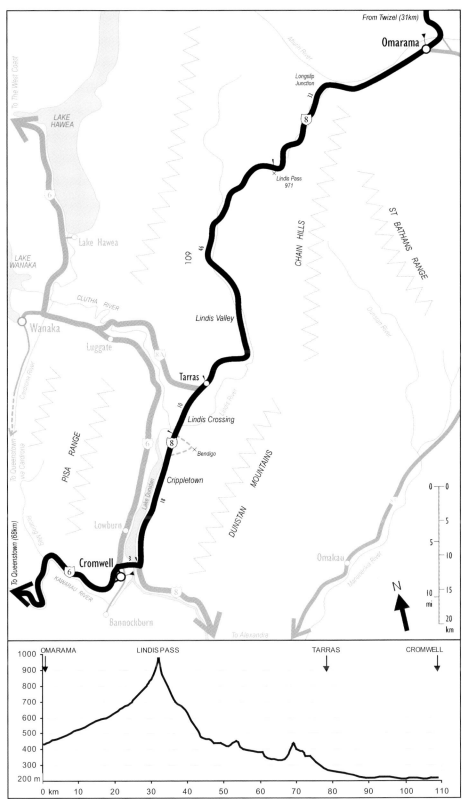

1983 or 1984 Old Blue, a 13-year old black robin, dies in the Chatham Is. When only 5 black robins were alive, her chicks were the only ones to survive and all black robins today can be traced to her and her mate, Old Yellow

159

dam the Electricity Corporation of New Zealand relocated many historic houses and shops to the new "Old Cromwell" above the lake, where the shops continue to serve as expensive tourist and craft outlets. The town has an excellent Information Centre that includes a small museum, in Cromwell Mall, with displays on the Clutha power projects and historical artefacts from the gold days. The town was originally known as The Junction, but was renamed after Irish prospectors fought with a Government survey team here, and subsequently put the curse of Oliver Cromwell on the area (Cromwell's actions in Ireland leaving him overwhelmingly hated by the Irish). The name stuck. The town library is next door to the Information Centre.

Cromwell is a town of about 2,700, which bills itself as the stone fruit capital of New Zealand. Summer roadside stalls make it easy to sample local peaches, plums, and apricots, amongst others. There are several campgrounds and numerous motel and hotel options. An interesting side trip from Cromwell is nearby Bannockburn, another old mining area, where there is a self-guided walk past old slucings and caves where miners once lived.

The Clyde Dam

Construction of New Zealand's largest hydroelectric dam project, at Clyde, has had a dramatic effect on Cromwell. When the reservoir was filled in 1992, water backed up through the Cromwell Gorge and formed a 20km long lake on Cromwell's doorstep, literally, with much of the old town having to be moved to accommodate it.

In September 1975, the Labour Government announced plans for a low dam at Clyde, 22km south of Cromwell. By December the following year the National Government of Robert Muldoon had upgraded it to a high dam as part of their "Think Big" scheme.

The blasting started in 1977, along with the first of numerous hearings on water rights issues. Other parts of the original Clutha Valley Development Project were shelved, but work on Clyde continued and by July 1982 the river had been pushed into a diversion channel allowing construction of the foundation. Geologists examining the foundation found a fault in the river channel that required a design change to include a flexible hinge in the dam that could accommodate movement on the fault.

By August 1989, 1,000,000m³ of concrete had been poured into the dam and filling of the reservoir was scheduled, however the discovery of additional landslides in the gorge resulted in a 2½-year postponement while remedial measures were undertaken to

prevent slides which could have blocked the lake or overtopped the dam. One of the largest of these was Cairnmuir Landslide, visible on the west side of the reservoir, about 7km south of Cromwell. This 20,000,000m³ slide, extending about 50m deep, was moving at 100mm/year before tunnels were dug below and drill holes were sunk into the slide to remove water.

Clyde Dam and powerhouse

Additional drainage measures were constructed on and around the slide and the area was replanted inside a rabbit-proof fence. This work resulted in the rate of movement at the toe of the slide slowing to 5mm/year in 1995, and continuing to slow since then.

The reservoir was finally filled to capacity in September 1993. The dam is New Zealand's largest concrete dam and the 4 generators in the powerhouse are capable of producing 432 megawatts, with room for 2 more generators if needed.

1984 Kiwi band Split Enz splits up

Camping;
Cromwell Top 10 Holiday Park, 1 Alpha St, Cromwell, Ph 03 445 0164 or 0800 10 72 75, T$15 ◆ The Chalets, 102 Barry Ave, Cromwell, Ph 445 1260, T$10, Cabin$30 ◆ Others; Bannockburn

Hostel;
Cromwell Motel, Cromwell (see motel/hotel)

B&B;
Cottage Gardens, 3 Alpha St, Cnr S.H. 8B, Cromwell, Ph 03 445 0628, S$60, D$90 ◆ Others; Cromwell, Bannockburn

Motel/Hotel;
Golden Gate Lodge, Barry Ave, Cromwell, Ph 03 445 1777 or 0800 104 451, S$95, D$180 ◆ Cromwell

Motel, Cnr Gair & Barry Ave, Cromwell, Ph 03 445 0373 or 0508 445 0373, Backpacker$25, S$50 ◆ Others; Cromwell

i;
i-Site, 47 The Mall, Cromwell, Ph 03 445 0212

Bike Shops;
Cycle Surgery, 48 The Mall, Cromwell, Ph 03 445 4100 ◆ Others; Wanaka, Alexandra

1900 km Between Omarama and Longslip Junction

1950 km Between Lindis Pass and Lindis Valley

2000 km Cromwell

1984 Roger Douglas becomes Minister of Finance. His radical economic policies are soon referred to as "Rogernomics"

161

CROMWELL TO QUEENSTOWN

Cromwell to;

Arrow Junction	42km	*44 58.6, 168 51.0*
Arrowtown	46km c, h, b&b, m/h	*44 56.3, 168 50.0*
Frankton	61km c, b&b, m/h	*45 01.0, 168 43.7*
Queenstown	68km c, h, b&b, m/h, i, bike shop	*45 01.9, 168 39.8*

This is a relatively short stage, which can be shortened further by bypassing the Arrowtown loop included here. However, Arrowtown is an interesting historical town that has maintained its gold-era charm, and is worth the ride (there is also a good campground there too, if you want to ride into Queenstown early the next day).

Leave Cromwell by taking State Highway 6 west. The road passes fruit stalls and is effectively flat for the first 7km or so, before entering the Kawerau Gorge. In the gorge, the road becomes gently rolling, then undulating. The scenery is stunning. The valley looks like a giant bread roll broken open. Jagged rock formations stick out of the canyon walls and the blue-green Kawarau River runs swiftly at the base. The road passes the Roaring Meg Power Station soon after entering the Gorge, followed by old mining areas and young vineyards on terraces above the river.

Near the southern end of the Gorge is the Kawarau Suspension Bridge. Built in 1880 to provide access to the surrounding mining areas, the bridge finally closed in 1963. These days

Roaring Meg Power Station on S.H. 6

tourist dollars are being mined at the bridge through New Zealand's longest running and most popular bungy jumping operation. AJ Hackett's illegal jump from the Eiffel Tower in 1986 proved a great business decision. He started offering bungy jumps here in 1988, and today the 43m leap is only one of numerous jumping locations in the Queenstown area.

43km from Cromwell is Arrow Junction, turn right here towards Arrowtown, a 4km ride off State Highway 6 (the detour through Arrowtown adds 7km to the stage compared to Cromwell to Queenstown direct on Highway 6).

The Arrow River, which flows immediately to the north of the town, was a frenzy of activity in the 1860's, as miners flooded into the area after the discovery of gold. The town quickly numbered several thousand but shrunk almost as quickly after the easily won gold had been removed. These days, Arrowtown's tree-lined main street, with its original miners cottages, is perennially featured in picture calendars of New Zealand - usually on an autumn month when the deciduous trees put on a colourful display.

Leave Arrowtown and follow the signs 7km back to State Highway 6, passing Lake Hayes to the right. 5km after rejoining Highway 6 the road dips and crosses the Shotover River. Shotover Jet have run their famous canyon-hugging jet-boat trips up this river since the 1960's and have sole rights to jet tours here. The road climbs the far riverbank and after a couple of kilometres reaches the outskirts of Frankton, which has numerous accommodation options, including campgrounds.

From Frankton, continue straight ahead on Highway 6A for the final 7km to Queenstown (turning left at the intersection of Highways 6 and 6A takes you on the next stage of the tour). Highway 6A includes one last climb before dropping into the heart of Queenstown.

1985 The first case of locally contracted AIDS is reported

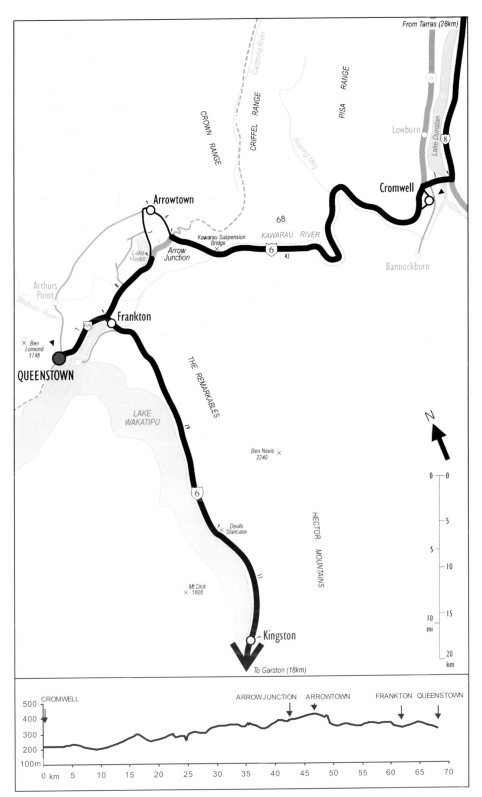

From Tarras (28km)

CROWN RANGE

CRIFFEL RANGE

Cardrona River

PISA RANGE

Roaring Meg

Lowburn

Lake Dunstan

Cromwell

Arrowtown

Kawarau Suspension Bridge

Lake Hayes

Arrow Junction

KAWARAU RIVER

68

6

42

Bannockburn

Arthurs Point

Shotover River

Frankton

6A

× Ben Lomond 1748

QUEENSTOWN

THE REMARKABLES

LAKE WAKATIPU

Ben Nevis × 2240

6

HECTOR MOUNTAINS

Devils Staircase

Mt Dick × 1808

Kingston

To Garston (18km)

N

0 — 0
5
5 — 10
15
10 mi — 20 km

CROMWELL   ARROWJUNCTION   ARROWTOWN   FRANKTON QUEENSTOWN

500
400
300
200
100m

0 km   5   10   15   20   25   30   35   40   45   50   55   60   65   70

Queenstown is unashamedly a tourist town but it's easy to forget about this because of its stunning location on the shore of Lake Wakatipu, surrounded by steep mountains. The town grew after Thomas Arthur and Harry Redfern, shearers on the Rees Station, discovered gold in the Shotover River in 1862. A full-on rush followed, with New Zealand and overseas miners converging on the area en-masse. By the early 1900's the boom had ended and Queenstown's population was under 200 again. For many years, the lake and surrounding rivers were the main transport routes. The road down the east side of Lake Wakatipu was completed in the 1936, and the road to Glenorchy was opened in 1962. Tourism, from the 1980's on, has been Queenstown's second boom industry.

Otago Gold

Just before Queenstown, State Highway 6 crosses the Shotover River, which early miners once called "the richest river in the World". When gold was found here in 1862 - a year when big strikes were happening all over Otago; at Bendigo, Dunstan, Cardrona, Macraes, Hyde, and on the Arrow River - it caused the biggest rush in Otago history. Stories of fabulous wealth easily won from the Shotover's bed, lured thousands of miners to the Queenstown area. Most passed through Dunedin on their way, making what was once a small port town into a sizeable provincial settlement.

Thomas Arthur and Harry Redfern started the rush to the lower Shotover a month after the Arrow River had been rushed. The two shepherds had panned for an hour or so and found 9oz of gold. After 2 months panning they had £4,000 worth of gold. Soon after, Dan Ellison and Hakaraia Haeroa were prospecting in the upper Shotover when Ellison's dog got swept away. He dived in to rescue the dog and ended up on a rocky point downstream staring, with his dog, at gold flecks in the rocky crevices. By the end of the day Ellison and Haeroa had 11kg of gold, worth £1,200.

The Otago gold rushes were started after a letter from Gabriel Read had appeared in the *Otago Witness* on 8 June 1861. Read described panning for gold on the Tuapeka River, a tributary to the Clutha in South Otago, and finding 7 ounces after 10 hours work - the gold sitting under a few feet of gravel on a soft slate and "shining like the stars in Orion on a dark frosty night". Within a month the rush to "Gabriel's Gully" seemingly emptied Dunedin to such an extent the *Witness* reported "...last Sunday the congregation at church consisted of the Minister and Precentor...". The Dunedin miners were soon followed by miners from the Victorian gold fields, and further afield.

About a year later, the focus moved from Read's Tuapeka discovery to the Clutha River itself when Horatio Hartley and Christopher Reilly arrived at the Gold Receiver's office in Dunedin with 40kg of gold. They were paid a reward of £2,000 to reveal the source of their find; the Molyneux River (now the Clutha) near, and up river of, Alexandra. The source of the gold was quartz veins, formed in Otago's schist and greywacke bedrock, from the Cretaceous (145 Million years ago) onward. These veins formed along faults and fractures, as hot, gold-bearing, fluids forced their way upward. Subsequent erosion concentrated the heavy metal into Otago's rivers, ripe for removal by pan or cradle. When alluvial gold became hard to find, hydraulic sluicing was used to blast old river deposits, which released the gold

Otago schist with quartz vein

but scarred the landscape - as seen at Bannockburn and in the Kawarau Gorge. Other miners sunk shafts into the quartz veins themselves, a more laborious method,

1986 The Russian cruise liner Mikhail Lermontov hits rocks near Cape Jackson in the Marlborough Sounds and sinks with the loss of 1 crew member

although one that became profitable from the 1890's after an effective cyanide leaching process was developed.

Otago's roughest gold town sprang up on the Arrow River. A solitary miner, William Fox, had been observed periodically coming into town and depositing large amounts of gold. Other miners would attempt to follow him but his habit of camping outside town and slinking away at night, leaving only an empty tent, ensured his secret spot was not immediately discovered (although his pursuers did find other profitable diggings while looking for him). Eventually, a Government geologist, Dr James Hector, found Fox in the Arrow Gorge. By that stage he had also been found by several other miners and a small community, sworn to secrecy, had grown under Fox's rule. When word got out, hundreds flocked to the Arrow and a canvas town sprang up. Billiard rooms, gambling halls, and brothels soon followed and order was only restored when armed police were stationed at the settlement.

The number of miners in Otago peaked in February 1864, at 18,000. New Zealand's gold production also peaked around this time, with 3¼ million ounces (nearly 100,000kg) produced between 1865 and 1870 (an average of about 20,000kg/year, compared to production in 2001 of 9,850kg). As the easily-won gold dried up many miners moved on to new rush areas on the West Coast and in Coromandel, and despite a second boom period from the 1890's when large bucket dredges were invented to scour the river bottoms, many settlements declined to ghost town status with just a few crumbling chimneys and scattered machine parts. "The Camp" (Queenstown) and "Fox's" (Arrowtown) survived.

Camping;
Arrowtown Holiday Park, 11 Suffolk St, Ph 03 442 1876, T$10, Cabin$40 ◆ Queenstown Lakeview Park, Brecon St, Ph 03 442 7252, T$24 ◆ Queenstown Holiday Park, 54 Robins Rd, Ph 03 442 6621, T$30 ◆ Others; Frankton, Queenstown

Hostel;
Poplar Lodge, 4 Merioneth St, Arrowtown,, Ph 03 442 1466, Dorm$20, S$50 ◆ Riverdown Guesthouse, 7 Bedford St, Arrowtown, Ph 03 409 8499, Dorm$24, S$50 ◆ Bungi Backpackers, 15 Sydney St, Queenstown, Ph 03 442 8725, Dorm$20, D$46 ◆ Deco Backpackers, 52 Man St, Queenstown, Ph (03)442-7384 Dorm$21, D$48 ◆ The Flaming Kiwi, 39 Robins Rd, Queenstown, Ph 03 442 5494, Dorm$20, D$80 ◆ YHA Queenstown, 48a Shotover St, Ph 03 442 7400, Dorm$25, D$100 ◆ Others; Arrowtown, Queenstown

B&B;
Rowan Cottage, 9 Thompson St, Arrowtown, Ph 03 442 0443, D$90 Others; Arrowtown, Queenstown

Motel/Hotel;
Mace Motel, Main Rd, Arrowtown, Ph 03 442 1825, S$90 ◆ 4 Seasons Motel, 12 Stanley St, Queenstown, Ph 03 442 8953, D$130 ◆ Amity Lodge, 7 Melbourne St, Queenstown, Ph 03 442 7288, D$126 ◆ Others; Arrowtown, Frankton, Queenstown

i;
Queenstown Visitors Centre, Clocktower Building, Queenstown, Ph 03 442 4100 or 800 668 888

Bike Shops;
◆ Bike Doctor, The Mall, Queenstown, Ph 03 442 8883 ◆ The Bike Fix Ltd, 106 Gorge Rd, Queenstown, Ph 03 441 2299 ◆ Others; Frankton

2050 km Between Arrowtown and Lake Hayes

QUEENSTOWN

Queenstown grew from a sheep station, into a gold mining town, and is now New Zealand's premier tourist resort, with year-round leisure and adventure activities on offer. The town's setting on the shores of **Lake Wakatipu**, surrounded by the steep slopes of the **Southern Alps**, is spectacular, and even the main campground and caravan park gets great views of the lake. The town's population is about 8,500 and there are a good range of services, including several bike shops, and plenty of cafes, tourist shops, and high-end boutiques.

The downtown area fronts Queenstown Bay, which is flanked by **St Omer Park** and **Queenstown Gardens** - the latter with a pleasant **lakeside walk** around the headland to Frankton Arm. The vintage steamship *TSS Earnslaw*, brought up in pieces from Dunedin and launched at Kingston in 1912, is a Queenstown icon which docks at **Steamer Wharf** (off Beach St). The ship offers dinner cruises and trips across the lake to Walter Peak Station, where there are **horse treks** and **farm demonstrations**. A **gondola** runs from the end of Brecon St to a vantage point and restaurant overlooking the town. A **bird park** near the base of the gondola has kiwis, other native birds, and tuatara (New Zealand's lizard-like living fossil).

Excursions, away from the downtown crowds, include; 4WD trips into **Skippers Canyon** (a road that includes the Gates of Hell and Fools Bend, and is banned by most rental car companies); trips to **Glenorchy** at the head of the lake (where several scenes from The Lord of the Rings movies were filmed); and day trips to **Milford Sound** and **Doubtful Sound** in the **Fiordland National Park**, a World Heritage area. **Tramping** (hiking) opportunities in the Whakatipu area are outstanding.

Queenstown offers plenty of adrenaline-inducing activities - most involving water or falling from various heights, and all quite costly, including; **jet-boat rides**, **rafting**, **river surfing**, numerous **bungy-jumping** options, **sky-diving**, **paragliding**, **skiing** (in winter), and **ballooning**.

1988 Cyclone Bola, a 3 day storm, causes over $100,000,000 damage

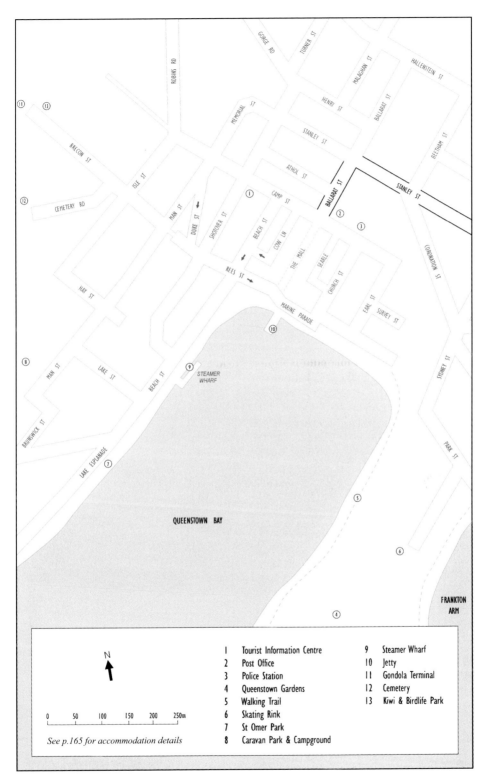

GORGE RD
TURNER ST
ROBINS RD
MALAGHAN ST
HALLENSTEIN ST
HENRY ST
BALLARAT ST
MEMORIAL ST
STANLEY ST
BEETHAM ST
BRECON ST
ATHOL ST
ISLE ST
CEMETERY RD
BALLARAT ST
STANLEY ST
MAIN ST
CAMP ST
DUKE ST
SHOTOVER ST
BEACH ST
COW LN
THE MALL
SEARLE
CORONATION ST
HAY ST
REES ST
CHURCH ST
MARINE PARADE
EARL ST
SURVEY ST
MAN ST
LAKE ST
BEACH ST
SYDNEY ST
STEAMER WHARF
BRUNSWICK ST
LAKE ESPLANADE
PARK ST
QUEENSTOWN BAY
FRANKTON ARM

N	

| 0 | 50 | 100 | 150 | 200 | 250m |

See p.165 for accommodation details

1	Tourist Information Centre	9	Steamer Wharf
2	Post Office	10	Jetty
3	Police Station	11	Gondola Terminal
4	Queenstown Gardens	12	Cemetery
5	Walking Trail	13	Kiwi & Birdlife Park
6	Skating Rink		
7	St Omer Park		
8	Caravan Park & Campground		

1988   The Government directed publisher of NZ's School Journals, age-
       specific readers with a distinct NZ flavour, is made into a Crown
       owned company

25 QUEENSTOWN TO ATHOL

Queenstown to;

Kingston	47km	c, m/h	*45 20.1, 168 43.1*
Garston	65km	b&b, m/h	*45 28.0, 168 41.1*
Athol	76km	c, m/h	*45 30.6, 168 34.5*

From Queenstown, Bluff is 219km to the south. This can be done in 3 stages, as described in this guide, with rides of 76km to Athol (a tiny stop), 82km to Winton, and 61km to Bluff. An alternative, if you are feeling fit, is to split the distance into two longer stages of 108km to Lumsden, and 111km to Bluff. Apart from Invercargill, the towns en-route are all small. The overnighting options at Athol are limited to a bed and breakfast, or a campground and lodge 1km north of town (Glenquoich Caravan Park & Lodge, Ph 03 248 8840), so check accommodation is available.

From Queenstown, backtrack 7km on State Highway 6A to Frankton and take State Highway 6 south following the signs for Invercargill. The road drops and crosses Kawarau River then follows the base of The Remarkables - a range of mountains that offer rock climbing and superb skiing in winter. The highest peaks are Double Cone and Ben Nevis. The area is dominated by Haast Schist, layered metamorphic rocks that originated as sediments on a 300-million-year-old sea floor that have been buried, baked, buckled and faulted into their present form. During the last major Ice Age glaciers flowed down from the surrounding mountains and converged in the valley now filled by Lake Wakatipu. Maori believed the slight rises and falls in the lake's level was from the breathing of a sleeping monster in the lake.

About 11km after Frankton the road nears the edge of Lake Wakatipu and climbs a ridge before rolling along for the next 29km to Kingston. There is one climb of note, known as Devil's Staircase, 29km from Queenstown. The road along the lake is twisty and tight, and with the tour buses that run south from Queenstown, riding requires keeping an eye on the road as well as the scenery.

Kingston is a small stop with a service station, store, and campground. It is most famous for being the northern terminus of the vintage steam train, the Kingston Flyer.

The Kingston Flyer

1989 Sunday trading begins

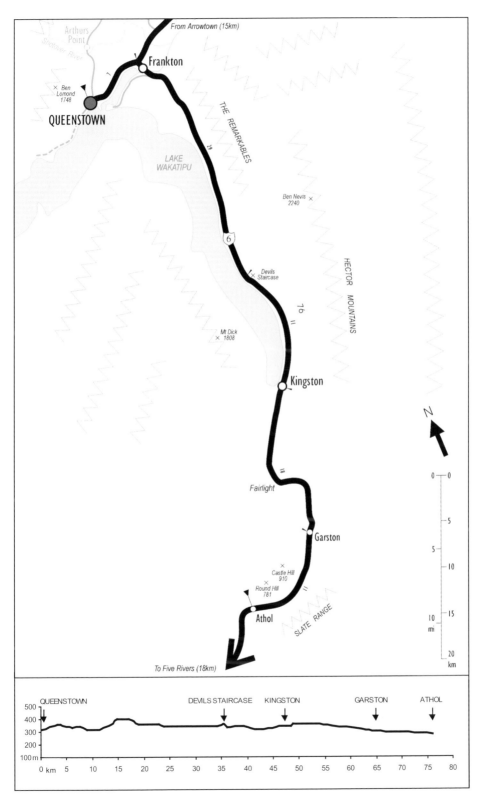

From Arrowtown (15km)

Arthurs Point

Shotover River

Frankton

× Ben Lomond 1748

▲

QUEENSTOWN

LAKE WAKATIPU

THE REMARKABLES

Ben Nevis × 2240

6

Devils Staircase

HECTOR MOUNTAINS

Mt Dick × 1808

Kingston

Fairlight

Garston

× Castle Hill 910

× Round Hill 781

Athol

SLATE RANGE

To Five Rivers (18km)

N

0 — 0

5

5 — 10

10 — 15

10 mi

15

20

km

500
400
300
200
100 m

QUEENSTOWN

DEVILS STAIRCASE

KINGSTON

GARSTON

ATHOL

0 km 5 10 15 20 25 30 35 40 45 50 55 60 65 70 75 80

1989 A second species of Tuatara, an ancient reptile with a primitive
"third eye" on the top of its head, is discovered

169

The train is a remnant of a service that operated from Kingston to Gore from the 1870's to 1950's. Two 1920's era locomotives tow restored wooden carriages between Kingston and Fairlight three times a day (during September to mid-May).

After Kingston, the route enters Southland province - the final district on this tour. The road to Fairlight continues as a series of short climbs followed by gentle descents. About 10km after Kingston the road meets the Mataura River, which it follows south, and the terrain becomes gently rolling. The Mataura is one of New Zealand's premier fishing rivers, with local and overseas anglers coming to Southland to fish for brown trout. The Mataura River is under a Water Conservation Order and the Southland Regional Council recently denied consents from irrigators who wanted to take water from the adjacent Riversdale aquifer, out of concern for sustainability of the waterway.

Garston, "New Zealand's Most Inland Village", is a small settlement, with a service station and pub. From here the route is flat to gently rolling to Athol, another small stop, with a café (albeit an expensive one) and a campground nearby.

Kiwi Icons

10 things visitors to New Zealand should know about, and aim to experience, before leaving the country;

Hokey Pokey Ice-cream

This is New Zealand's second most popular flavour (after vanilla) and has been a national icon for over 50 years. A combination of vanilla ice-cream and bits of hokey-pokey (a toffee made from melting sugar and golden syrup, then adding bicarbonate of soda to dramatic effect) - makes for a great treat after a hot day's riding.

Swanndri® bush shirts

Since 1913 these tough, weather-resistant, woollen shirts have been standard fare for farmers, fishermen, footy fans and generations of kiwis heading into the outdoors. See *www.swanndri.co.nz*.

Bic Runga and Brooke Fraser

Runga's 1997 debut album *Drive* became the biggest selling local album in New Zealand recording history. Fraser's 2003 debut, *What to do with daylight*, went seven times platinum and gave the 19-year-old singer-songwriter 4 No.1 hits in New Zealand.

Watties® Baked Beans

A low-fat favourite - full of protein and fibre to fuel your cycling too. New Zealanders enjoy baked beans for breakfast, lunch, and dinner. This brand was started by James Wattie in Hawke's Bay in the 1930's.

Footrot Flats

Cartoonist Murray Ball's Wal and Dog live on Footrot Sheep Farm, and have appeared in New Zealand newspapers since the 1975. A great insight into New Zealand and New Zealanders - from a dog's perspective.

1990 The 4 crew of the capsized trimaran Rose Noelle reach Great Barrier Island, 119 days after the boat flipped on a voyage from Picton to Tonga

Feijoas

Not even a native to New Zealand, but many kiwi kids grew up with one of these trees in their backyard. A knife and teaspoon are all that is needed for a meal of the guava-like fruit which ripen between March and June, or try feijoa jam year-round.

Greenstone

Known as pounamu and held in the highest regard by Maori. Found in limited quantities, mainly on the West Coast, it is illegal to take raw greenstone out of the country, but a carved pendant on a leather or woven flax necklace is a beautiful souvenir of New Zealand.

Fairydown® and Macpac®

These kiwi outdoor equipment manufacturers have been around for decades and make excellent quality gear, which has been battle tested on NZ's toughest tramps, and alpine adventures here and overseas. Several young NZ brands make quality gear too.

The New Zealand Listener

This weekly general interest and news magazine has been published in New Zealand since 1939. Originally a guide for radio listeners, it now includes television, arts, and event listings, but more interestingly, editorial and literary content with a distinctly New Zealand flavour.

Pavlova

This dessert of airy meringue is made from egg whites and sugar (in a decidedly difficult combination to get right), and topped with cream and fresh fruit - usually strawberries or kiwifruit. Australians may argue this is their creation but Kiwis claim otherwise. Low fat, but high sugar.

Camping;
Kingston Motels & Holiday Park, Kent St, Kingston, Ph 03 248 8501, T$18, Cabin$25, Motel$70 ◆ Glenquoich Caravan Park & Lodge, 24 Avon St, Athol, Ph 03 248 8987, T$10 (no cooking facilities), Lodge S$35, D$60

B&B;
Menlove Homestay, 17 Blackmore Rd, Garston, Ph 03 248 8516, S$50, D$80

Motel/Hotel;
Kingston Motels & Holiday Park, Kingston (see camping) ◆ Garston Hotel, S.H. 6, Garston, Ph 03 248 8820 ◆ Glenquoich Caravan Park & Lodge, 24 Avon St, Athol (see camping)

2100 km Between Frankton and Kingston

Athol to;

Five Rivers	18km		*45 37.4, 168 27.5*
Lumsden	32km	c, b&b, m/h, i	*45 44.3, 168 26.5*
Dipton	53km		*45 53.9, 168 22.3*
Winton	82km	c, m/h, i, bike shop	*46 08.5, 168 19.5*

State Highway 6 from Athol to Winton is mostly flat to gently rolling with a downhill trend, apart from two significant hills; Jollies Hill, 9km after Athol, and Josephville Hill, 9km after Lumsden. The tour continues through the pastures of Southland Plain, which receive just the right amount of sun and rain to make them some of the most productive farmland in New Zealand.

Jollies Hill is a stiff 2km climb, followed by a 2km descent, then, immediately after, another 1km climb before the route drops and becomes gently rolling again.

Five Rivers is the turn-off for many of the tour buses, which head to Te Anau and Milford Sound (72km and 193km distant, respectively). There is a service station at the intersection. Lumsden is another 14km south.

Lumsden is a small community of about 450 residents. The town has a motel, hotel, campground and unmanned Information Centre. After Lumsden, the route parallels the Oreti River, another prolific trout fishing river, which flows south to Invercargill and discharges to Foveaux Strait. The first 9km after Lumsden are flat, before the road starts a steep 1.5km climb over Josephville Hill. There are good views from the top; over the Southland Plains, Oreti River, and

Hokonui Hills, Southland

mountains beyond. This area is part of the Hokonui Hills, rugged bush-clad ranges famous for hidden stills and Hokonui moonshine whisky in the mid-1800's. The route drops to gently rolling countryside around Dipton, where there is a service station (if you ask for tap water here the locals' advice is to "…run it first. It tastes like rust but is good…"). The final 29km to Winton includes a service station and store at Centre Bush, 9km before Winton.

Winton is a town of several thousand, serving the surrounding farming district. There are several accommodation options in town, including the 1861 Winton Hotel, and you may be able to camp at the local Golf Club, where they have power points for camper vans.

Winton Hotel

1990 13 people are killed by a lone gunman in a shooting spree at Aramoana

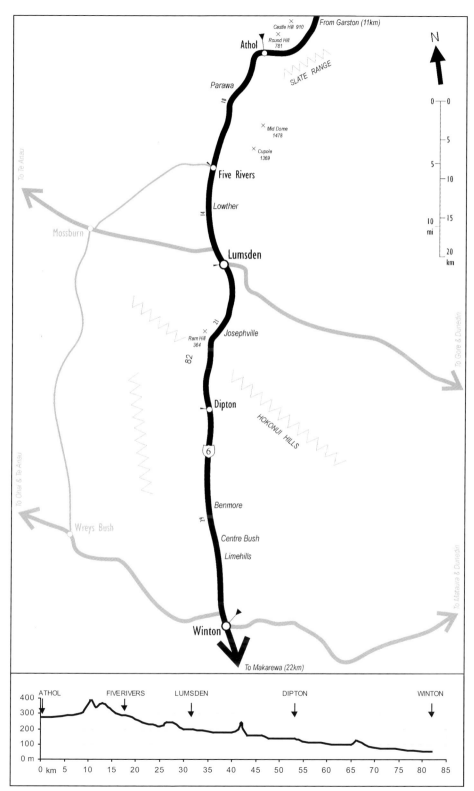

From Garston (11km)

Castle Hill 910
Round Hill 781

Athol

Parawa

18

SLATE RANGE

N

0 — 0

5

5 — 10

10 — 15
mi

20
km

Mid Dome 1478

Cupola 1369

Five Rivers

To Te Anau

Lowther

14

Mossburn

Lumsden

21

Josephville

Ram Hill 364

82

To Gore & Dunedin

Dipton

HOKONUI HILLS

6

To Ohai & Te Anau

Benmore

19

Wreys Bush

Centre Bush

Limehills

To Mataura & Dunedin

Winton

To Makarewa (22km)

ATHOL   FIVE RIVERS   LUMSDEN   DIPTON   WINTON

400
300
200
100
0 m

0 km 5 10 15 20 25 30 35 40 45 50 55 60 65 70 75 80 85

*1990 Peter Hillary reaches the summit of Mt Everest, 37 years after
his fathers' historic ascent. He climbs it again in 2003 - the
50th anniversary of the first climb*

Minnie Dean

Minnie McCulloch, a widow with two small children, arrived in New Zealand from Scotland in 1868. She married Charles Dean, and by the time Minnie's own children were grown the couple had moved to Winton, where she was known for taking in unwanted babies and young children. The sad truth about Minnie Dean was discovered in 1895, when the bodies of several infants were found buried in her flower garden and it was established she was running a "baby-farming" operation for cash. She was the only woman to be hung in New Zealand.

For the mothers of illegitimate children there were few options in Victorian New Zealand, and Deans - who placed newspaper ads (using a false name) describing herself as childless, and offering unwanted children a home - may have seemed like a good option. Deans also made false applications to adoption agencies with the same offer; for a financial consideration, children would be taken care of, no questions asked. When it came to collecting the children, Minnie usually made a train journey.

The Dean's lived on a 22-acre property outside Winton known as "The Larches". After their original 2-story house burnt down, they were reduced to living in a weatherboard shack with up to 10 foster children at a time. Periodically, Minnie's husband and working-age adopted daughter would arrive home to find a child gone, after Minnie had apparently secured a suitable home for them. The police had actually visited The Larches a number of times, after the deaths of several children, although these were determined to have been by natural causes, and no obvious child neglect was evident.

Police began having suspicions about Minnie after publicity on the issue of Baby-Farmers (unscrupulous women taking unwanted babies for money) and a baby advertisement under a false name was traced to the Dean's address. A guard on the Dipton to Lumsden train was interviewed and remembered a woman matching Minnie's description, with a child, getting on the train but noticed only the woman got off. Police inquires located a Dunedin woman who identified Minnie as the woman she had dropped her newborn granddaughter off with and gave a description of the clothes the baby was wearing at the time. Minnie denied ever having met the woman. A search of the Dean's house turned up the baby clothes and, after a Constable noticed the flowers in the flowerbed appeared to be just stems pushed in the ground, the bodies of a new-born and a one-year-old girl were found in a shallow grave. Charles and Minnie Dean were arrested. A third body was found in the garden several days later.

Charles Dean seemed genuinely horrified by the discoveries and following a Lower Court hearing charges against him were dismissed. Only one charge was filed against Minnie; the murder of 1-year-old Dorothy Carter. Her trial commenced in the Invercargill Supreme Court on 18 June 1895. During the trial it was established that arrangements had been made for Dorothy to be adopted by a "Mrs Cameron, The Larches, East Winton". Dorothy was picked up at Bluff, on behalf of Mrs Cameron by a "Mrs Grey", later identified as Minnie Dean. The poison register at Bluff pharmacy recorded that Mrs Grey purchased a quantity of the poison laudanum. Two days later Minnie told her husband she going away with Dorothy for a trip. She boarded the Invercargill-Kingston train with Dorothy and a large hat-box. It was during the several days she spent travelling the area by train that the guard noticed Dean exiting the train without a child. A porter testified how unusually heavy the hat-box had been. Dean had continued travelling, meeting the Dunedin grandmother and taking possession of the new-born, before returning to Winton, childless, and telling her husband the hat box contained bulbs she would plant the following day.

A post-mortem of Dorothy Carter indicated laudanum poisoning. Another critical piece of evidence, despite Dean's protested innocence, was her inability to provide names or addresses for any of the parents of children she had supposedly found homes for.

Minnie Dean was buried in an unmarked grave in Winton cemetery - 8 feet down instead of the usual 6 feet under.

Camping;
Lumsden Camping Ground, Cnr S.H. 6 & Albion St, Lumsden, Ph 03 248 8816, T$18 ◆ Winton Golf Club Sub Station Rd, Winton, Ph 03 236 8422 (call to confirm)

B&B;
Josephville Gardens, S.H. 6, Lumsden, Ph 03 248 7114, D$140

Motel/Hotel;
Lumsden Hotel, 6 Diana St, Lumsden, Ph 03 248 7099, S$38, D$55 ◆ Lumsden Motel, 5 Hero St, Lumsden, Ph 03 248 7099, D$85 ◆ Paramount Motel, 342 Great North Rd, Winton, Ph 03 236 7681, S$70, D$80 ◆ Winton Hotel, 218 Great North Rd, Winton, Ph 03 236 7315, S$50, D$70 ◆ Central Southland Lodge, 232 Great North Rd, Winton, Ph 03 236 8413 ◆ Others; Winton

i;
Lumsden Information Centre, c/- Five Finger Craft Inc, Diana St, Lumsden, Ph 03 249 7241 ◆ Winton

Library and Information Centre, 11 Meldrum St, Winton, Ph 03 236 0407

Bike Shops;
Winton Mowers & Chainsaws, 301 Great North Rd Winton, Ph 03 236 8585

2150 km Between Athol and Five Rivers

2200 km Between Dipton and Winton

1991   A landslide on the east face of Mt Cook lowers NZ's highest peak 10m, to 3,754m

175

27 WINTON TO BLUFF

Winton to;

Makarewa	22km		*46 20.0, 168 20.8*
Invercargill	31km	c, h, b&b, m/h, i, bike shop	*46 24.8, 168 20.8*
Bluff	61km	c, b&b, m/h, i	*46 36.8, 168 21.4*

The last stage is pleasantly flat, with only a few minor hills, although as you get nearer Invercargill the road gets noticeably busier with cars and trucks. The route continues across the Southland Plains and there are several small settlements, which are mostly loose collections of houses with no services, before Invercargill.

As you approach Invercargill, The Bluff - the 265m hill at the tip of the South Island, which Bluff township is named after - becomes visible. Past that, the peaks of Stewart Island can be seen on clear days.

Dee St is Invercargill's main street; lined with old buildings and wide enough to turn a Cobb & Co. coach around. Queens Park is the city's premier park and is worth visiting (go left off Dee St onto Gala St on the way into town. The entrance is ½km on the left). The Southland Museum, Art Gallery, and Visitor Information Centre are in the park, along with botanical gardens and sports fields. The museum includes details on Invercargill's Scottish connections (many of the old streets are named after rivers in the Highlands), as well as Maori and natural history - even a live tuatara exhibit. Invercargill is a major South Island city, with a population of 46,000 and a full range of services.

Continue down Dee St, past the war memorial, and rejoin State Highway 1, the road you started on at Cape Reinga, for the final 30km to Bluff. The road passes the industrial edge of town and poorer suburbs, then skirts the New River Estuary. 10km out of the city the road is back into farmland and scrub, with flax lining the road and the 137m high stack of Tiwai Point Aluminium Smelter, opposite Bluff, off to the left. Australian and Japanese interests own the smelter, which uses about 500,000 tons a year of alumina from Queensland and produces 2% of the world's aluminium. The process uses a huge amount of electricity and was the principal reason the Manapouri hydroelectric power station was built in Fiordland.

Soon after passing the estuary to the right the road meets Bluff Harbour on the left. The harbour is the base for Bluff's fishing fleet, and the departure point for ferries to Stewart Island. Above the port, the slopes of The Bluff are dotted with houses that get a regular wind battering.

A famous Kiwi spot on Bluff's main street is "Fred and Myrtle's Paua House"; paying homage to one of New Zealand's tastiest molluscs. The walls are covered with thousands of paua shells, and other things paua, and until they passed away a few years back, Fred was happy to receive visitors in his lounge and point out distinctive shells with his walking stick. The family still allows visitors to view the house.

After passing the few shops that comprise Bluff's main street, the road crests a gentle rise. On the other side, State Highway 1 curves down and abruptly ends at Stirling Point. There is a small carpark with a signpost similar to the one at Cape Reinga, a memorial to Captain William Stirling, and a plaque quoting a Psalm.

Plaque at the end of S.H. 1

1992 NZ votes to replace the First-Past-the-Post electoral system with Mixed Member Proportional representation

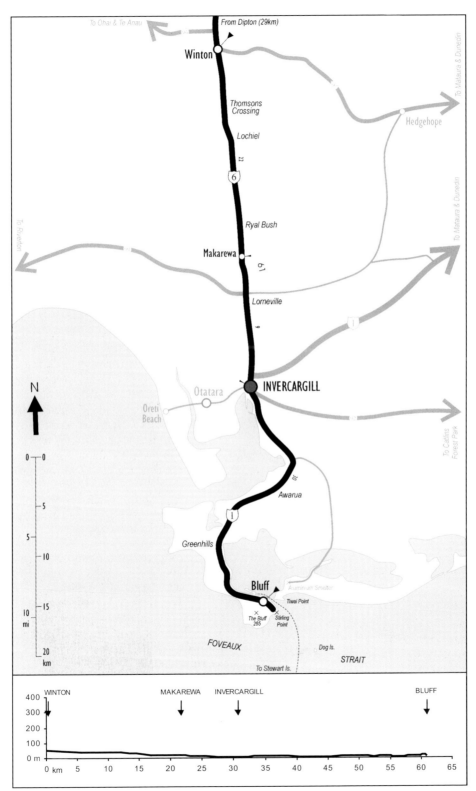

From Dipton (29km)

To Ohai & Te Anau

Winton

Thomsons Crossing

Lochiel

6

Ryal Bush

Makarewa

61

Lorneville

6

To Riverton

N

Otatara

Oreti Beach

INVERCARGILL

To Mataura & Dunedin

Hedgehope

To Mataura & Dunedin

1

To Catlins Forest Park

Awarua

10

1

Greenhills

Bluff

Aluminium Smelter

Tiwai Point

× The Bluff 265

× Stirling Point

FOVEAUX

Dog Is.

STRAIT

To Stewart Is.

0 — 0

5

5 — 10

10 — 15
mi

20
km

400
300
200
100
0 m

WINTON

MAKAREWA

INVERCARGILL

BLUFF

0 km   5   10   15   20   25   30   35   40   45   50   55   60   65

1992 Jacinda Amey - snorkelling at Campbell Is. when a colleague loses an arm in a shark attack - waits until the shark moves away then pulls the man to shore. She is later awarded NZ's highest bravery honour; The NZ Cross

Pelham Rock lies just below the surface a few hundred metres off Stirling Point - claiming 4 ships between 1864 and 1913. Dog Island is about 5km offshore, marked by a lighthouse. The larger, more distant, island to the southeast is Ruapuke - a major settlement for South Island Maori in the 1800's, when it was home to the Ngai Tahu chief Tuhawaiki (also known as "Bloody Jack"), a great rival of Te Rauparaha. The mountainous landmass to the south is Stewart Island, New Zealand's other main island. Details on Stewart Island are on p.180. Options for getting back to Invercargill from Bluff, other than riding, are on p.37.

Bluff Oysters

If you arrive in Bluff during the annual Oyster and Southland Seafood Festival, be prepared to sample oysters which the locals consider are the best in the world.

Bluff oysters have been dredged in Foveaux Strait since the 1870's, with demand for these fat molluscs far outweighing supply from the early days. Growing to about 10cm in diameter, "Bluff" or Flat oysters *(Tiostera chilensis)* are actually found in several places around New Zealand, in lesser numbers, and overseas. They differ from the more common Pacific oyster (which probably arrived from Japan on ships' hulls in the late 1960's, and was discovered in 1971) and the native Rock oyster (which lives in the north of the North Island) by, effectively, caring for their young. Non-Bluff oyster species have a carefree spawning, involving females releasing millions of eggs - so many that the water can look cloudy - and males releasing sperm, which fertilise some of the eggs into larvae. [Interestingly, oysters spawn as male when they are young, and become female as they grow older]. The larvae then float around as plankton for a month, before finding a suitable surface to attach to, where they are referred to as "spat". By contrast, Bluff oyster females produce far fewer eggs. The ones that are fertilised are sucked in through the oyster's filter feeding system and recognised as offspring, rather than food. Once inside the shell, the larvae are brooded for about a month before being spurted out at a stage where they are more likely to attach to the seafloor and survive. At 2 years old Bluff oysters are at a size suitable for harvesting.

The first harvests of Bluff oysters were off Stewart Island, back when stocks were so plentiful locals say that boats could be beached on the shallow oyster beds and the shells shovelled aboard at low tide. As the inshore stocks were fished out, deeper beds were found that fishing boats out of Bluff targeted with dredges. By 1963, the demand for Bluff oysters had resulted in overfishing, and New Zealand's first fishery quota was introduced - 170,000 sacks (about 140 million oysters). [Nowadays, strict, and highly valuable, quotas are in place for most commercial fish species in New Zealand].

In subsequent years, the Bluff oyster quota steadily dropped, as dredging continued

to shrink the beds. Then, in the mid-1980's, fishermen started noticing some of the dredged shells had a black watery oyster inside, or no flesh inside at all. The culprit was identified as the parasitic protozoan Bonamia, which can enter the shell when the oyster sucks its young back in. No one is sure if the parasite was always present, but in low numbers, or if it has somehow been introduced, but the effect on the fishery in the 1990's was dramatic, with estimated oyster stocks dropping from over a billion, to under 300 million. From 1992 to 1995 dredging was cancelled altogether.

Although Bluff oyster numbers have increased, the disease is still an issue. In March 2003 the Minister of Fisheries announced the commercial quota for the season (March to August) would be halved for the year, from 15 million oysters to 7.5 million,

1992 There are over 1,000,000 overseas visitor arrivals for the year

and beds which were predominantly smaller oysters could be not be dredged.

The value of the Bluff oyster harvest has resulted in researchers at the University of Auckland and NIWA (the National Institute of Water & Atmospheric Research) studying the possibility of growing Bluff oysters elsewhere in New Zealand, through aquaculture. Pacific oysters, which grow quickly to a large size (so quickly in fact they can smother the slower growing native Rock oysters), are a multi-million dollar aquaculture industry in New Zealand, and the researchers hope the same will be possible for the Bluff variety. If farming elsewhere in New Zealand does prove feasible, it may spell the end of the current frenzy at the start of the Bluff oyster season, which sees oysters flown around the country to customers willing to pay $19 a dozen. Although, the question would be; "Are farmed Bluff oysters, really Bluff oysters?"

Camping;
Invercargill Caravan Park, 20 Victoria Ave, Ph 03 218 8787, T$8, Cabin$30 ◆ Invercargill Holiday Park, 77 McIvor Rd, Ph 03 215 9032, T$24 ◆ Bluff Motor Camp, Gregory St, Ph 03 212 8704, T$5, Cabin$15 ◆ Others; Invercargill

Hostel;
Southern Comfort, 30 Thomson St, Invercargill, Ph 03 218 3838, Dorm$20, S$42 ◆ Kackling Kea, 225 Tweed St, Invercargill, Ph 03 214 7950, Dorm$20, D$48 ◆ Tuatara Lodge YHA 30 Dee St, Invercargill, Ph 03 214 0954, Dorm$23, D$50 ◆ Others; Invercargill

B&B;
Lovett Lodge, 31 Duke St, Gladstone, Invercargill, Ph 03 218 6060, S$50, D$100 ◆ The Lazy Fish, 35 Burrows St, Bluff, Ph 03 212 7245 or 021 211 7424, D$120 ◆ Others; Invercargill, Bluff (see info.)

Motel/Hotel;
Balmoral Lodge, 265 Tay St, Invercargill, Ph 03 217 6109, S$90, D$110 Queens Park Motel, 85 Alice St, Invercargill, Ph 03 214 4504, D$88 ◆ Foveaux Hotel, 40 Gore St, Bluff, Ph 03 212 7196, S$40, D$70 ◆ Others; Invercargill, Bluff

i;
i-Site, 108 Gala St, Invercargill, Ph 03 214 6243 ◆ The Little Inn by the Sea, Stirling Pt, Bluff, Ph 03 212 7575 (also B&B accommodation)

Bike Shops;
Wensley Cycles, 53 Tay St, Invercargill, Ph: 03 218 6206 ◆ Others; Invercargill

2250 km Between Makarewa and Invercargill

2277 km Stirling Point, Bluff

1993 Professor Fred Hollows, dedicated to cheap, life changing, eye treatment for indigenous people in Australia and Asia, dies

179

STEWART ISLAND

Most New Zealanders never make it to Stewart Island, the nations third largest island. It is an interesting place to visit and since the daily ferry leaves from Bluff, it's worth making the 30km boat trip across if you have time (Stewart Island Experience Ferries, Ph 03 212 7660). Alternatively, you can make the trip by plane from Invercargill (Stewart Island Flights, Ph 03 218 9129).

There are only a few kilometers of road on the island, so don't plan an extensive cycle tour, although a bike is still a good way to get around. You can also hire scooters or take one of the scenic bus tours offered. Stewart Island is a wildlife and wilderness gem, and the island includes NZ's newest National Park; Rakiura National Park.

Captain Cook briefly skirted the island in 1770 and thought it was connected to the South Island. The island was named after William Stewart, who explored it in 1809 then returned to set up a trading post and timber mill in 1825 (the venture failed and he was later jailed for his debts). These days, the population of fewer than 500 is supported by fishing and tourism.

The only sizable settlement is Oban, in Halfmoon Bay, which has a number of shops, cafes and restaurants, a museum, and a 6-hole golf course. Basically, Stewart Island is a good place to escape the mainland, relax, and enjoy beautiful scenery. The coast is a mix of sandy beaches and rocky inlets with a bush backdrop. Paterson Inlet, to the south of Oban, has a number of small islands, including Ulva Island - one of several predator-free islands around Stewart Island where endangered native bird recovery programmes are being undertaken. Tours to Ulva Island are available. Stewart Island is also a great place to see kiwi in the wild, and night-time tours are run. At the Muttonbird Islands, off the turbulent southwest coast, and a few other islands around Stewart Island, Maori have traditional rights to seasonally harvest Muttonbirds - the fatty chicks of the Sooty Shearwater.

Inland, Stewart Island is mountainous and there is good tramping (hiking) for the well equipped, although be prepared for muddy trails. A popular multi-day track runs along the northern coast, past the highest point on the island, Mt Anglem (980m), returning to Oban via the Freshwater River.

Other activities on offer include sea kayaking, scuba diving, nature tours, hunting, boat trips, and fishing. There are plenty of accommodation options including several camping areas, hostels, a hotel, motels, B&B, and house or cottage rentals.

◆   ◆   ◆   ◆   ◆

Camping;
Stewart Island Backpackers, Ayr St, Oban, Ph 03 219 1114, T$8

Hostel;
Innes Backpackers13 Argyll St, Oban, Ph 03 219 1080 ◆ Stewart Island Backpackers, Ayr St, Oban, Ph 03 219 1114, Dorm$20, D$72 ◆ Ann's Place, 55 Horseshoe Bay Rd, Oban, Ph 03 219 1065

B&B;
Jo and Andy's B&B, 22 Main Rd, Oban, Ph 03 219 1230, S$40, D$60 ◆ Thorfinn Charters & Accommodation, Butterfield Beach, Ph 03 219 1210, D$75

Hotel;
South Sea Hotel and Motel, Elgin Tce, Halfmoon Bay, Ph 03 219 1059, D$80 ◆ Bay Motel, 9 Dundee St, Halfmoon Bay, Ph 03 219 1119, D$130 ◆ Rakiura Retreat Motel, 1.6km from Oban, Ph 03 219 1096, D$95 ◆ Others; Oban

i;
Stewart Island Visitor Information Centre, Main Rd, Halfmoon Bay, Ph 03 219 0009

1994 A protester chainsaws the lone pine tree on Auckland's One Tree Hill although the tree survives

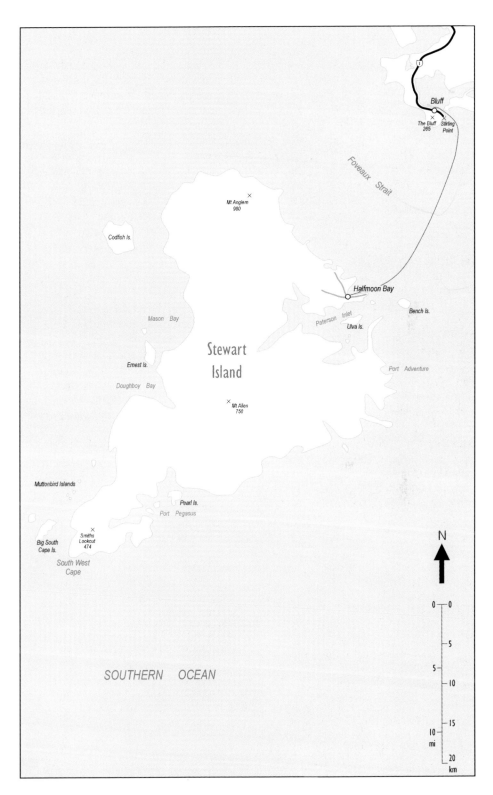

Bluff

The Bluff
265

Stirling
Point

Foveaux Strait

Mt Angiem
980

Codfish Is.

Halfmoon Bay

Bench Is.

Mason Bay

Paterson Inlet

Ulva Is.

Stewart
Island

Port Adventure

Ernest Is.

Doughboy Bay

Mt Allen
750

Muttonbird Islands

Pearl Is.

Port Pegasus

Big South
Cape Is.

Smiths
Lookout
474

South West
Cape

N

SOUTHERN OCEAN

0 — 0

5

5 — 10

15

10 —
mi

20

km

1994 Lee Tamahori's film version of Alan Duff's book "Once
Were Warriors" is an eye-opener for many kiwis, and
wins an award at the Venice Film Festival

APPENDIX A: TEMPERATURE AND RAINFALL

Cape Reinga

Month	Jan	Feb	Mar	Apr	May	June	July	Aug	Sept	Oct	Nov	Dec
Av. Min. (°C)	12	13	12	11	9	7	6	7	8	8	9	11
Av. Max. (°C)	24	25	24	22	20	18	17	17	18	19	21	23
Av. Rain (mm)	58	68	65	96	102	118	120	109	80	67	56	53

Auckland

Month	Jan	Feb	Mar	Apr	May	June	July	Aug	Sept	Oct	Nov	Dec
Av. Min. (°C)	12	12	10	8	6	4	3	4	5	7	8	10
Av. Max. (°C)	27	27	25	23	20	18	17	18	19	21	23	25
Av. Rain (mm)	70	87	79	98	118	130	135	115	96	96	84	77

Chateau , Mt Ruapehu

Month	Jan	Feb	Mar	Apr	May	June	July	Aug	Sept	Oct	Nov	Dec
Av. Min. (°C)	1	2	0	-1	-4	-5	-6	-6	-4	-3	-2	0
Av. Max. (°C)	23	22	21	17	14	12	11	12	14	18	18	21
Av. Rain (mm)	200	194	171	219	266	271	265	248	243	260	250	251

Wellington

Month	Jan	Feb	Mar	Apr	May	June	July	Aug	Sept	Oct	Nov	Dec
Av. Min. (°C)	8	8	7	5	3	2	1	1	2	4	5	7
Av. Max. (°C)	25	25	24	21	18	16	15	16	18	20	22	24
Av. Rain (mm)	81	81	85	100	122	125	139	122	100	106	88	91

Blenheim

Month	Jan	Feb	Mar	Apr	May	June	July	Aug	Sept	Oct	Nov	Dec
Av. Min. (°C)	6	5	4	1	-2	-3	-3	-3	-1	0	2	4
Av. Max. (°C)	31	30	28	25	21	18	17	18	21	24	27	29
Av. Rain (mm)	50	44	45	56	68	56	62	65	49	55	46	46

Christchurch

Month	Jan	Feb	Mar	Apr	May	June	July	Aug	Sept	Oct	Nov	Dec
Av. Min. (°C)	6	5	3	1	-2	-3	-3	-3	-1	1	2	5
Av. Max. (°C)	31	30	28	25	21	17	17	18	22	25	27	29
Av. Rain (mm)	55	42	54	56	75	62	71	53	47	47	46	58

Lake Tekapo

Month	Jan	Feb	Mar	Apr	May	June	July	Aug	Sept	Oct	Nov	Dec
Av. Min. (°C)	2	2	0	-2	-5	-7	-8	-7	-5	-3	-1	1
Av. Max. (°C)	28	28	26	22	17	13	12	14	18	22	24	27
Av. Rain (mm)	50	40	44	53	56	50	51	51	53	51	48	50

Queenstown

Month	Jan	Feb	Mar	Apr	May	June	July	Aug	Sept	Oct	Nov	Dec
Av. Min. (°C)	5	5	3	1	-2	-4	-4	-3	-1	0	2	4
Av. Max. (°C)	29	28	26	21	17	14	13	15	18	22	24	27
Av. Rain (mm)	73	56	71	75	74	62	55	56	70	83	68	62

Tiwai Point, Bluff

Month	Jan	Feb	Mar	Apr	May	June	July	Aug	Sept	Oct	Nov	Dec
Av. Min. (°C)	6	6	5	3	0	-2	-2	-1	0	2	3	5
Av. Max. (°C)	25	24	25	21	16	14	14	16	17	20	23	24
Av. Rain (mm)	93	59	90	101	112	99	94	69	98	93	81	88

Note: Data are approximate averages for selected locations. Conditions are likely to vary outside these averages, and it's always possible you could strike a significantly hotter, colder, or wetter month. Average min. (or max.) temps are the average of the lowest (or highest) temperatures in each month.

1994 The concept of Te Araroa, The Long Pathway - a walking route between Cape Reinga and Bluff - is announced. With completion is expected in 2008, marker posts have started to appear on some sections

APPENDIX B: ADDITIONAL INFORMATION

Useful Reading;

The Penguin History of New Zealand. Michael King. Penguin Books 2003

The Reed Field Guide to New Zealand Birds. Geoff Moon. Reed Publishing 1992

Essential NZ Short Stories. Owen Marshall (Ed.) Godwit 2002

The Reed Field Guide to New Zealand Geology. J. Thornton. Reed Books 1997

The New Zealand Weather Book. Erick Brenstrum. Craig Potton Publishing 1998

The Bicycle Touring Manual. Rob van der Plas. Bicycle Books Inc. 1998.

The Bible, New Living Translation. Pocket-size New Testament. Tyndale House 1996

New Zealand's Great Walks. Pearl Hewson. Hodder Moa Beckett 1996

Internet Sites;

www.immigration.govt.nz How to get into NZ

www.linz.govt.nz Maps of NZ

www.mountainbike.co.nz Includes a section with daily postings from cyclists on tours of NZ or planning to tour NZ

www.ltsa.govt.nz NZ Road Rules

www.nzherald.co.nz NZ's largest circulation daily newspaper

www.doc.govt.nz Department of Conservation

www.tepapa.govt.nz The Museum of NZ

www.nzhistory.net.nz On-line history of NZ

www.thehungreypeople.org Sponsors rickshaws in India to provide families a way to make a living

www.cyclingnz.com National organisation for road and mountain bike events and racing

APPENDIX C: NEW ZEALAND LANGUAGE 101

Some common Maori words that make up place names;

iti	small	puke	hill
kainga	village	rangi	sky
kare	ripples	roa	long
kato	floodtide, pluck	roto	lake
kohe	talk nonsense	taka	turn, prepare, roll
manga	stream, branch	tane	man, husband
mata	swamp	tapu	forbidden, sacred
moana	sea, lake	te	the
motu	island	toto	bleed, blood
nga	the (plural)	wai	water, river
nui	big	waka	canoe
one	mud or sand	whaka	towards
pa	protected village	whanga	bay
papa	flat		

The word Maori has traditionally been written as shown throughout this guide. Variations sometimes seen include Māori, Maaori, or Mäori.

Taumatawhakatangihangakoauauotamateapokaiwhenuakitan atahu, a hill in Hawke's Bay, is thought to be the second longest place name in the world (a Welsh location having a slightly longer name). It means something like; "The top of the hill where the great husband of heaven, Tamatea, caused plaintive music from his flute to descend on his beloved"

Colloquial Kiwi;

Bach (pronounced batch):	Holiday home
Barbie	BBQ
Bludger	Parasitic individual
Caravan	Camping trailer
Campervan	RV
Crikey dick	Wow
Dag	Funny guy
Dairy	Corner store
Dunny	Toilet
Hard yakka	Hard work
Have a yarn	Have a chat
Ice block	Popsicle
Knackered	Very tired
Motorway	Freeway
Petrol	Gasoline
Push bike	Bicycle
Rattle your dags	Hurry up
Smoko	Rest break
Stuffed	Very tired
Take-aways	Fast food
Tiki tour	Indirect (often scenic) route
Torch	Flashlight
Whinger	Incessant complainer
Gidday	Hello
Yak, Yack	Chat

APPENDIX D: METRIC CONVERSIONS

DISTANCE

To convert kilometres to miles multiply by 0.621
To convert miles to kilometres multiply by 1.61

To convert metres to feet multiply by 3.28
To convert feet to meters multiply by 0.305

km	=	miles		miles	=	km		m	=	ft		ft	=	m
1		0.62		1		1.61		1		3.28		1		0.31
2		1.2		2		3.2		2		6.6		2		0.6
3		1.9		3		4.8		3		9.8		3		0.9
4		2.5		4		6.4		4		13.1		4		1.2
5		3.1		5		8.1		5		16.4		5		1.5
6		3.7		6		9.7		6		19.7		6		1.8
7		4.4		7		11.3		7		23		7		2.1
8		5		8		12.9		8		26.2		8		2.4
9		5.6		9		14.5		9		29.5		9		2.8
10		6.2		10		16.1		10		32.8		10		3.1

WEIGHT

To convert kilograms to pounds multiply by 2.20
To convert pounds to kilograms multiply by 0.455

kg	=	lbs		lbs	=	kg		g	=	oz		oz	=	g
1		2.2		1		0.46		1		0.35		1		28.4
2		4.4		2		0.9		2		0.7		2		57
3		6.6		3		1.4		3		1.1		3		85
4		8.8		4		1.8		4		1.4		4		114
5		11		5		2.3		5		1.8		5		142
6		13.2		6		2.7		6		2.1		6		170
7		15.4		7		3.2		7		2.5		7		199
8		17.6		8		3.6		8		2.8		8		227
9		19.8		9		4.1		9		3.2		9		256
10		22		10		4.6		10		3.5		10		284

To convert grams to ounces multiply by 0.35
To convert ounces to grams multiply by 28.4
1 British ton = 1019kg (2240lbs) and 1 US ton = 910kg (2000lbs)
To convert British tons to US tons multiply by 0.893

VOLUME

To convert litres to US gallons multiply by 0.264
To convert US gallons to litres multiply by 3.79

litre	=	US gal		US gal	=	litre
1		0.26		1		3.79
2		0.5		2		7.6
3		0.8		3		11.4
4		1.1		4		15.1
5		1.3		5		19
6		1.6		6		22.7
7		1.8		7		26.5
8		2.1		8		30.3
9		2.4		9		34.1
10		2.6		10		37.9

(1 litre is 1.5 US pints, and 1.8 UK pints)
(1 imperial gallon = 4.55 liters (1.18 US gallons))
(To convert US gal. to imperial gal. multiply by 0.845)
(1 cubic m = 35.3 cubic ft, 1 cubic ft = 0.0283 cubic m)

TEMPERATURE

To convert °C to °F multiply by 1.8 and add 32
To convert °F to °C subtract 32 and multiply by 0.555

°C	=	°F		°F	=	°C
50		122		120		49
45		113		110		43
40		104		100		38
35		95		90		32
30		86		80		27
25		77		70		21
20		68		60		16
15		59		50		10
10		50		40		4
5		41		30		-1
0		32		20		-7
-5		23		10		-12
-10		14		0		-18
-15		5		-10		-23

1995 Multi-sport athlete Steve Gurney wins the first of his 9 Coast-to-Coast race victories

APPENDIX E: AUCKLAND AIRPORT TO CITY MAP

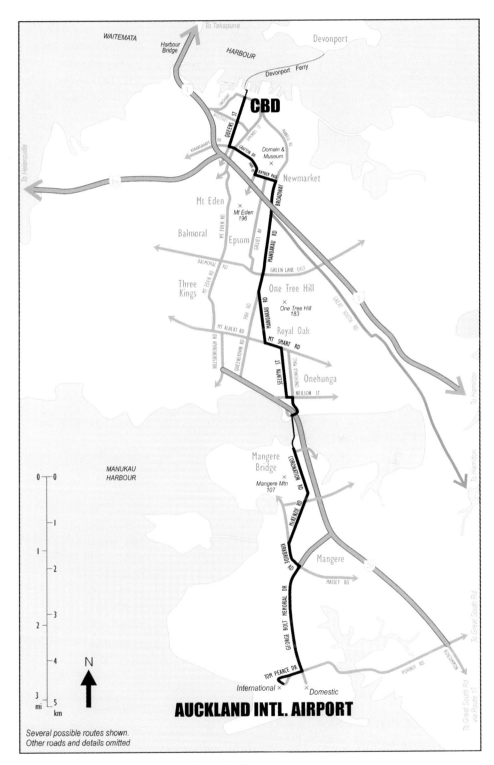

Several possible routes shown.
Other roads and details omitted

INDEX

Pages with colour photos in **bold**

*1996 After the first MMP election NZ First holds the balance of power.
Leader Winston Peters decides to form a coalition government
with National and becomes deputy PM*

1997 Dead rabbits found near Cromwell indicate rabbit calicivirus disease (RCD) has been smuggled into NZ for use as a biological control agent

*1999 Helen Clark, an MP since 1975, is the first woman elected
Prime Minister, leading NZ's fourth Labour Government*

2000   There are 3,100,000 registered motor vehicles in NZ and the average car is estimated to emit 2.8 kg of CO₂ and 1 kg of CO every 10km

191

*2000 A NZ art dealer offers works he attributes to Paul Gauguin for sale. Critics
say they are by Karl Sim, a 77-year old previously convicted of forging
Goldie paintings who changed his name by deed poll to Carl Fedor Goldie*

2001 Thieves murder NZ's most respected sailor, Peter Blake, on his yacht near the mouth of the Amazon

*2002 Graeme Hart, a one time tow truck driver and panel beater
who left school at 16, becomes NZ's first billionaire*

2003 There are over 2,000,000 overseas visitor arrivals for the year

*2004 Pre-eminent NZ historian Michael King dies in a car crash on
a notoriously dangerous section of S.H.2 in the Waikato*

199

www.epicguides.co.nz

A guide for Britain's most famous long-distance cycle tour, following mostly quieter roads. This tour incorporates some of Britain's most beautiful and interesting areas including; the Cornish coast, the Roman towns of Bath and Chester, the Lake District, and Scotland's Highlands and brooding locks. Includes photos every 25 miles from Land's End to John O' Groats.

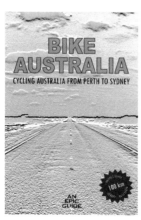

This epic guide for experienced cycle tourers covers Australia from the Indian Ocean to the Pacific, following main roads. It passes through remote wilderness areas, Australia's rural heartland, and the cities of Perth, Adelaide, and Sydney - a total of four of Australia's six states. A highlight of the trip is the Nullarbor Plain, a vast expanse, beautiful in its own isolated way. Includes photos every 100km across the country.

FEEDBACK

Hopefully this guide had the information you needed for an epic tip to tip tour. If we've missed something or something significant has changed since publication - we'd like to hear. We'd also like to hear how you found the route, any comments on services along the way, and your ideas on others routes or countries you'd like to see Epic Guides for. Contact us at biker@epicguides.co.nz or via mail at Epic Guides, P.O. Box 31053, Milford, New Zealand.

2004 Sarah Ulmer wins the 3000m individual pursuit at the Athens Olympics, riding a world record 3 min 24.537 sec (an average of 52.8 km/hr)

The Hungry People

A portion of the purchase price of this book goes to this Australian-based charity - the world's largest provider of cycle rickshaws to poor Indian families. They have gifted over 13,000 bikes that enable families to have a debt free, income producing, small business to permanently support themselves. For more information see *www.thehungrypeople.org*

◆　　◆　　◆　　◆　　◆

About the Author

Born and raised in New Zealand, Paul started cycle touring while studying at Auckland University. He has undertaken long-distance tours in a number of countries and currently works as a geologist in Auckland.

2005 In a guest letter to the Automobile Association's magazine, Robert Ibell, from the Cycling Advocates' Network, suggests introducing a Safe Passing Gap law to aid cyclists

201

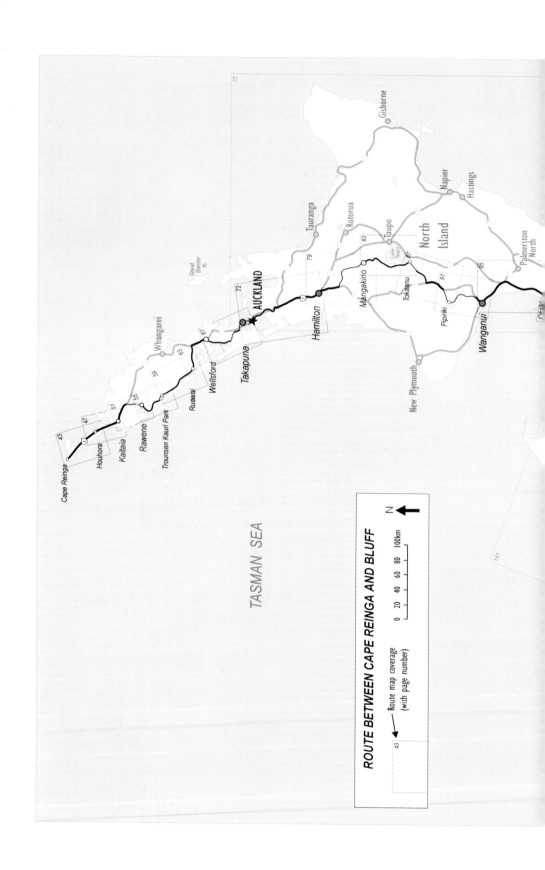

ROUTE BETWEEN CAPE REINGA AND BLUFF

Route map coverage
(with page number)

0 20 40 60 80 100km

N

43

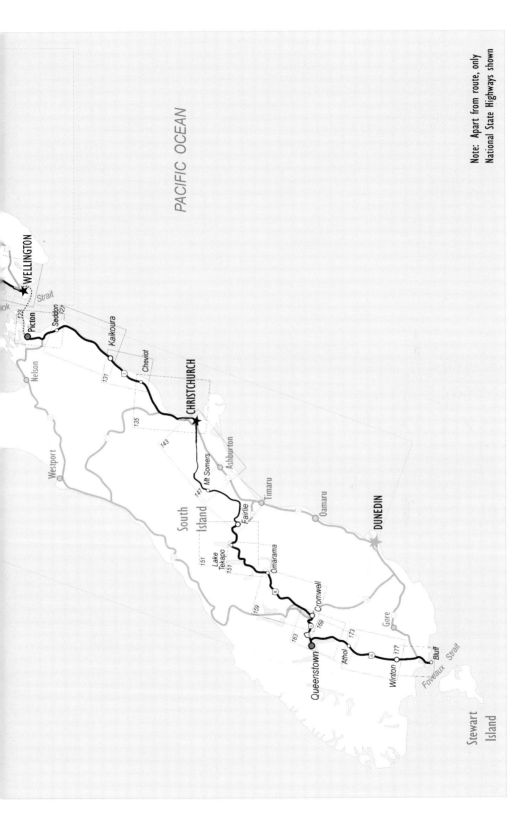

PACIFIC OCEAN

WELLINGTON

Picton

Strait

Seddon

Kaikoura

Cheviot

CHRISTCHURCH

Nelson

Westport

South

Island

Mt Somers

Ashburton

Timaru

Fairlie

Oamaru

DUNEDIN

Lake
Tekapo

Omarama

Cromwell

Gore

Queenstown

Athol

Winton

Bluff

Foveaux Strait

Stewart
Island

Note: Apart from route, only
National State Highways shown

Baldwin Street, Dunedin - a cyclist's nightmare - is reputedly the steepest street in the world.